'Brilliantly witty'

KT-134-835

'This should be nominated for the Booker prize ... it's a really funny book but it's actually more than that ... it blows my postmodern mind'   DAVID BADDIEL

'The funniest book of the year and possibly all time'
                                          *****Heat

'Pure comic genius'   Independent

'A magnificent comedy creation'; 'The significant celebrity book this year'   Guardian

'The best book of the year ... without peer ... I urge people to go out and buy it'   DANNY BAKER

'This book is a genuinely hilarious read'   Shortlist

'A rare treat ... painfully funny in that inimitable Alan way'
                                    **** Sunday Express

'As a parody of celebrity autobiography, it's sound; but as a sustained piece of comic writing, it's outstanding'
                                        **** Time Out

'I, Partridge might just be the funniest book I've ever read. Proper laugh out load moment on every page'
                                      RICHARD BACON

I, PARTRIDGE

WE NEED TO TALK ABOUT ALAN

With Rob Gibbons, Neil Gibbons, Armando Iannucci and Steve Coogan

HARPER

HARPER

An imprint of HarperCollins*Publishers*
77–85 Fulham Palace Road,
Hammersmith, London W6 8JB

www.harpercollins.co.uk

First published by HarperCollins*Publishers* 2011
This paperback edition 2012

1

Picture Credits: Page 1, top © Albanpix Ltd/Rex Features, bottom courtesy of author;
page 2, top © Getty Images, bottom courtesy of author; page 3 © Adrian Sherratt/Alamy;
page 4 © BBC Photo Library, inset © Tim Rooke/Rex Features; page 5 © Colin Mason/
LFI/Photoshot; page 6 © Fremantle Media Ltd; page 7, top & bottom left © BBC Photo
Library, bottom right © Brian Rasic/Rex Features; page 8, left © David Pearson/Alamy,
right © Andy Drysdale/Rex Features; page 9 © Justin Canning/Comic Relief; page 10,
top © BBC Photo Library, bottom © Ken McKay/Rex Features; page 11 © BBC Photo
Library; page 12, left © Hera Food/Alamy, right © BBC Photo Library; page 13, left ©
Alvey and Towers, right © BBC Photo Library; page 14 © BBC Photo Library; page 15,
top © BBC Photo Library, bottom © Yuri Arcurs/Alamy; page 16 © Baby Cow
Productions/Fostersfunny.co.uk

A catalogue record of this book
is available from the British Library

ISBN 978-0-00-744918-7

Printed and bound in Great Britain by
Clays Ltd, St Ives plc

MIX
Paper from
responsible sources
FSC™ FSC® C007454
www.fsc.org

CONTENTS

***

For Fernando. And Denise.

ACKNOWLEDGEMENTS

***

Pete Gabitas (1958–2005)
Norfolk Range Rover
Dave Millicent
William 'Bill' Oddie
Steven Eastwood
All those who have ever doubted me – you only made me stronger
Alvin Krysko (1986–2009)
HRH Prince Charles
Lynn Benfield

FOREWORD

***

ALAN PARTRIDGE IS A DJ who presents *Mid-Morning Matters*. He is hard-working and enthusiastic, with a broad appeal to our regional listenership. He has worked at the station since 2009 and was previously employed by its sister station Radio Norwich.

I have always found Alan to be honest and trustworthy and a relatively good ambassador for the station and for Gordale Media as a whole.

Alan is smart, punctual and his attendance record is very good, with an average of 1.5 sick days taken per year of employment.

I would have no hesitation in recommending him.

Regards,

Andy Powell

MD, Gordale Media

INTRODUCING
WHAT FOLLOWS

***

Hi, Alan. Tell me – what is this page?
It's the introduction to my book.

Written as a short interview with yourself?
Yes.

That's brave and unusual. Why?
Well, questions and answers are my bread and butter; my meat and drink; my sausage, beans and chips. I'm an accomplished broadcaster, presenter and interviewer. Chat is what I do.

You're not going to write the whole book like this, are you?
No.

What do you want the book to say?

That I am Alan Gordon Partridge, a respected broadcaster, but also so much *more* than that. Son to a dead father, father to a living son, TV personality, businessman, brand, rambler, writer, thinker, sayer, doer. I think that's everything.[1]

And today?

Today, I'm the presenter of *Mid-Morning Matters*, an award-worthy weekday morning-thru-lunchtime radio show on North Norfolk Digital – North Norfolk's best music mix. In fact, you join me in my studio, as I scribble these opening thoughts in the 3 minutes 36 seconds of downtime I enjoy as a record plays.[2]

So what can people expect from the book?

They can expect quality throughout and excellence in places. These memoirs are a serious, thoughtful and grammatically sound body of work, a welcome antidote to the kind of crank 'em out, pile 'em high shit-lit that passes for most modern autobiographies.

Examples?

Well, put it this way. In terms of craftsmanship, it's less Bewes, Madeley, Parsons and more Clancey, Archer, Rushdie. What's more, it's accessible enough to capture a market as wide as that of Rowling, Brown, Smith, McNab, Lama[3].[4]

---

1 I also have a daughter.
2 Hue & Cry's 'Labour of Love'. I thought I'd choose a song from their debut album as it's one I've heard of, something I can't say about any of the songs from their subsequent 15 albums.

3 Rodney. Richard. Tony. Tom. Jeffrey. Salman. Joanna. Dan. Wilbur. Andrew. Dalai.
4 This is a footnote, by the way. I'll be using these to pepper and garnish the body copy, so keep an eye out for them. Or as I say: If you see a number, look down under! Which either rhymes or nearly rhymes.

Is there anything in the book that 'breaks the mould'?
Yes, a soundtrack. I spent three days with my 'iPod' creating a list of tracks that would provide the perfect mood music to accompany my life.

My publishers HarperCollins said that this wasn't necessary. In fact they specifically told me not to bother, as they weren't willing to pay for the production or dispatch of a CD and certainly weren't going to seek clearance from, or pay royalties to, the artists I'd chosen.

But they can't stop me providing you, the reader, with a list of songs plus directions as to where in the book they should be played. You'll find the tracklist on page 311. My instructions can be found within the text. Please note: the soundtrack is mandatory.

What kind of research did the book involve?
Content: six consecutive afternoons of remembering. Style: reading ten pages from each of the writers mentioned above.

And have you been honest?
Searingly honest. Brutally honest. Painfully honest. Needlessly honest. Distressingly honest. HarperCollins asked for full disclosure and that's what I delivered. I've opened myself up (not literally), put my balls on the line (not literally) and written it all down (literally).

Having read your book, I see you've had your fair share of run-ins. Indeed, Phil Wiley's behaviour at school and in Scouts seems particularly sickening. Do you agree with those people who say that he's proven himself to be a pretty scummy human?
Phil Wiley. [Chuckles] In all honesty? I don't give the guy a second thought. I just let bygones be bygones.

And what about Nick Peacock and his cowardly refusal to give you the Radio Norwich breakfast show, even though it leaves a sour taste in the mouth of even the most casual observer? That **must** *rankle?*

Look, Nick did what he did. I'm fairly zen about the whole episode.

Given the success of this book, there'll be a pretty loud clamour for a follow-up. Are you ready for that?

I take whatever comes my way. I roll with the punches and I ride the tsunami of life.

Does the book have an ISBN number?

Yes, I insisted on it.

What is it?

You'll find it on the back of the book. But for ease of reference it's ISBN-10: 0007449186 and ISBN-13: 9780007449187

Thanks, Alan.

Goodbye and *God bless.*

1.

BEGINNINGS

***

WHEN I WAS EIGHT years old, I suffered a nose bleed so profuse and generous, I bolted from the schoolyard and sought solace in the first-class countryside of Norfolk.

Nose bleeds were a pretty common feature of my childhood, caused variously by physical exercise, spicy food, bright sunlight, embarrassment, dairy, shouting (hearing or doing) and fiddling with my nose. And my school friends were wise to it. More impressively, they'd worked out that they could induce a haemorrhage themselves, by tethering me to the roundabout with the strap of my own school bag and letting the centrifugal force do the rest. (Unbowed, I refused to accept this affliction and would sneak into the yard alone after school and subject myself to a few turns of the ride once or twice a week. This went on until I developed enough tolerance to prevent the bleeding, at the age of about 16.)

But this nose bleed was hefty, brought on by a perfect storm of country dancing, hot weather and the high pollen count. As it spread and dried on my face and neck, I knew I couldn't face the juvenile tittering of my class colleagues.

Which is how I came to wander the leafy idylls on the outskirts of Norwich.[5] Had this been 2011, I'd have probably returned to the school with some Uzis to give my classmates something to really laugh about, but this was a different – and better – time. So I walked though the countryside, and I bathed in the majesty of nature in quite a mature way for an eight-year-old.

It was quiet, peaceful. The only soul I encountered was a lady rambler, who literally ran when I smiled at her. (The bleeding was *very* profuse.)

Eventually, I found myself stood at the verge of a copse, directly in front of a tree. I didn't remember approaching it, but there I was, standing and gawping at a single tree. Why, I thought? Why this tree? What is it about this simple field maple that makes it stand out from the others? It's not the biggest, the strongest, the coolest, the best at PE. Why am I being hauled into the tractor beam of this tree over and above the millions of other ordinary trees? I guess it had a certain something. At ease with itself and blessed with a gentle authority, it had class and spunk.[6]

---

5 *Press play on Track 1 of the soundtrack.*

6 In more ways than one, as it transpired. Years later, I took a walk to this place at dusk and saw a teenage couple sullying my memory of that tree with some pretty vigorous frottage. I was going to run at them with a stick, but in the end I didn't.

Then it hit me (the thought). It's me, I exclaimed. I am that tree. I personify its stand-out quality. Some people might say that's arrogant. Arrogant? Actually, accurate.

What's made me different from the others? How – and these were pretty much my exact words, even at the age of eight – did I come to be born with this aura of otherness, this *je ne sais quoi*?[7]

I stood and looked at the tree, and thoughts tumbled around my head like trainers in a washing machine. What made me thus? What made me thus? What made me thus?

And as the memories swirled around like the trainers I mentioned in the previous paragraph, all that could be heard was the pitter-patter of blood – my nose was still *piddling* the stuff – as it dripped from my nose and chin and on to my shoes. Pitter-patter, pitter-patter, pitter-patter …

***

Pitter-patter goes the rain on the window. Pitter-patter, pitter-patter, and outside cars zoom up and down the road, some of them dropping down to second to turn right into Gayton Road. On the pavement, people hurry and scurry, both to and fro. A clap of thunder – BAM! – and some really gusty wind. Everyone agrees it's a pretty dramatic evening all round.

Pan right. It's a hospital room. A clammy pregnant woman lies spread-eagled on the bed and is about to produce pitter-patter of her own. She's not going to wet herself – although that's often a distressing side effect of childbirth. I'm referring to the pitter-patter of children's feet. 'Stand back,' says the midwife. 'Her contraptions are *massive*. Get ready!'

'Looks like Anthony Eden's about to be named Prime Minister,' mutters a nurse as she strolls past the door. 'And

---

7 'I do not know what'.

Chelsea are about to win the First Division title!' replies an orderly, almost certainly not educated enough to follow politics. In the corner of the room, 'Rock Around the Clock' by Bill Haley blasts from the radio quietly.

You see, this wasn't now. It's then. The present tense used in this passage is just a literary device so that this next bit comes as a surprise. The scene is actually unfurling in 1955! The hospital? The Queen Elizabeth Hospital in King's Lynn. The sweaty woman? Mrs Dorothy Partridge, my mother. And the child's head slithering from her legs? It belongs to me. The child was I, Partridge.

'You've done it! Brilliant pushing!' says the midwife. She holds the newborn aloft like a captain lifting a fleshy World Cup. And then the child throws his head back and roars the roar of freedom. The noise is relatively nonsensical but no less intelligent than most babies would produce. In fact, probably a bit more switched on than average.

In many ways, the proud wail that burst from my lungs was my first broadcast. Delivered to an audience of no more than eight, that still equated to an audience share – in the delivery room at least – of a cool 100%. Not bad, I probably thought. Not bad at all.

***

As I write these words I'm noisily chomping away on not one, but two Murray Mints. I've a powerful suck and soon they'll be whittled away to nothing. But for the time being at least they have each other. For the time being, they are brothers. Which is more than could be said for me, for I was an only child. I will now talk more about being an only child.[8]

---

8 *Press play on Track 2.*

Why my parents never had more kids I don't know, though as a youngster I'd often lie in bed wondering. Maybe it was financial reasons. Maybe I'd bust Mum's cervix. Maybe Dad had just perfected the withdrawal method.

But I would have loved a little brother to play football with or bully. I'd rush downstairs every Christmas morning and rip open my presents, hoping against hope that one of the boxes contained a human baby. It rarely did. In fact it never did.

The sad fact was, my parents (although *not* Communists) were unconsciously adhering to the same one-child-only policy espoused by the People's Republic of China. And, like billions of Chinese children, I consequently had to endure a home life of intense loneliness.

This meant there was extra pressure on me to be sociable. I didn't have a motto growing up, but had I done it would almost certainly have been 'I'd love some friends, please'. But maybe in Latin.

I'd look on with longing as I saw my fellow children greedily enjoying their friendships. I remember being especially jealous of a lad called Graham Rigg. Graham was too cool for school (though he did still attend). He'd not only been the winner of the sports day slow bicycle race for three straight years, he was also the first boy in our class to properly kiss a girl. There'd been cheek pecks before, not to mention inter-sex handshakes, but he was the first kid in the playground to 'go French'. None of the rest of us could figure out where he'd learnt to do this, but the general consensus was 'from porno films'.

Eight-year-old Jennie Lancashire was the cock-a-hoop recipient, and she was rightly grateful.[9] But when I look back I

---

9 By the way, update on the Murray Mints: one's already gone, the other is a shadow of its former self.

often think how fortunate it was that Graham was the same age as her, because if he'd been 20 years older he would have been up in Crown Court. And quite right too!

I bumped into him for the first time in decades the other week. It was at the returns desk in my local Homebase. We were both taking back kettles (him – faulty filament; me – didn't like colour).

'Still French-kissing eight-year-olds?' I said, pointing an accusing finger at his potentially paedophilic mouth.

'No,' he replied.

'Good,' I said. Then for extra emphasis I said it again, but slightly more slowly. 'Gooood.'

I'd made my point. Anyway, after that, talk naturally turned to motor vehicles and I was bowled over to learn that Graham had been the first person in Norwich to own a car with a catalytic converter. From playground lothario to environmental trailblazer in under 50 years. It quickly dawned on me that here was a man whose number I needed to take, but before I had the chance he'd collected his refund, mimed taking his hat off to me and disappeared off into the sunset/down the paint aisle.

***

Without love (parental or matey) to sustain me, I turned to myself, Alan Partridge, for comfort. Eager to keep myself occupied, I was from a young age deeply inquisitive. Learning was my friend; knowledge, my bosom buddy. Indeed, in my quest for self-education, I once put a bumblebee in the freezer. It was to see if I could freeze it and then bring it back to life. I couldn't. Of course I couldn't, it was dead.[10] (I put it in a

---

10 Bear in mind, this was the late 60s. Everyone was experimenting. We'd just put a man on the moon, anything seemed possible. In this case, of course, it wasn't. But then we didn't have Google. If you wanted to find out if something was possible you had to try it for yourself. Terrible business.

matchbox, like a biodegradable bee casket. Then just chucked it in the bin. I never told my mother.)

And so, this young, neglected but resourceful young man would guzzle down knowledge like other kids would guzzle down fizzy pop. Or full-cream milk. Either works. For a time, I was fixated with butterflies – an interest that my father did much to encourage. We'd go into the garden on a summer's evening and when we saw the gentle flitter-flutter of a butterfly, he'd smash it to the ground with his tennis racket.

'Fifteen love!' he'd roar. Either that or some other tennis-related phrase. ('Advantage, Dad' was my favourite.) 'You know what you need to do now, Alan,' he'd continue.

'Yes, father. I'm to collect the remains, piece them back together and do my utmost to identify the genus.'

Sometimes I could actually do it too, but more often than not (particularly when Dad used his textbook backhand slice), you would have needed dental records to identify the dead. Still, world-class interactive learning.

But don't be deceived by this seemingly intimate tale of fatherliness. (In fact, I probably shouldn't even have put that bit in.) No, above all else, overriding everything, was the dark heart at the core of my parents' parenting which meant that, as I think I've said, my home life was one of neglect and sadness.

Mother was cold, distant. After school, between the ages of 13 and 14, I would routinely have to let myself into the house, where I'd be on my own, unfended for, for a minimum of 45 minutes, before she came home from working in a shoe shop. She'd console me by gifting me the latest shoe-cleaning merchandise, and to this day I've always had an affection for shoe trees and shoe horns.[11]

---

11 Of which more later! (possibly)

And then there was Father. Like most men of his generation he'd returned from war a changed man. He signed up on the day of his 17th birthday. 'Mum,' he'd said chirpily, 'I'm off to save a Jew or two.'

It was April 1943 and he'd had quite enough of the idiots with the swastikas (and they *were* idiots). I remember asking him once over breakfast what it had been like. But his eyes glazed over and he just took another bite of his boiled egg. It was a bite that seemed to say, 'Son, I don't want to talk about war, because I've seen soldiers decapitated like in *Saving Private Ryan*.'

'The only soldiers I want to talk about are the ones I dip in my boiled egg, which coincidentally has also been decapitated!' his next bite seemed to add. This was typical of my dad – or would have been if he'd said it – because he'd often have dark thoughts rounded off with a little joke.

He wasn't an easy man, though. Mum said he came back from the war with a rage that never went away. She said he was still just very angry with Mr Hitler. Yet it was me that suffered the consequences. Let's just say Poppa had a hand like a leather shovel.

What made it all the more galling was that it wasn't even me that had carried out the Final Solution. The closest I'd ever got to the extermination of the Jewish race was teasing Jon Malick about his big nose. But (a) I didn't even know he was Jewish. And (b) it was pretty massive. You could have hung your washing off it. They say your nose is one of the few things that keeps growing throughout your life. Jon will now be 56. Good god.

The only thing that softened the blow (metaphor) was that I was at least being beaten with a degree of excellence. My father was a naturally gifted corporal punisher. The quality of the blows was always the same, whether administering them with his right hand or his left, whether he was alone or had Mum screaming at him to stop, whether we were in the privacy of the home or out at a charity treasure hunt organised by Round Table.

I couldn't wait for the day when I was big enough to turn round and thump him in the tummy or set fire to an Airfix Messerschmitt and put it behind his bedroom door so he'd be intoxicated by the burning plastic.

You see, it wasn't just physical abuse. The torment was sometimes psychological. I still bear mental scars from him trimming our privet hedge and then making me go and collect the cuttings in the rain. Well, I've got a saying: 'Be careful what you do, because some day something similar might happen to you.'

And you know what? It did, because financial difficulties in later life meant he ended up as a casual labourer in his 60s. I allowed myself a wry smile at that. You may think it's cold of me to be glad of his occupational misfortune just because he had me collecting privets, but let me tell you this: he made me do it *four times*, in as many years. On another occasion, he made me clear out the garage on a sunny day.

But I never have turned round and thumped him in the tummy or set fire to an Airfix Messerschmitt before putting it behind his bedroom door so he'd be intoxicated by the burning plastic. Why? Well, I guess resentment fades with time. Also he's now dead. And the last thing I've got time to do is exhume, and subsequently duff up, the cadaver of a loved one. There'd be a heck of a lot of paperwork, for one. Plus I really need to take the car in for a service. Must do that next week.[12]

***

---

12 *Press play on Track 3.*

'Ah, but at least your parents didn't split up,' you might be crowing. 'You're lucky in that respect, Alan!'

I shake my head slowly and smile. You see, my parents' marriage wasn't as stable as their long list of wedding anniversaries might suggest. And that in itself was unusual and upsetting.

Of course, these days the institution of marriage is in crisis. It's crumbling like an Oxo cube. I don't have the exact figures to hand,[13] but it's probably correct to say that half of all marriages end in separation. Take the royal family. Elizabeth and Phillip – solid as a rock; Charles and Diana – crumbled like an Oxo cube. Charles and Camilla – rock; Andrew and Fergie – Oxo. Edward and his wife[14] – rock; Anne and Mark Phillips – Oxo. You see, exactly one in two.

'Marriage is dead!' I shouted to the listeners of *Mid-Morning Matters*, not six weeks ago.[15] Then I paused for dramatic effect and to finish my mouthful of sandwich. 'Someone inform the relatives. Time of death: 2011. Cause of death … well, why don't you play Quincy? Get in touch and let us know why *you* think marriage passed away.'

It turned out to be a really insightful phone-in. Dealing with unemployed listeners five days a week, I'm still sometimes pleasantly surprised that they can be brainy. Regular caller Ralph laid the blame at the door of the Mormons. Other less angry listeners put it down to the rise of contraception, E-numbers giving us attention deficit, and tax law, while my assistant texted in to say it was a symptom of terrible ungodliness.[16]

---

13 Internet's down.
14 Internet's still down.
15 Time of me writing, not time of you reading.
16 Didn't read it out.

Me? I put it down to a combination of all these factors. Apart from the one about ungodliness. And the one about Mormons. Whatever your view, in the last hundred years there must have been more divorces than marriages.

Fifty years ago things were kinda different though. It was as rare to see a divorce as it was to see a four-leaf clover or a black chap in a position of authority. If only things had stayed that way.[17]

Now, I'd thought my parents' union was in the rock-solid camp. But I was wrong. Because one night something happened that threatened to turn my world upside down like one of those paperweights with fake snow inside. It was an incident that made me have a terrible, terrible thought. What if the rock of their marriage was actually a rock made ... of Oxo?

***

I woke with a start. At first I assumed I'd trumped myself awake again – it was summer time so there were lots of fresh vegetables in our diet. But as I listened through the darkness, I realised that something far worse was going on. My mother and father were having the row to end all rows.

A sudden shot of fear ripped through my pre-pubic body. And now I did do a trump. The noise fizzed out of my back passage like a child calling for help. That child was me. I cupped my hands behind my ears creating a sort of makeshift amplifier. *Look and Learn Magazine* was right – it really did work.[18] But still I couldn't quite hear everything. I shut my

---

17 Divorces.
18 It's a technique I still use to this day when talking to quiet people at cocktail parties.

11

eyes in the hope it might make me hear better, like they say it does for blind people.

'I've told you, there's no point keeping those. They're not tax-deductible,' my dad thundered.

'I think you'll find they are,' raged my mum like some sort of feral animal (a badger with TB perhaps).

'They're not. You only get VAT back on lunches outside of a 50-mile radius from your place of residence. You effing bitch,' he seemed to add, with his eyes, I imagined.

'Alright, fine, I'll get rid of them then,' sobbed my mum, her fight gone, her spirit crushed like a Stu Francis grape.

Then the door was shut. Or was it slammed? It was hard to know for sure as I'd now opened my eyes, thus depriving myself of the hearing boost conferred on me by blindness. I curled up on my bed like a foetus (though admittedly, quite a large one) and cried like a baby (again, large). 'Please Lord, make it stop,' I snivelled. 'I'll do anything you ask of me (within reason and subject to getting permission from my mum). Just don't let them break up.' Like an Oxo cube, I could have added.

And with that, I went off to the bathroom to clear my head, not to mention my nose.

Yet miraculously, when I went down to breakfast the next morning, there was no mention of the bitter war of words that had waged so fiercely just hours before. The nightmare that had threatened to rip my world apart like an experienced chef portioning up a ball of mozzarella had somehow been averted.

It was 25 October 1962, and on the other side of the Atlantic, President 'JFK' Kennedy had just pulled the world back from the brink of nuclear war. Could I just have experienced my own personal Cuban Missile Crisis?

Yes, I could have.

***

And so, in summary, mine was a childhood of undeniable hardship – a chilling and far-from-delicious cocktail of neglect, solitude, domestic strife, and abuse.[19]

I was, if you like, A Child Called It. This was Alan's Ashes. A protagonist dealt a really shoddy hand by hard-hearted parents. (They're dead now and my mum's sister Valerie, who disputes my version of events pretty vociferously, has gone medically demented so I'm really the gospel here.)

But it wasn't all foul-tasting. For example, I remember the intense joy I felt when my father slipped on some cake and cracked his head open. It was the day of my ninth birthday, and as I sat effortlessly reading a book aimed at 11–12-year-olds, I heard a commotion. It was my father.

'Delivery for Mr Partridge! Delivery for Mr Partridge!' he was saying.

He meant me, rather than himself, and although he could have eliminated the obvious ambiguity by saying 'Alan Partridge' or 'Master Partridge', my instincts told me that he was using the third person, so probably did mean me.

I ran into the kitchen. And there was my father – normally so cruel, as I think I've made abundantly clear – holding a cake. It was a ruby red birthday cake, with my name piped on to it in reasonably accomplished joined-up writing. I could barely contain my excitement – more at the cake than the writing. I adored cakes, but was only allowed to eat any on special occasions such as after meals. I began to run over, licking my lips as I sprinted.

---

19 Naysayers have suggested that I'm dramatising details of my early years because my publishers were concerned that my childhood was boring. How wrong they are. If anything I'm bravely playing down some of the hardships I faced in a way that critics might choose to describe as 'stoical'.

Although blessed with cat-like co-ordination, something made me lose my bearings. Perhaps I'd been pushing myself too hard with the book for 11–12-year-olds and my brain was scrambled. Whatever it was, I misjudged my proximity to the table and clattered against it. The cake fell from it and smashed on to the floor in a hail of crumbs and redness and cream.

My father surveyed the scene, his face slowly crumpling with anger. He crouched down, taking the weight of his body on his two haunches and then he addressed me: 'You'll never amount to anything,' he said. 'You're that to me.'[20]

On the word 'that', he held his finger and thumb one, maybe two, centimetres apart as if to say 'not very much'.

I didn't know what to say, my mind blasted by the twin concerns of spilt cake and parental cruelty. He turned to go and put one of his angry feet on to the remains of the cake. This acted as a lubricant, destroying any traction his foot might have had with the floor. It shot forward and, with his balance now a distant memory, he came crashing to the floor. His back took the first hit, smashing against lino and cake with a bang – 'bang'. His rump was next – 'doof' – followed by his skull – 'crack'. And for a second he was motionless, before blood began to spill from the back of his head.

As my father lay on the ground, the tension – much like the physical integrity of Dad's skull – was broken. Suddenly, all the years of neglect, which could easily make a book in its own right and definitely a film, were lifted. The hardship, the

---

20 Auntie Valerie, who was there that day, is adamant that Dad said absolutely nothing of the sort. But, like I say, this is a woman who often forgets her own address, so you can strike her testimony from the record.

loneliness, the disappointment squeezed out of my eyes in the form of hot salt tears. Was I crying or laughing? I didn't know. All I knew was that these tears felt like a monsoon on a parched African savannah to the delight of a proud but easy-going black farmer. Pitter-patter, pitter-patter.

***

Pitter-patter. Pitter-patter. I'm back at that tree as an eight-year-old child, my nose still bleeding (but it should scab up in a few minutes). All those childhood thoughts are racing through my mind, even though some of the incidents above haven't yet happened, so would have only raced through my mind in a very vague form.

These hard hardships, testing trials and tricky tribulations are the things that have made me who I am. Like this tree, I am different. I have staying power, strength, nobility, staying power and the ability to 'branch' out.

I wait for the bleeding to stop. It has done ... now. The cathartic, cleansing effect of rapid blood loss has made me feel elated.[21] And I return to school to face what proved to be a pretty massive bollocking. I didn't care. Something had been ignited in me.[22]

I still return to that tree once a year. It's been bulldozed now to make the car park of Morrison's. I like to think it was

---

21 This was a feeling I would come to know well in later years. Major blood loss has been a close friend of mine – be it the kind I've endured (impaling my foot on a spike before a sales presentation, sneezing blood over a nun's wimple) or the kind I've inflicted (punching a commissioning editor, shooting a guest). And on each occasion, the initial regret has been swiftly replaced by a joyous high, brought on by relief, defiance or morphine. In this case: it was a brand new sense of purpose.
22 Metaphor.

pulped to make the very pages you're reading now (a huge long shot, admittedly).

But still I stand there each year, smack bang in the middle of a disabled parking bay, and remember its leafy majesty. We've both had our knocks (my TV career was bulldozed by a short-sighted commissioner who I'm *delighted* to say is now dead), but we retain that indefinable quality of excellence. And I think back to that turning point, that fulcrum of my early years when I first fully realised what I had, where I was going, and who I was. I was Alan Partridge.

2.
SCOUTS AND
SCHOOLING

***

I JOINED LORD BADEN Powell's army of pre-pubescents – and it *is* an army – in the heyday of the Boy Scouts. In those days we were truly legion. Some say there were close to a million UK scouts in the early 1960s, a terrifying proposition if you imagine them all running at you across a field or chanting 'Ging Gang Goolie' again and again and again and again, but slightly louder each time.

Even among such a vast number, I stood out as a quite outstanding officer in the North Norwich district, (HQ'd in Costessey). I excelled at outdoor tasks, mastering knots that could (theoretically) lash a small boat to a jetty or splice together a child's shattered leg; identifying clues to help me track a stricken comrade; spotting dock leaves from 50 paces.

But I was even more adept at the domestic chores that Scouting taught. I could embroider badges on to the shirts of every scout who asked and was an absolute whizz at buffing shoes, tying neckerchiefs and adjusting woggles.[23]

I might as well admit now, before any member of my troop publishes a counter-memoir, that I never mastered fire-lighting. I admit that – I couldn't do fires. I could build them into sturdy wigwams of sticks and newspaper, no problem. But I found it very, very hard to make them catch fire. In fact, I still can't, which is why gas BBQs are such a blessed relief.

I'm often asked, what do Scouts *do*? Well, although highly trained and physically fit, Scouts are not invited to defend Britain in international conflict. Instead, much of our effort went into the production of our annual Gang Show – my first taste of showbiz.

My aptitude for knot-tying meant that I was called into action as a stage-hand, hoiking up scenery panels and then lowering them down again. I was good at it and felt no real calling to be on stage … until the night of our first show.

Scout Leader Dave Millicent was MC. Smartly dressed and with his hair parted to one side, he worked the crowd beauti-fully and introduced each turn with real panache. He was, in a very real sense, a presenter that night. And it was at the show's pinnacle – as he cued up the backing track to 'Crest of a Wave' and told them to 'take it away' – that I think I first knew what I wanted to be. I wanted to *present*.

Many years later, I contacted Dave and asked him to co-present my show on hospital radio, but he said he didn't want to do it and didn't remember who I was. Still, he was a good man and a very talented Scout.

***

23 Not racist.

What most appealed to me about the Scouts was that it was a true meritocracy. If you were diligent and resourceful and attended each week, you could orienteer your way to the very top. I'm proud to say I achieved the rank of Patrol Leader in no time, with six good Scouts under my command.

You'd think that this would automatically confer on me a bit of respect and obedience from others in the patrol. Sadly, many in the troop felt the Scouting hierarchy only applied during our weekly meetings. One member of the troop, Phil Wiley, was in my class at school – and his behaviour towards me, a superior officer, was quite, quite shameful.

On one occasion, he stole my swimming trunks, dropped them in a urinal and laughed. This was in front of the whole class, many of who(m) were in my troop. Of course, I couldn't let this slide, and ordered him to rescue and wash them. He sniggered. I took a breath.

'Do as I say,' I said calmly.

He began to walk away.

'Do as I say, Scout Wiley,' I boomed.

'What did you call me? Scout Wiley?'

He laughed again and indicated to the rest of the class that I was mentally defective, by twirling a finger by the side of his head. Well, this was rank insubordination.

'Do as I say. I'm your Patrol Leader!'

'Oh my god …' he attempted, weakly.

'I *am* your Patrol Leader.'

'You are such a tit.'

'I *am* your Patrol Leader!'

'Fuck off.' He *actually* said that to me.

'I *am* your Patrol Leader! I *am* your Patrol Leader! I *am* your Patrol Leader! I *am* your Patrol Leader!'

I continued to shout this until I was the only person left in the changing rooms, and then I fished my trunks from the well of piss with a fountain pen, and showered them off for a few minutes before repeatedly hurling them against a wall to release the excess liquid. Yes, I'd had to save my trunks from someone else's urine, but I'd left my class colleagues certain of one thing: I *was* the Patrol Leader.

The following week, I reported Wiley to Scout Leader Dave and was told not to tell tales, which didn't really bother me much at all. (Wiley left the troop shortly after and his school work began to decline markedly. Without the discipline and brotherhood of the Scouting Movement, he drifted into a spiral of underachievement, culminating in his having sex with a lab technician. Because of pregnancy, she gave birth to a child, although Wiley has as close a relationship with it as you or I do.)

***

I treasured my involvement with the Scouts – of course I did. But it didn't compensate for the absence of love and affection I received in my home life. That is a fact.

Do you believe in guardian angels? I do.[24] Not the winged ones you see in films. As I've often explained to my assistant (a Christian female), as well as being aerodynamically unfeasible, wings sprouting from the shoulder blades would pull the ribcage backwards and gradually suffocate the angel – a cause of death that's similar, ironically, to that of crucifixion.

No, by guardian angels I mean 'nice people'. And I do believe in them. (Although I reserve the right to be deeply suspicious of anyone who is unilaterally kind to me.)

---

24 *Press play on Track 4.*

My guardian angels were the Lambert family. They took me in when I had nowhere to go. They gave me food and shelter and love when my own parents had deserted me. I remain forever in their debt.[25]

I was temporarily fostered by this kindly family in 1961. As family friends who were friends with our family, theirs was a loving home and I stayed for more than three weeks, returning home only because Mum and Dad had come back from their holiday in Brittany and it was time to go.

This was the first time I'd experienced the warmth of a caring family. Not for them the bickering over VAT receipts or making their children pick up privet cuttings in the rain. Instead, I was treated like a human being.

The father, Trevor, was an asthmatic, but what he lacked in being able to breathe quietly, he more than made up for with his parental skills. He always found time to not hit his children and I remember thinking that was tremendous.

'Got to say, Trevor,' I remember announcing, on my second day there, 'you have a wonderful way with your kids. You're a credit to yourself. I for one am impressed.'

'Thanks, Alan,' he said.

'Yes, that's lovely of you, Alan.'

I turned to see Mother Lambert, better known as Fran, handing out fresh milk and cooked cookies to her three children: Kenneth, Emma and Sheila. The children were marginally older than I was (and remain so to this day) but they reached across the age divide to show me friendship and good will.

But it was Fran who was the chief supplier of love. From day one, I was clasped to her bosom – not literally. Not literally at

---

25 Disclaimer: Not in any legal sense.

all. There was no suggestion of any sordid behaviour. Please don't think there was, just because I've created the image of my face being pulled towards an older woman's breasts. No, I don't want you to take away even a residual inkling that this was a family marred by a proclivity for child molestation. I'm in two minds now whether to keep this paragraph in at all, in case the denial of any wrongdoing makes you think there's something that needs denying. There isn't. They were a lovely family. Kept themselves to themselves and neighbours have said they seemed perfectly normal. Actually, that makes them sound worse.

I was happy there and saw no reason why I couldn't stay among the Lamberts for the rest of my life. But the nature and length of my stay there hadn't been adequately explained to me. And so it was that one cold summer's morning, I looked up from a genuinely difficult jigsaw puzzle to see my mother and father standing there, my coat in Mum's hands. I burst into tears.

The Lamberts cried too (inwardly) as they waved me off. Mum and Dad thanked their counterparts. 'Say thank you, Alan,' Mum said.

'Thank you,' I snivelled.

'Don't mention it,' said Trevor Lambert. 'You can come and stay any time you like.'

I stopped crying. 'Pardon?'

'Come and stay any time you like.'

And with that, I was driven away. But my life had been touched by guardian angels – their kindness ringing in my ears like chronic tinnitus. I pressed my hand against the window like they do in films and at this point the director might like to do a slow fade to black.[26]

***

26 *Press play on Track 5.*

'Smelly Alan Fartridge! Smelly Alan Fartridge!' The words spewed from my classmates' mouths like invisible projectile sick, landing in my ears and ending up caked all over my shattered self-esteem. My inner confidence must have reeked.

Short of doing me in with a blade (it wasn't that sort of school), there was nothing that these educationally slow children could have done to hurt me more. But still they shouted.

'Smelly Alan Fartridge! Smelly Alan Fartridge! He loves his mum, he lives in her bum. You think that's bad, you should smell his dad. Smelly Alan Fartridge!'

It was agony on so many levels. For starters, they were bellowing over the sound of English teacher Mr Bevin – academically suicidal given that mock exams were just weeks away, and a personal affront of Mr Bevin who, although timid and stuttering, knew his onions, English-wise.

For mains, it was the dunderheaded wrongness of what they were saying: I did not smell. I was a keen cleanser, diligently showering each day and making sure that my body, privates, face and mouth were stench- and stain-free. If I smelt of anything, it would have been Matey (now Radox) and Colgate.

And for afters, their catcalls were a depressing reminder of my own father's suffering. Having signed up to the 2nd Battalion of the Royal Norfolk Regiment in World War II (for my money *the* 'Great War'), he learned that a sloppy administrator had spelt his surname: PRATridge (my capitals). The consequent teasing and name-calling he received at the hands of his comPRATriates (my caps) cut him deep. The horror of war. Up there with trench foot and being attacked with guns.

Smelly Alan Fartridge. Say it to yourself a few times. Pretty annoying isn't it? About 3% as clever as it thinks it is, it's a piece of infantile wordplay that most right-minded abusers would dismiss as rubbish but which a small minority of backward Norfolk underachievers repeated again and again and again and again.

They were led by one child whose name I can barely even remember. In fact, his name was Steven McCombe. You won't have been able to tell, but I had to think for ages then, between the words 'name' and 'was', so insignificant is he in the roll call of people I've encountered.

McCombe – let's not bother with first names – was, and I'm sure is, a grade A dumbo. He could afford to lark around in class, so certain was his fate as a manual worker – the kind who'd never have cause to rely on school teachings unless it's for the tie-break round of a pub quiz (where the top prize is some meat).

McCombe didn't just squawk 'Smelly Alan Fartridge' at me a few times. His was a campaign of petty abuse that was awesome in its length and breadth. Between 1962 and 1970, McCombe – and again these are events that bother me so little my brain has filed them under 'Forget if you like' – waged an impressively consistent war on me. This frenzied attack on me and my rights took several sickening forms: he stole, interfered with, and returned my sandwiches; he mimicked my voice when I effortlessly answered questions in class; he removed my shorts on a cross-country run and ran off fast; he reacted hysterically when I referred to a teacher as 'mum'; he threw my bat and ball into a canal; he spat on my back; he daubed grotesque sexual images on my freshly wallpapered exercise books; and, in a sinister twist, he tracked the progress of my puberty, making unflattering comparisons to his own and the majority of my classmates'. This was psychological torment that few could have withstood. I withstood it.

One day, I decided enough was enough, so I plucked up the courage to confront him for an almighty showdown. It was

5pm on a wet Tuesday and I took a deep breath and went for it.

'Oi,' I said. 'McCombe.'

He hesitated. 'What?'

'Watch it, mate.'

A pause. The guy was rattled. 'What?'

'I said watch it. Watch what you say and watch how you say it, you snivelling little goose.[27] You might find you push some-one too far one day and they unleash hell in your face.'

'What?'

'Stop saying "what". Listen to me. You're going to start showing me a bit of respect, buddy boy. Or you will reap a whirlwind. The days of infantile name-calling and sexually explicit graffiti are over. It stops. *Right?*'

'What? I can't hear you, mate.'

'I'm not your mate.'

'What?'

This was infuriating. I unwrapped my jumper from the mouthpiece. Oh, I forgot to say, this was on the phone.

'Just watch it, McCombe.'

'Who is this?'

'See you around.'

'Is this Partridge?'

I hung up. My point made. My parting shot – 'See you around' – had sounded particularly menacing. I would have said 'See you in school', but we'd both left a few years before. And 'around' sounded more threatening anyway.

McCombe had left school at the first opportunity, his mind-less decision-making conducted almost entirely by a hormone-addled penis desperate to impregnate the first chubby cashier

---

27 Not sure why I said goose or what I meant by it.

it could slip into. Sure enough, McCombe and Janice have a litter of four children, not much younger than they are. Way to go, guys.

McCombe worked for several years in the warehouse of British Leyland before a back injury scuppered his forklift-truck driving. He now lives on disability allowance in Edgbaston and has gained a lot of weight. No prizes for guessing which of us is the 'Smelly' one now.

Interestingly, McCombe's career-ending back complaint is so cripplingly debilitating, he can only manage the three games of tenpin bowling per week, a fact that may or may not have been documented and photographed by my assistant.

The dossier may or may not have been passed on to Birmingham City Council. And I may or may not be waiting for a reply, although this is the public sector so I shan't be holding my breath!

The divergence between our two lives (mine: successful, his: pathetic) is best illustrated in our choice of garden furnishing. I've enhanced my lawn with a rockery. McCombe has chosen a broken washing machine.

And what a pair he and Janice make. I spoke with her once, when she asked me what I was doing outside their house,[28] and her language was *appalling*. Very aggressive woman.

McCombe rarely, if ever, strays into my consciousness now. But in some ways I thank him. The ribbing that he orchestrated – and to be fair there were probably others involved too[29] – has given me a thick skin that has served me well. I

---

28 I'd stopped to let the engine cool down when I was in the Birmingham area looking for Pebble Mill, and coincidentally it happened to be on their street.

29 Andy Bendell, Joe Cowes, Alan Holland, Richard Toms, Justin Parker, Noel Scott, Daniel Groves.

grew a teak-tough, metaphorically bullet-proof hide, essential in the very real warzone that is broadcasting.

I could give you three examples right now of times that the 'Smelly Alan Fartridge' barbs have stood me in good stead. When Bridie McMahon (failed TV presenter who you won't have heard of) pointed out on air that an anagram of Alan Partridge is Anal Dirge Prat, sure, I wanted to shove her in the face, but had the self-discipline not to. When formerly significant TV critic Victor Lewis-Smith described my military-based quiz show *Skirmish* as 'a thick man's *Takeshi's Castle*', I wanted to hurt him physically, but had the restraint not to. I just left 60 abusive voicemails on his mobile (plus 12 on Valerie Singleton's *for which I have apologised*. She's above him in my contacts list.) There's probably a third example too. But the point is, the inane taunts from my school days had given me strength and perspective.

An addendum: in 1994, I was named *TV Quick*'s Man of the Moment. At the same time, McCombe contracted glandular fever. Needless to say, McCombe, I had the last laugh. And I'm still having it.

3.
EAST ANGLIA
POLYTECHNIC

***

'O-O-O-OPEN IT,' STUTTERED MY mother, nervously.

'Y-y-y-yes, open it,' said Dad, frightened.

'Cool it, cats,' I breezed. (This was the 70s.)

In my hand was a golden envelope[30] containing the most important pieces of paper I'd ever clutched: my A-level results.

Rectangular in shape and with my full name typed across it in ink, it looked important because it was of real import(ance). The foldable flap hugged the back of the sheath tightly, bound together in a solemn, gummy embrace. Unable to slip my nail beneath its coagulated clasp, I nodded to myself. I was going

---

30 I think it was golden anyway.

to have to tear the paper along the top fold. I did so and then reached inside to extract the papery contents.

'W-w-w-w-what does it s-s-s-say?' my parents whispered in absolute unison.

I opened it as gingerly as a rookie bomb disposal operative would open a fat letter bomb in a crèche. In a funny sort of way, the contents were just as explosive as a powdered acetone peroxide. They spelt the difference between me attending tertiary education and being consigned to the heap marked 'Don't have A-levels', and that was a mound of slag I did *not* want to be on.

Like the bomb disposal man[31] mentioned above, I swallowed hard and began to remove the letter within the 'lope. A single bead of sweat sprinted down my face, skirting round my temple and pausing at the jaw before throwing itself to its death.

I pulled the paper out further, until I could make out the letters it bore, letters that had been formed into words by a kindly typist. I gulped again and looked at my parents, before emitting a sigh.

'Bad news,' I muttered. 'Your son has failed … at failing his exams!!!'

They were confused momentarily by the clever double negative, so I added: 'I passed!' (The it's-bad-news-ha-no-actually-it's-good-news technique is one I've always enjoyed. It was really pioneered by David Coleman on *Question of Sport* when he'd tonally suggest Bill Beaumont had got an answer wrong … only to reveal at the end of the sentence that he'd got it right! The judges on ITV's *X Factor*[32] use a similar technique to reveal that a singer has made it to 'boot camp'.)

---

31 And it's always a man.
32 A modern-day *New Faces* in which the audience wear t-shirts with the contestants' names on them.

My parents were elated. Mum patted me and Dad joined me in one of the first high-fives that Norwich had seen.

'I passed!' I kept saying. 'I passed them both!'[33]

The exact grading isn't important. Suffice to say, I was the proud owner of two shiny A-levels and *nobody* could take them away from me.[34]

***

1974 was a crazy, hazy time for Alan Partridge. The Sixties had come to East Anglia and it was a time of free thinking, free love and in my case free university accommodation.

I was quite the man about Norwich,[35] striding confidently through the dreaming spires and hallowed halls of East Anglia Polytechnic – whose alumni included news woman Selina Scott and meteorology whizz Penny Tranter – and soaking up all the knowledge that this seat of learning had to offer.

The free accommodation? Well, enigmatically, I had decided to stay not in the woodworm-infested squalor of university halls, but to commute in from my home (my parents' home). Although misinterpreted by some of my peers as reluctance to cut the apron strings and live independently, the decision to reside at home was a canny marshalling of my resources. It enabled me to avoid the scruffiness of my shaggy-haired, sandal-wearing colleagues. By using my 'rent money' wisely, I was never less than beautifully shod.

Of course, it also meant that I was something of a 'mystery man' on campus. While my fellow students lived in each other's pockets and played out their debauched lifestyles for

---

33 I'd actually taken three but obviously I didn't count the one I dropped.

34 *Press play on Track 6.*

35 Sometimes called 'Naughty Norwich'.

all to see, I was far less known. I'd be glimpsed at the back of lecture halls, ghosting through the student union with a glass of cider or shushing idiots in the library. And then I'd be gone. This all added to my aura. As did my idiosyncratic dress sense. Thick-knit zip-up cardigans, flared brown corduroys and shiny black pepperpot brogues set me apart from the long-haired layabouts who bore an uncanny resemblance to the Guildford Four and some of the Birmingham Six – Irish long-haired layabouts 'wrongfully' convicted of bombing England.

It was a time of sex, drums and rock and roll, and these three things (or four things depending on whether you count 'rock and roll' as one item or two) provided the backdrop to a very crazy time. I know for a fact that I would have developed a pretty impressive booze habit and had full sex had it not been for the fact I was expected home for 6 to 6.30.

You'll notice I said 'full sex'. Oh, I'd dabbled alright. Gentlemanliness prevents me from recounting some of the early incidents involving my nascent but powerful sexuality, but suffice to say, I was no frigid. I did quite a lot of kissing, some of it vigorous enough to chap lips (mine and hers). On other occasions, I enjoyed erotic and informative afternoons with a student whose essays I was writing. Years ago, I'd have been too prudish to discuss these sexual experiences in print, but hitting 50 has given me a new candidness. I'm happy to recall those eye-opening afternoons, with me and Jemima sitting bollock naked on her bed – me exploring her body with my quivering hands while she coquettishly feigned indifference by reading album sleeves or smoking.

Young I may have been, but I was confident enough to speak my mind. This strutting, young, cockcertain Alan would often dish out compliments as he perused and felt her body.

'You're a really busty woman, Jem,' I once said. 'One of the bustiest on campus.'

'Thanks,' she said through her cigarette.

'You've got quite a long torso, but your legs aren't in the least bit thick. Believe me, if I didn't have lectures, I'd love to kiss your back from top to bottom and from side to side. Also diagonally.'

Things like that.

And I knew how to party. Typically, I'd press a blade crease into my cords,[36] comb my thick hair past my ears like a glossy hat (the style at the time) before pitching up fashionably late to a house party, where my appearance through the frosted glass of the door would provide hushed whispers of anticipation inside.

Perhaps subconsciously aware that I'd soon become a disc jockey (DJ), I'd bring albums with me and sit in front of the record player, treating my fellow carousers to the latest cuts. And what cuts! You couldn't pigeon-hole me if you tried. The Swingle Singers, Nana Mouskouri, John Denver, The Seekers, The New Seekers, and then I'd throw them a curveball with some Steeleye Span. And all the while I'd sing along at a steadily increasing volume. (My warm tenor actually improved many of the tracks, some of which were marred by the rock stars of the time adopting a screechy higher register.) I'd do all this while getting roaring drunk on a Watneys Party Four – it was four pints of foaming beer in a can or, with Shaw's Lemonade, six pints of shandy. What's more, I knew a lot about my selected artists and would regale the fellow partygoers with interesting facts about the artists we were listening to.

_____

36 You could have sliced cucumber with it, were it not for the lint.

On one occasion, I woke up to find my records had disappeared, no doubt pilfered by a new convert to my fresh rock sounds. Although it was only 9pm, the party had completely wound down, with guests no doubt annoyed into leaving by the noisy party going on next door.

Fun as these times were, I'd begun to grow disillusioned with university life. My relationship with Jemima had burned brightly (certainly on my part), but our encounters stopped when we had a blazing row (ah, the passion of youth) on the subject of female armpit hair on which I had – and have – pretty trenchant views. I'm in full agreement that women should enjoy sexual equality with men and not feel expected to live up to an unrealistic ideal, but if you're a lady and you don't shave your pits, you look like a ruddy bloke. End of.

To be honest, the end of this affair came as a blessed relief. I'd experienced a COLOSSAL sexual enlightenment, learning much about my own capabilities and the ins and outs of female anatomy, but Jemima was undeniably one of those uppity, over-confident types who think they can live by their own rules. Listeners to my current radio show (don't worry, we'll come to that!) will know that I actively relish the regimented parameters and enforced norms of broadcast media.

Smoking 'doobies', buying books second-hand and getting out of bed after midday is all well and good (it isn't), but it's far from productive. These people might be able to tell you which French films John Luc Picard was in, but I bet you any money they wouldn't be able to reattach a stop cock if it came loose. *Utterly* useless people.

My measure of success – and it's stood me in pretty good stead over the years – is how well someone would cope in the post-apocalyptic aftermath of a nuclear war. Trust me, when it comes to staving off radiation poisoning, repopulating the human race or restoring some semblance of sanitation, having an encyclopaedic knowledge of subtitled films is going to be pretty low on the agenda. I'd much rather stand shoulder to shoulder with someone whose video collection featured one video of *The Goonies* and another of *The Tuxedo* with Jackie Chan but who was a Polish plumber.

That's why students and their incessant status quo bashing are so wrong. Challenging convention should be left to those of us who truly understand convention – and you can only understand convention if you've stuck rigidly to it 99% of the time. That's basic.

I regretted going to university deeply. Education is clearly important (we're repeatedly told by those who have a vested interest), but it's borderline self-indulgent to devote several years of your life to a single subject. That kind of blinkered obsession with one topic at the expense of all others doesn't sit easily with me. I say that as a man who can gen up on any subject to university standard in an hour and then chair a radio phone-in on it that informs *and* entertains. Wikipedia has made university education all but pointless.

My mind was already on the next exciting stage of my life. What would I become? How would I make my mark? I still didn't know. But as I bellowed from a park bench to everyone and no one after another Party Four one night – 'Alan Partridge is coming!' (The same phrase I'd hear shouted up the stairs when I turned up at parties.)

4.

CAROL

***

THUMP, THUMP, THUMP, WENT my heart, like Phil Collins hitting one of his drums. My breathing was shallow, my limbs were shaking and my sweating palms were crying out for the absorptive powers of a chamois leather. I don't think I'd ever been so nervous.

The date was 13 April 1978 and I, Partridge was about to be wed. My intended? A female by the name of Carol Parry.

Our relationship was to be given full legal status in St Edmund's Church in the Norfolk village of Caistor St Edmund. We'd been to visit the previous summer and had both fallen madly in love with the place – Carol for its pretty graveyard, its cherry blossom and its old-world charm; me for its ample parking and easy access to junction 5 of the A47.

Of course there were limitations too, most notably the lack of wheelchair access. And while all of our guests were able bodied, the marriage was still nine months away – ample time for one (or more) of them to be involved in a serious road traffic accident or develop a degenerative brain disease.

In the end we decided to follow our hearts and book it. Besides, we figured that if anyone did end up paralysed come next spring, our two ushers – one taking the feet, the other the hands – could easily carry them into the church in a safe and dignified manner.

The intervening months passed in a blur, until suddenly the day had come. I rose early, breakfasted on an egg medley (one poached, one boiled, one baked), changed and headed off to St Edmund's. I got there with just two hours to spare. For what seemed like an eternity I wandered around the grounds of the church, killing time, trailed by an almost constant stream of – without wishing to be crude – my own bum gas.

Soon enough, though, the guests arrived. I smiled to myself as I noticed that none had succumbed to any form of disability. And as the clock struck three minutes past eleven, a hush fell over the congregation. There, at the end of the aisle, was Carol. Clad in a pleasant white dress, her lace veil glistening in the sunlight like some sort of semi-transparent burka, she really did look a thousand dinars.

Half an hour later, and despite a ceremony which I felt had been deliberately marred by the vicar's lisp, we were man and wife. But as I locked lips with my comely bride, tasting her distinctive spittle in my mouth, little did I realise that we would never be this happy again.[37]

***

---

37 With the exception of a Hoseasons holiday to Bournemouth in 1979. Consistently excellent intercourse.

There'd been girls before,[38] of course there had (look at me for goodness sake!), but no one like Carol. Carol just 'got' me.

We'd met in southern Norwich at a local café called Rita's. I was at polytechnic at the time and had popped in for a bite to eat (Rita made some of the best toast around) on my way back from Scottish country dancing practice.

I placed my order – 'Toast please, Rita. Just been to dancing' – handed over my dosh and took a seat at my usual table. As I plonked my aching limbs down on the chair (SCD had been horribly gruelling this week), I saw a young lady/old girl stood nearby. She was fashionably turned out and had brown hair that was so glossy it genuinely wouldn't have looked out of place at a dog show. Immediately I wanted to know more.

In her right hand, she had a cup of tea. And in her left, she didn't. But something about the way she was looking at that cuppa didn't add up. She seemed somehow disillusioned. Yes, the tea had that layer of scum that comes from adding the water before the milk, but something inside me said it wasn't that. I just had to find something to say to her. But what?

Suddenly my mind, normally so richly populated with premium quality chat, had gone completely blank. She turned to go, the swirl of her glossy hair revealing a neck bejewelled with moles. It was now or never. But just as I thought I'd missed my chance, it was as if I went into auto-pilot. Before I knew what I was doing, I had gone over and started talking to her.

'Tea and coffee are okay,' I said, casually. 'But they're not the be-all and end-all. Surely there's room in life for a third caffeinated beverage option?'

---

38 *Press play on Track 7.*

Suddenly I came out of auto-pilot. What the hell was I doing?! In the ten years since I'd come up with that view, how many people had ever agreed with me? I'll tell you how many – zilch. At best it provoked an indifferent grunt, at worst it had cost me friendships. It was chat suicide.

Or so I thought.

'I know,' she said, her brown hair even glossier in close-up. 'I've been saying the same thing for years.'

Cha-ching! Instantly my confidence returned to its normal level. Then just carried on soaring; soaring like an eagle that didn't care if it went so high that it blacked out. Within seconds I found myself sharing another of my ace theories – that it was time to go beyond salt and pepper and begin the search for a third primary condiment.

This time she disagreed (she actually got quite angry), but it didn't matter. By now a bond had been formed, a bond that nothing – save for 16 years of attritional bickering and one pretty choice piece of philandering (hers, see Chapter 15, the bitch) – would ever be able to undo.

***

Those first couple of years flew by like a car doing 50 in a 30 zone. Maybe even 60 in a 30 zone. Depends who you ask. We were the principals in our very own Norwich-based Hollywood romcom. She was a thinking man's Meg Ryan, I was a non-Jewish Billy Crystal.

We soon moved in together, and it was when we did that I took another giant leap into the warm waters of adulthood. A gentleman doesn't dwell on such things, but let's just say that when two healthy and hygienic adults enjoy two bottles of wine on an empty stomach, strip naked, lie on the kitchen floor and place their genitals within spitting distance of one another, there are going to be fireworks.

I'll admit that there was a certain awkwardness to those early romps. Whereas I was flying my first sorties into sexual territory, Carol had been hymen-free for the best part of six years. My caution didn't last long, though, and within about three months I was able to perform my duties quietly, competently and with a minimum of fuss.

With things continuing to go well, it seemed only logical (I sound like Spock!) to proceed to the next step – marriage. So, in early 1977 I cycled the 26 miles to Carol's parents' house to meet with her father and request his daughter's hand in marriage. But when I got there I was on the receiving end of an almighty curveball.

'Hello, Alan,' said Carol's dad, Keith.

'Hello, Alan,' said Carol's mum, Stella, not bothering to think of a greeting of her own.

Within seconds, I had nodded back at them. I would have spoken, but I'd just cycled the equivalent of a full marathon.

'What brings you out this way?'

I put my hand up as if to say, 'Give me a minute, will you, Keith? I've just cycled the equivalent of a full marathon.'

Yet no sooner had I got my breath back than I spotted something truly incredible. Sat on the lawn, as bold as brass, was a brand new FlyMo. Now not only did I not know Keith was getting a FlyMo, I didn't even know he was *considering* it.

I was completely floored. This machine was science fiction brought to life. It was based, of course, on the original design for Sir Christopher Cockerell's hovercraft. And you really did get a sense of that – apparently it simply glided across the turf, as light as a feather, as nimble as a ballerina. I'd even heard rumours that owners didn't mind the back-breaking job of collecting up the cuttings afterwards. And that speaks volumes. Clearly, it was an honour to mow with.

Of course I was so distracted by this turn of events that I never did get his permission. I did make another attempt the following month, though. I faxed through a request to his office. But I'd got the extension number wrong and it went to a different man.

***

The most profound moment of my life was still to come, though.[39] And I'll never forget the moment I heard the news.

I was banging about in the cellar, trying to find a pewter tankard that a friend of mine, Pete Gabitas, had suggested could be worth a fair bit of money. Sweaty, angry and pretty pissed off, I was not in the best of moods. Carol approached with a glass of lemonade, but it was homemade and I preferred the bottled fizzy kind so I took it without saying anything. Straight away, she looked hurt and I could tell she was troubled by something.

'Out with it, Carol,' I said. 'I'm trying to find a ruddy tankard here.'

'Alan,' she said. 'I've fallen –'

Freezeframe!

Let me tell you something about Carol. Over the years I spent with her, I learnt that 'I've fallen' was an opening gambit that could go one of two ways. One was very good, the other very bad. There was no middle ground. On the bad side, the sentence could end, '... off some step-ladders' or '... out of love with you'. On the good? '... for one of your practical jokes' or ...

---

39 *Press play on Track 8.*

Unfreeze!

'… pregnant.'

She was with child, and I was to be a dad. I'm told that some men have written entire books about the experience of becoming a father. And while that's clearly too much, there's certainly plenty to be said on the subject.

This child, my first, was Fernando. He was conceived in January 1980, the same month that President Carter announced a grain embargo against the USSR. Carol and I had been hiking and stopped for a toilet break behind a large boulder on Helvellyn. One thing led to another and soon we'd taken off our Gore-Tex trousers[40] and were having, for want of a better phrase, full sexual intercourse. (I should add that before getting 'hot and heavy' we'd moved a good metre due east of the piddle zone.)

As to how it happened? Well, Carol hadn't been on the pill, so I can only hazard a guess that the prophylactic had got punctured in the cut and thrust of what was some fairly robust lovemaking. Not that we cared. We were to be parents! In just under nine months I would be welcoming a child into the world in much the same way as I would one day welcome the guests on to my primetime BBC chat show. Namely, very warmly indeed. (And ideally with the musical backing of a 22-piece house band.)

The early stages of the pregnancy were equally tough for both of us. For the first ten weeks Carol suffered from almost incessant nausea, not to mention frequent bouts of oral vomiting. While, for my part, I was having hell's own job getting a reasonable quote for a new fan belt.

---

40 But not our boots – there was a fair bit of shingle underfoot.

Eventually, though, things settled down (I ended up going with NDB Autos on King Street) and we could begin to enjoy learning about the different stages of the foetus's growth. One week it was the size of a pea, another a walnut, then a plum, an apple, a beef tomato, by which time the novelty of being able to equate my child's size to the mass of a common fruit or vegetable had really started to razz me off.

When the birth came, though, I have to confess that I didn't find it especially traumatic. After all, I'd been through it myself some 25 years earlier, and that experience (see page 3) *seemed* to stand me in good stead. Carol, on the other hand, wasn't quite so keen. It took her two days and two nights to deposit our first-born from her loins. But finally, almost as if he knew there were only minutes left on my car-park ticket, Fernando Partridge was born, weighing in at 9lbs 4oz (roughly the size of nine one-pound bags of sugar).

There he was, his skin covered in a thick film of my wife's innards. Tears streamed down my face. I was so happy I wanted to shout it from the rooftop. But at the same time I knew that that afternoon's downpour would have made the slate tiles so slippery that achieving any kind of purchase would have been impossible. Equally, I was acutely aware of the car-parking situation mentioned above.

After a while (a bit too long actually) I was awarded my child and I cradled him against the crook of my elbow. He was well swaddled so I didn't have to worry about getting any of Carol's guts on my shirt. We stood at the window, me and my son, my son and I. The night sky was straining to get into the room but couldn't because of the glass. I could at least protect him from that.

I looked up at the starry night and knew what I must do. I closed my eyes and began to sing very, very quietly, for the first time, to my infant son.

'There was something in the air that night, the stars were bright, Fernando. They were shining there for you and me ...'

And at that point, I broke down. To this day, my inability to sing the full chorus irks me because I'd just realised that I could change the next bit, 'for liberty', to 'for Carol P', which I thought would be quite nice. But I'd turned to look at Carol and she looked so happy and proud, it made my throat constrict and fill up with tears. I handed the child back to a nurse and ran off to the toilets so I wouldn't be seen, throwing my head back on the way to shout, 'I'm a *father*, you *mothers*!'

I also have a daughter, whose birth invoked similar feelings.[41]

---

41 Denise.

5.

HOSPITAL RADIO

***

IN 1967 I MISDIAGNOSED myself with cancer of the ball bag. In every other respect I was a perfectly normal youth – I was active, I had a good diet, I was pubing well – but one day I found a lump.

For three long days, I felt the cold hand of death on my shoulder. Lost in the depths of despair I tried to figure out what I had done to deserve this. I wasn't an evil person. The worst thing I'd ever done was kick a pig.[42] It's not even as if I wanted to live a particularly long life. As a child I would have been satisfied to reach my mid 30s. To be honest, I just wanted to best Christ.

---

42 School trip to Heston Farm, 1964. I maintain it was self-defence.

Yet it seemed I wouldn't get the chance. As I sat in the doctor's waiting room, I pulled out a notepad and began to draw up my final will and testament. It was almost as if, even at the age of 12, I was somehow aware of the tax implications of dying intestate.

But before the pencil lead had dried on the paper, I was spared. A quick medical fondle by Dr Armitage had identified that the suspected tumour was nothing more sinister than an infected paper cut – a result, I later realised, of a clandestine word-search puzzle done under my duvet after lights off. The heat from my head-mounted caver's torch had made it impractical to continue without removing my jim-jams. And it was then that I must have nicked my scrotum.

I may have cheated death on that bitter February morn, but I had learnt a valuable lesson. I had learnt what it felt like to stare death in the face (and also what it felt like to have its cold hand on your shoulder). And I believe it was this knowledge that helped me make such an unmitigated success of my first job in broadcasting (read on).[43]

***

Snowflakes fell from the sky like tiny pieces of a snowman who had stood on a landmine.[44] My wipers scurried across my windscreen, back and forth, back and forth, back and – my god, was that the time? I had just five minutes to get to work. And so help me god, nothing (other than perhaps the weather,

---

43 *Press play on Track 9.*
44 If he was particularly unlucky it would have been a Bouncing Betty. These horrible little devices are designed to spring three feet into the air before exploding and inflicting the maximum number of casualties on an enemy. I think they've won awards.

the roadworks at the top of Chalk Hill Road, and the distance I still had to travel) was going to stop me.

For the last three years I had been a hospital radio DJ at St Luke's in Norwich. It was a smashing little hospital and many of the people who went in there didn't end up dead. I loved my job, though. And despite being unpaid, I'd been quick to negotiate free parking and the right to jump the queue in the canteen – this never went down well, but the patients were often too weak to oppose me.

But I hated being late, because the inmates needed me. And while no one would be silly enough to claim that my trademark mix of great chat, decent pop and amusing home-made jingles could take *all* their pain away, it did take the edge off and was definitely more helpful than homeopathy.

Six minutes later I pressed the red button and spoke into the mic(rophone).

'Whoa! Yeah! Call off the search party. I'm *here*. It's one minute past eight and this is Alan Partridge! Or should I say the *late* Alan Partridge! Perhaps not, because that would suggest I was dead. And I am not! But here's a list of people who are …'

You'll notice from this that I had a much brasher broadcasting style in my early days, my speech peppered with laughs and shouts and whoops. Soon after *Good Morning Vietnam* came out, I'd even begin shows with the holler: 'Gooood morning St Luuuuuke's!!!!!!' However, I was upbraided for this and told it called to mind a war zone littered with the injured and diseased – which was precisely why I'd thought it was so appropriate.

As DJing gigs go, it was far harder than people realise. Yes, you have a captive audience, but you also have a listenership that is almost exclusively poorly. And that makes song selection a delicate business. One wrong step and you could instantly offend a fairly meaty percentage of patients. Just take the number one singles from my first year in the job, 1975. Almost all of them were capable of upsetting someone. Art Garfunkel's 'I Only Have Eyes for You' (the recently blinded); David Essex's 'Hold Me Close' (burns victims); The Stylistics' 'Can't Give You Anything' (the terminally ill); Tammy Wynette's 'Stand By Your Man' (paralysed women, paralysed homosexual men).

In my time at the hospital, I was broadcasting live during the deaths of some 800 patients. It's a record that stands to this day. Industry awards and repeated praise from *TV Quick* magazine are all very well, but it gives me immense pride to think that the final voice those 800+ people heard may have been mine, as I read the traffic and travel or introduced a clip from my favourite *Goon Show* LP.

I spent 94 wonderful months behind the mic at St Luke's. But by autumn 1983, much like most of the patients on the Marie Curie wing, my days were numbered. I guess I always knew that as word of my competence leaked out across Anglia, my head might be hunted. And so it was that in September I answered the phone to local media mogul Rich Shayers.

'Alan, you've done your time on hospital radio. It's time to spread your wings.'

'What, like a bird?' I asked, keen to know more.

'I'm starting a new station and I want you on board.'

'Will I get loads of salary?' I blurted. I was young and unsure how to phrase questions relating to remuneration.

'Just swing by my office tomorrow and we can hammer all that out.'

'Great,' I replied. 'I'll bring the hammers!' And with that, my career changed forever.

But there was to be a moving post-script to this chapter in my life. And I'll tell you about it now. At my leaving do, with the party in full swing, I stopped the music, climbed atop a chair and gave the hospital staff an emotional, heartfelt guarantee. I pledged, no matter how famous I became, that while there was still air in my lungs, I would come back and do my show for a minimum of one week every year.

I may not have been able to donate money, but in some ways I was able to donate something far more powerful. I was able to donate chat (to a maximum value of one week each year). And with that, I picked up my coat and left the building, the warm applause of my colleagues still ringing in my ears like a big church bell.

Sadly, circumstance has meant that I've not been able to get back to the hospital in the intervening 31 years. In the main that's down to me – work commitments have made it simply unfeasible. But for the record I'd like to point out that the hospital is not entirely blameless itself. In 2001 it moved to a new site around the corner from the University of East Anglia. The studios from where I used to broadcast my show were reduced to rubble. And I think most reasonable people would agree that by allowing that to happen the NHS Trust effectively voided my promise.

6.
LOCAL/
COMMERCIAL RADIO

***

RICH SHAYERS HAD CONVINCED me to do something more worthwhile than providing a soothing backdrop of music and companionship for those in need[45] – so I'd accepted his offer of a job DJing for a fledgling station. The set-up reminded me very much of the buccaneering can-do spirit of Radio Caroline – maverick disc jockeys flouting regulations to give listeners something new and fresh. My job wasn't on pirate radio – that would have been a criminal offence. It was the in-store radio station for a branch of record shop Our Price.

It was a pilot scheme way, way, way, way ahead of its time (indeed, it folded within weeks). But the team! It's my

---

45 *Press play on Track 10.*

privilege to say that these were some of the most dazzling young broadcasters I've ever had the pleasure of working with. They were scientific in their understanding of good radio – they were radiologists.

Check out this roll call.

Paul Stubbs. An aficionado of US shock jocks and personality DJs, he sadly never knew what he had. He left the business shortly after Our Price and now works for Hertz car rental. Still follows the US game and is a fountain of knowledge on call-ins and quiz ideas. Invaluable.

Phil Schofield. Phil was always the baby of the group and had a snotty-nosed quality that we bullied out of him. Now better known as the presenter of TV's *This Morning*, Phil was back then a bit of a know-it-all and was brought down a peg or two by off-air pranks such as having his new shoes filled with piss. There was no smoking gun/dripping willy, so Stubbs got away with it. It was a tough time for Phil and he never talks about it. Phil, if you're reading, why not give me a call?

Jon Boyd. That voice! Warm, reassuring and deliciously transatlantic, Jon later turned his back on radio and has made quite the name for himself as a voiceover artist with, by his own admission, a pretty limited range. His voice can be heard in the lift of an art gallery in Bath. He tells me he takes women there and then mimes the words 'Doors Closing' or 'Third Floor' over the sound of the recording. Freaks them out. Cracking SOH.

Brian Golding. 'Bonkers' Bri combined a wacky sense of humour with a genuine mental illness and went on to co-host *Drive Time* on Signal Radio before killing himself in 1991.

***

As a team, I think we all knew then that we had something special, and that sense of worth was a shot in the arm for a young, thrusting Alan Partridge. With that shot – easily as powerful as an intravenous drug like 'heroin', 'smack' or 'gear' – I was driven to go out into the world of broadcasting and succeed. Nothin' was gonna stop me!

***

1984–1987. Not much happened here.

***

It's 1988 and a young, side-parted young radio reporter is pinning a pretty rude lower-division football manager down on his team's disgraceful disciplinary record.

'Six red cards in as many games,' says the reporter. 'Why do you continue to tolerate this culture of hooliganism?'

The manager tries to worm his way off the hook by disputing the figures. 'They're yellow cards,' he says, 'And that's actually a pretty good behaviour record.'

But the reporter has the figures written down on a notepad and won't be deterred. In the end, the manager loses his rag – 'You bloody idiot' – pulls the top off the microphone and throws it at the reporter, but it doesn't hurt anyway because it's made of grey foam. The reporter broadcasts the story that night. It was, everyone agreed, great radio – and although the reporter had to issue a full apology and retraction for the red/yellow card error, it burnished his reputation as one to watch.[46]

That reporter was Alan Partridge. The manager? The name escapes me, but it must have been fairly local because I remember being pleased I'd driven there without stopping for a toilet break. I can't remember what he looked like either or what colour his team played in, just that he had a strong regional accent and used such a hilarious mix of tenses – 'he gets the ball and he's gone and kicked it' – that he sounded like a malfunctioning robot at the end of a space-fi movie.

So what had happened to me? How had I gone from the cosseted glamour of Our Price radio to the snarling, balls-out toughness of sports reporting? Well, I'd always been a keen sports fan. It seemed to me that the world of sport – with its reliance on stats, facts, trivia and rules – provided modern man with certainty and structure. Just as a well-fitting jock-strap cups the cock and balls of a sportsman, so sport cradled me. You know where you are with sport. It's good.

And it's all so logical. Watch a play by Shakespeare or go to a modern art gallery, and no one has the faintest idea what the hell is going on.

Take Shakespeare. Not a play goes by without one character whispering something about another character that is *clearly audible* to that character. By virtue of the fact it has to be loud enough for the audience to hear it, it's inconceivable that it can't also be heard by the character in question. It's such an established technique in Shakespeare's canon people just think no one will notice. Well I've got news for you – this guy did.

Sport, on the other hand, is straightforward. In badminton, if you win a rally, you get one point. In volleyball, if you win a

<hr>

46 Listen to.

rally, you get one point. In tennis, if you win a rally, you get 15 points for the first or second rallies you've won in that game, or 10 for the third, with an indeterminate amount assigned to the fourth rally other than the knowledge that the game is won, providing one player is two 10-point (or 15-point) segments clear of his opponent. It's clear and simple.

But that wasn't what catapulted me to local radio glory. No, what catapulted me to local radio glory was the fact I'd been uninvited to a wedding at the eleventh hour (reason not given), and had a day to kill. Happily, I received a call from a friend called Barry Hethersett, who moonlit as a radio reporter on Saxon Radio in Bury St Edmunds. He'd heard I was free that day and asked me to fill in on his slot because he had to attend the funeral of one his parents. I agreed and he gave me a lift to the station, dressed in a smart suit but wearing a buttonhole flower, which I felt was in bad taste.

I was introduced to the station controller, Peter Crowther, very much one of the old school,[47] and a man who could make or break careers like *that*.[48] Eager to validate my sports credentials, I'd dug out a prize-winning thought-piece (or essay) I'd written on sport as a schoolboy. Labelled 'brilliant' by one of the finest headmasters I've worked under, the piece took as its starting point the truism that there are lots of sports, each of them different from each other, before providing a pretty thorough breakdown of the main ones and peppering it with facts and figures. Faux-leatherbound, I brought it with me.

Crowther read the first page with bemused interest before – in a clear indication that he was still on the sauce – bursting out laughing. Very much one of the old school. But it was a

---

47 Biographical shorthand for: alcoholic.
48 I just did a click with my fingers.

laugh that said, 'Boy, this guy's good.' I'd proved I knew the subject inside out.

Within the hour, I was broadcasting to the whole of east East Anglia, reading out sports reports direct from Teletext, 'throwing' to a pre-recorded interview with a 15-year-old cycle champ and then reading out greyhound racing results, which I later learnt had been made up by the still-laughing Crowther.[49]

Hethersett – perhaps still crushed by the death of his mother or father – never returned to Saxon Radio. And they wouldn't have wanted him anyway. I'd shown my mettle and taken to it like a duck to water. (Or, as former Olympic swimmer Duncan Goodhew says, 'like a Dunc to water', which isn't that funny but forgivable as Duncan continues to be an inspiration to hairless children nationwide.)[50]

Sports reporting was a dizzying but exhilarating slog.[51] I was spending my Saturday and Sunday afternoons at horse trials, football matches, squash tournaments ... I was becoming a familiar voice on radio and, yes, people wanted a piece of me.

I ascended the career ladder like a shaven Jesus ascending to his rightful place in the kingdom of Heaven. I was poached by Radio Broadland (Great Yarmouth), Hereward Radio (Peterborough), Radio Orwell (Ipswich) and eventually Radio Norwich.

---

49 He explained that this was 'radio tradition', and I diligently kept the practice up until years later at Radio 4, when I was challenged about the existence of Wetwipple Dog Track. A subsequent BBC disciplinary was only made bearable by the presence of the kindest BBC HR adviser to ever discipline me. NB – false greyhound racing results are *not* a radio tradition.

50 I once retorted with 'Alright! Keep your hair on!' (He has chronic alopecia.) He wasn't that impressed.

51 *Press play on Track 11.*

There, my brief extended beyond sport to a bi-monthly[52] magazine show called *Scoutabout*, which I took over from amateur DJ and Scout obsessive Peter Flint.

'Fall in, Troop! Fall in!' I'd shout into the microphone. And then as the specially commissioned theme music ended with a rom-po-pom-pom, I'd say, 'Aaaaaaaat ease.' And the show – a high-spirited hour aimed at Boy Scouts and to a smaller extent Girl Guides – would begin.

It was great, great fun, but my sports reporting was obviously my top priority. As such, I became a valuable and well-known asset to Radio Norwich. The controller there, Bett Snook, was a chain-smoking woman who sounded like a chain-smoking man whose chain smoking had called for an emergency laryngectomy.

She gave me some solid gold advice. 'Dickie Davies, Barry Davies, Elton Welsby, Jimmy Hill, David Coleman, Tony Gubba, Ron Pickering, Ron Atkinson, Bob Greaves, Stuart Hall, Gerald Sinstadt. What do they have in common?'

'They're all sports broadcasters,' I said. 'Some more successful[53] than others.'[54]

'And what's the difference between them?' She sat back in her chair, smoking her cigarette using her mouth.

'Some are more successful[55] than others,'[56] I repeated.

'No, more than that. Think about it. They're different *types* of sports broadcaster. Some are anchors, others commentators, some are analysts, some are reporters.'

---

52 'Bi-monthly' is a funny word. Twice a month or once every two months? In this case, it depended on audience demand. Mainly the latter.
53 Dickie Davies.
54 Elton Welsby.
55 Barry Davies.
56 Tony Gubba.

I realised what she was getting at.

'Alan, it's all very well being Norwich's Mr Sport [which I was]. But you're spreading yourself too thin. Work out what it is in sport you want to be, and then be the best at it.'

So I did. And I was. I became the best sports-interviewer-cum-reporter/anchor on British terrestrial television.

***

In 1990, I was fortunate enough to see a steward badly hurt at an archery competition. In a funny kind of way – and at first, it was very funny – this single mishap provided the spring-board to a career at what was, in my view, the biggest publicly funded broadcasting corporation in the United Kingdom. The BBC.

I'd been extremely reluctant to report on the contest, but had agreed to cover it live as Taverham Archery Club was playing host to the British Archery Championships that year and this was apparently a big deal for Norfolk.

'Whether you regard it as an ancient art form, a woodland hunting technique or just a big version of darts, this is *archery*,' I boomed. 'And we'll be following every twang, whoosh and gadoyng of what is shaping up to be a *classic* British Archery Championships.'

It was sports broadcasting with real panache, that much should be obvious, but it was nothing out of the ordinary. That was until, mid-way through the event, second favourite Chris Curtis accidentally discharged his bow and it issued a rod of arrow into the arm of a female steward. (And for the billionth time, I didn't *accuse* Curtis of being drunk, I merely speculated that he *might* be drunk.)

Suddenly, I was hurled into the middle of a breaking news story. This was live radio and all ears were literally on me.

'The poor woman's wailing like a banshee over there and, as concerned officials gather round her to stem the flow of blood and presumably discuss what, if any, rule has been broken, I'll do my best to describe the scene.

'Basically, archers are standing round chatting – none of them have approached the stricken victim, but that's what archers do. If this was in the wild, the archers would stand there high-fiving each other while the carcass was retrieved by a young bushwacker or loyal gun dog.

'Not that she's dead. She's hit in her upper arm, which must come as some relief. If it'd been her neck, it would have been curtains for both her and the rest of the afternoon's archery action, coming to you live from Taverham.

'And while the lady steward squeals like an impaled but quiet pig, I can tell you she's gone into shock – you can see that from here. The colour's drained from her and she's all a-quiver. And actually … like "a quiver", she has an arrow in her.

'Erm … it's an unusual sight, certainly. A person lying there with a big rod coming out of them, like a human kebab or – if you prefer – some kind of lady lolly. And a not unattractive lady lolly, I must say. One that I'm sure every man here would dearly like to lick.

'But that's not to in any way trivialise what is clearly a distressing situation.

'Er … St John's ambulance are nearby. Not doing anything, of course, but I'm not sure they're trained to administer medical care. They're to a real paramedic what the Salvation Army is to a special forces soldier. Still, they look smart enough.

'And the arrow's out! The arrow is out! It's been plucked from the woman like a pointy Excalibur. Well done that man …

'Right. Next to shoot is Mark Allen ...'

When I played the tape back to Carol the next morning, she agreed (in an uncharacteristically effusive show of support) that it had been 'a powerful and moving broadcasting *tour de force*'.[57]

And she wasn't the only one impressed. With my commentary played out on BBC radio news bulletins up and down the land, I was thrust into the national limelight. Suddenly, I was hot property.

And so it was that, six months later, I was included on a round-robin circular memo to BBC reporters, asking for applications to join the team of a new Radio 4 current affairs show. I was a wanted man!

---

57 My words. Her agreement.

7.

JOINING THE BBC

***

I'M STANDING IN FRONT of a building that is literally steeped in history. Behind me is London's swanky Regent Street, home to the Café Royal, Hamley's toy store and a genuinely impressive two-storey McDonald's.

Ahead of me, as I say, is a formidable structure, headquarters to broadcasting magnificence. Inside its browny-coloured walls are rooms, studios and cupboards that have played host to some of the greatest moments in broadcasting: *Just a Minute*, *Gardener's Question Time*, John Birt's 55th birthday party.

I'm about to start work for an organisation that needs absolutely no introduction, qualification or explanation. Reader, I'm about to work for Radio 4, the BBC1 of UK radio.[58]

***

─────────────

58 *Press play on Track 12.*

Before this big break, I'd been to London before: once for Carol's birthday when she was going through an 'unfulfilled' phase and had ideas above her/Norwich station, and another time when I had to pick up a cagoule that had found its way on to the Charlton Athletic team bus after a fractious post-match interview.

But working in the capital? This was quite unexpected. I'd received the good news during an intervention – Carol's brother Tim was drinking too much, so we'd effectively ambushed him in our lounge – and I was pleased that my own success could in some small way deflect attention from his enormous failings. To provide a bit of levity, I left the room for a moment and came back in wearing a bowler hat and umbrella, saying 'I'm going to work in London!' while marching up and down. I thought that was absolutely hilarious. After a stern word from Carol, the intervention continued in earnest and I'm delighted to say it was a success. Tim's barely touched a drop since then, apart from wine.

Although it was a Sunday, I thought it best that I telephoned every one of my Radio Norwich colleagues to tell them I'd been plucked for national stardom and I'd be leaving Norwich. It was best they found out from me, as I knew that the loss of the station's Mr Sport would hit them hard. Most of them took it well and showed tremendous stoicism, displaying almost no emotion.

I began to make arrangements for my new life. But it was only after I'd completely cleared my desk weeks later that I found out that *On the Hour* was to be a weekly show, which meant that we were only required in London on a Friday.

I spoke to the station controller of Radio Norwich, quickly unresigned and set about returning the items to my desk. There were a few snide remarks from colleagues but I was unperturbed, glad even, that I'd made the error, as the process of clearing and then restocking my workspace was an absolute pleasure. It allowed me to conduct a full stationery audit, think seriously about the strategy and ergonomics of my desk, and devise a new layout that was fresher, simpler and more logical.

The telephone was switched to the far left, on the grounds that I tended to wedge the receiver under my left jowl and use my right hand to scribble notes or gesticulate. To that end, my pen jar and notepad were migrated from the leftermost reaches of the space to a new position, just by the right hand. The computer monitor – previously slap bang in the middle – was perched in the right-hand corner, angled jauntily in my face's favour. Snacks and chocs were housed in a new Tupperware box in the top drawer, a radical departure which freed up a good quartile of the desk's surface. Staplers, hole punches, sticky-backed plastic, Post-it notes: gone, in a hard-headed cull of underused items. The angle-poise was placed – nice touch, this – on an adjoining cabinet, not impinging on the desktop at all and casting its beam from an unusual angle which gave a quality of light that was genuinely different from that of the desks of Elaine Clark (news), or Sophie DeVault (weather).

It was a pared-down and original layout that was user-friendly and looked good too. I've tried several other designs since but have honestly never bettered this one. If I have the time, I'll sketch it out and put it in the appendix, entirely free of charge.[59]

---

59 For years, I guarded the Alan Desk Design jealously, but in 2007 I concluded reluctantly that I was never going to successfully monetise the concept and so I made it – and this isn't arrogant – into my gift for the world.

It all felt like a fresh start for me. A new city, a new job, a new desk system, even a new brother-in-law who could speak clearly and wasn't over-affectionate with my kids. I was cockerel-a-hoop.

***

Radio 4's *On the Hour* was a weekly news programme with seriously big balls. It made *Newsnight* look like *Newsround* and *The Nine O'Clock News* look like *Newsround*. If other shows were a normal-sized packet of crisps, *On the Hour* was very much a grab bag. And for those of you unfamiliar with the denominations of crisp bags, that means it was large.

It was a serious break for me and I knew it.[60] I'll never forget my first week in the job. On the morning of the show I'd arrived at London's [CHECK NAME OF STATION] with nothing other than a Slazenger back-pack, a selection of snacks and sandwiches, a spare shirt and tie, a notebook, pens, pencils, pencil sharpener, first aid kit, an emergency 50p for the phone box and (I hoped) a glint in my eye.

I hopped on the tube and made my way over to the BBC. (By the way, for anyone reading this overseas or in Wales, the 'tube' is a means of public transport.)[61] The show was to be recorded in the august surroundings of Broadcasting House. And what a building! As soon as you walked through the

---

60 *Press play on Track 13.*
61 Comprised of a hidden network of mysterious subterranean tunnels – how did they get there? Where do they end? – it's at work for 18 hours a day hurtling busy Londoners around their capital at almost twice the speed of walking. Meanwhile at night, with all the humans gone, it is said that the station platforms become a place for the capital's innumerate rats to gather for bouts of high-energy unprotected sex. It's basically dogging for rats.

doors, you could tell these people knew what they were doing. Quite simply, the place stank of news.

But this reek of pure BBC quality only added to my sense of apprehension. With only an hour to go until the opening editorial meeting, nerves fluttered around my stomach. It's a hard feeling to describe but it was almost as if someone had put moths in my tummy.

It was of some comfort to me that I knew one of the team already. *On the Hour* was edited by the redoubtable (love that word) Steven Eastwood. I'd met him when I came up to London for my job interview. Things had begun, as they so often do at the BBC, with a handshake.

'That's a good handshake you've got there, Alan.'

'Thanks,' I replied. 'I practise it in front of the mirror.'

'And how was your journey?'

'Real good, thanks, Stephen,' I said, briefly forgetting that his name was actually spelt 'Steven'.

'So tell me, young man, how much do you want this job?' he probed.

'What's it out of? Ten?'

But Eastwood didn't want a number – if he had, my answer would have been ten, maybe eleven – he just wanted to see a flicker of true passion. Thankfully for me, that's exactly what he saw. And incredibly that was all it took – along with a 90-minute interview, a written exam, a series of psychometric tests and the submission of a full portfolio of my work – for him to offer me a job. Well from that moment onwards, our professional relationship went from strength to strength to strength to strength to strength.

On a personal level things were slightly different. He and I were just chalk and Cheddar. At the height of the show's popularity I was receiving five, sometimes six, pieces of fan mail a quarter. It was pretty relentless and if I'm honest, I think it stuck in Eastwood's craw. Sure, I tried to build bridges from time to time. I'd take him to the BBC bar and order us each a pint of bitter and a meat-based sandwich. But he'd take a few sips (of his drink) before claiming he was 'dead drunk' and needed to go home.

Maybe it was possible to get drunk that quickly. I've certainly heard it said that Chinamen can't hold their booze. But all these years later, when I think back to those aborted evenings out, there's one tiny detail that just doesn't add up: Eastwood wasn't Chinese.

Okay, he had a soft spot for a portion of Chicken Chow Mein on a Friday night. But, be honest, who doesn't? And besides, even the most berserk Sinophile would struggle to argue that ingesting industrial amounts of egg noodles actually makes you Chinese. No, Eastwood was from Hertfordshire, and there was nothing anybody could do about it.

But as I made my way to that first editorial meeting, I knew I still had my fellow reporters to wow. Questions tumbled around my head like trainers in the washing machine I have mentioned on two previous occasions. Would I pass muster? Would I cut the mustard? Would I pass the mustard?

I was panicking. There was no point spending my time conflating two well-known phrases or sayings into a third that, while making grammatical sense, had no value as a metaphor. Or was there? I thought for a moment. No, there definitely wasn't.

Somehow I needed to chill the eff out. If I was a drug-doer I would probably have spliffed myself into the middle of next week. But I wasn't (although – full disclosure – I had taken two paracetemols from my first aid kit and administered a splodge of Savlon to an ankle graze sustained at London's [CHECK NAME OF STATION].)

In the end I sorted myself out by using a simple but effective visualisation technique taught to me by either Paul McKenna or Russ Abbott, I forget which. Hang on, no, it was Ali Bongo. Taken from the teachings of Buddha (I'm guessing here), the idea is to imagine yourself as someone with the characteristic you desire. In the case of Bongo, he would think of a cuddly old cat lying in the sunshine. Before a big show he would spend 15 minutes purring, licking his imaginary paws and hanging his head over a bin trying to bring up fur balls. And by the end of it? He was as cool as beans.

For me, though, cats weren't the answer. No, the answer was Roger Moore. I locked myself in a toilet cubicle and spent the best part of a quarter of an hour visualising myself in *A View to a Kill*, taking on the evil Max Zorin, sailing under the ocean in a submarine disguised as an iceberg and having it off with Grace Jones, the first black woman I have ever slept with.

And by the time someone started banging on the door wondering what all the noise was about, I had reached a zen-like state of calm. As it turns out, though, I was right to be anxious about the editorial meeting. There were some seriously large-brained people in that room. Those in attendance included Christopher Morris (anchor), Rosie May (environment), Kevin Smear (roving reporter), Peter O'Hanraha-hanrahan (economics editor) and yours truly (sport, plus the Paralympics).

I picked a chair and sat down quietly and effectively. It was a good start but I needed to do more. I took a deep breath and prepared to introduce myself. But as soon as I heard the level of their chit-chat, I froze. They were using words, ideas and concepts that you simply never heard in Norfolk. Not even in Norwich.

I resolved to keep my mouth shut until I'd acclimatised. Phrases swirled around the room. 'Where does Labour stand on that?' 'It's over for Milosevic.' 'Alan, could you pass the biscuits?' 'This Rodney King thing is going to be massive.' 'GDP's down by 0.5% this quarter.' 'Alan? The biscuits.' 'The Home Office aren't going to comment apparently.' 'Fine, I'll get them myself then.'

How in the name of holy living heck was I going to bust my way into this conversation? I don't know, I answered, inside my head. On the table next to me was the tea urn. Now this was a plus point because I loved tea urns. Still do. There's something very reassuring about the concept of hot beverages dispensed from a lovely big drum.[62] Of course your problem with any kind of communal drinks station is the sugar bowl. People put the spoon back in the bowl after stirring in their sugar. No problem with that, you might think. Well think again. The residual moisture acts as a caking agent, forming the granules into unsightly asymmetric clumps. Worse still, those clumps are stained a grubby brown by the tannin-rich tea. Not nice, not nice at all.

And let's not forget the germ issue. Putting a damp spoon back in the bowl is the tea-drinking equivalent of sharing a needle. And I did *not* want to end up with the tea-drinking equivalent of AIDS.

Instantly it struck me that if their 'thing' was intimidating intellect, my 'thing' could be beverage-related hygiene. Of course I later remembered that I already had a 'thing',

---

62 For a long time I'd actually lobbied to get one at home. Carol and the kids had said no. With the best will in the world, those kettle-crazed Luddites wouldn't know progress if it came up and scalded them in the face.

namely sport (plus the Paralympics). But I wasn't thinking straight, which should go some way to explaining what happened next.

Kevin Smear (roving reporter) approached. This seemed somehow appropriate because while the others had stayed where they were, he had quite literally roved over.

'Hello, Alan.'

'Hello.'

'Guys, I'm just saying hello to Alan.'

The rest of them nodded in my direction, using their heads.

'What are you doing sat over there?' said Rosie May (environment).

'Nothing much,' I smiled. 'Just thinking that you lot have probably got tea AIDS!!'

Wham! I knew it was a winner as soon as it'd left my lips. If you'd stuck me in a room with a typewriter for ten years I would never have come up with one that good. But in that room, fuelled by nothing other than raw nerves, out it plopped, fully-formed and ready to go.

Of course it wasn't a winner at all. Not being privy to my train of thought, they had no idea what this 'tea' prefix was. As far as they were concerned their new colleague had just accused them all of having AIDS. Yet they didn't have AIDS. And though the colourful lifestyle of one of them certainly put him in the 'at risk' category, he wouldn't go full-blown until 2003.

No, I was wrong to suggest they all suffered from a terminal beverage-based illness, whether that was tea AIDS, coffee cancer or hot chocolate tumours. I was so ashamed by my behaviour that I retreated into my shell like a turtle would if it realised it was about to have a car reverse over its head. (And for the record, Fernando shouldn't have let it out of its cage in the first place.) And it was in my shell that I would stay for most of my time on *On the Hour*.

To be honest, you'd find this unfriendly attitude across the whole BBC News and Current Affairs team. It saddened me because the department was populated by heroes of mine, faces I'd watched time and again on the news while eating my dinner: pork chops and gravy, beans on toast, hot pot, chicken pie and chips, maybe even a *coq au vin*, sometimes just a quick can of soup. Any meal, it doesn't matter really. I've just realised I'm listing things I have for dinner when I should be listing faces I'd seen on the news. But I'm just saying I'd seen these people on the news and respected them. But their reassuring televisual demeanour was, I realised, a facade. In person, they didn't like to mingle at all. Not even with each other.[63]

So yes, in London, I was very much in my shell. But back in Norwich, things couldn't have been more different. Anyway, this chapter's over now.

---

63 Many was the time I'd see Nicholas Witchell sitting all alone in the canteen. It was a shame, because years later I realised we both shared a love of collecting butterflies. He has an enormous collection in his London flat. I like to imagine that after a hard day following the royals, he returns home, sits in an armchair with a mug of cocoa and waits as his entire herd of butterflies greet him by flitter-fluttering their way over and landing on his naked body. But I know for a fact this can't happen because his entire collection is dead, each one attached to a display case with a single pin through the heart.

8.
A MIGHTY BIG FISH FOR A POND THIS SIZE[64]

***

'WHO ARE YOU? I don't bloody know you any more!'

Carol was shouting at me, tears streaming down her ruddy[65] cheeks, as I tried to barge past her. She grabbed at my jowls, imploring me to look at her. But she was right. This was a different Alan Partridge and he wasn't in the mood.

I eased her out of the way and put the takeaway menus – the glossy food-describing documents that she'd so carefully placed in my hands – back into the top drawer. It should have been second drawer down but I wasn't thinking straight.

---

64 *Press play on Track 14.*
65 This isn't swearing. Her cheeks were host to several burst blood vessels.

She swung me around and fanned some of my breath into her nostrils. 'Have you … been drinking??' Her voice was shaking. I turned away. I'd had a half-bottle of wine – I don't remember the colour – on the train back home and was out of control.

Friday would usually have been our takeaway night, but tonight I wasn't hungry – I'd been in the BBC club, enjoying a buffet put on to celebrate 26 years of *Tomorrow's World*. (For the uninitiated, the BBC club is a subsidised bar-cum-restaurant, laid on by licence fee payers for the talent and crew of the BBC alike. It provided a public-free environment for BBC staffers to carouse and unwind, to share ideas and to complain about working conditions. It was where a star-struck Alan Partridge would buy a sandwich most days in the hope of spotting Esther Rantzen, Andy Crane, Karl Howman.)

This was a new experience for me. I was starry-eyed, my mind addled with possibility and adventure, recognition and more adventure. Which is how I found myself seduced that night by the lure of glamour, sausage rolls and a chat with Maggie Philbin.

Not many people had turned up to the soiree – the 25th anniversary in 1990 had been a much bigger do – but I had lost track of time, arguing with Howard Stableford about the possibility of time travel, and had missed my usual train. On the next scheduled service, I thought I'd wash down the rolls with a drink. Frig it, I said aloud, why not? I work hard, it's Friday night and I want a glass of wine (still can't remember the colour).

I had some crisps as well, and the sliced potato snacks had lopped a fair bit off my appetite. I didn't want a bloody takeaway. I wanted another slice of quiche and another half of bitter. I wanted to be back in the BBC club, the happy filling in a Kate Bellingham/Judith Hann sandwich, not sat in with Carol as she decorates her face with spare rib sauce.

And when she handed me the menus, my response had been withering. 'I'm not peckish. I don't want to eat a take-away meal tonight.'

That's when she shoved me and burst into uncontrollable (but still annoying) sobs. 'Who *are* you? I don't bloody know you any more!'

Yes, reader, London had changed me. My career was going stratospheric, with millions of radio listeners hungrily eating the sound of my voice as it fed them sports-centred info. It was all so new to me. New and intoxicating and fun.

I slumped in front of the TV and Carol sat next to me, ordering a takeaway for one. Armed with a new understanding of London broadcasting, I was able to provide a kind of Director's Commentary on current affairs TV shows, pointing out what the presenters ordered from the BBC club, if they were taller/shorter than they appeared on TV and generally providing helpful info on the production process. Carol said nothing.

Sue Cook appeared on screen, and in my tipsiness I began to talk in gushing terms about her. She'd always reminded me of Jeff Archer's wife, Lady Archer. Sophisticated and demure. But having got to know her a little bit, I'd realised she had a wonderful sense of humour and had a loathing of other presenters that I found quite wonderful. I mentioned this to Carol and she ran to the bedroom, really fast and loud. I climbed into bed next to her and thought it prudent to say nothing. You really can't win with Carol sometimes.

I muttered something about heading off early the next morning to test drive the new Rover 800 with Gary who directs the Superdrug commercials and she just looked at me.

'Don't you know what day it is?'

I mentally rifled through the roller deck of red-letter days: birthdays, anniversaries, deaths. And then it hit me. I stumbled into the bathroom, splashing my face with water so cold it made me go 'Ah! Ah!' with each splash.

Tomorrow was the day of the Royal Norfolk Show, and we were to man the Elizabethan craft fair in period dress. This was a Partridge family fixture, absolutely utterly unmissable. And not just out of duty – we always had a really great day, adding '–eth' to our words to sound more Elizabethan and having a bloody good laugh about it.

Carol was right. What had I become? A Royal Norfolk Fair-forgetting ogre of a man. I slumped into the shower (which was just a curtained-off area at one end of the bath), decided not to turn it on and sobbed.[66]

***

If you'd told me in the late 80s that one day my local branch of Tandy would shut its doors to the public so that Alan Partridge could browse its electricals in peace, I'd have thought you were mad. If you'd told me that they would do this at the height of the Christmas shopping period, I'd probably have spat on your back. Yet in December 1993 and December 1994 and December 1995, this is exactly what happened. The question of course, is how …

There was no doubt about it, Carol was on the money. I had become a monster. It was as if I was one kind of person in my London life (not a monster) and an altogether different type in my Norwich life (a monster). And I'd guess that the transition between the two would have taken place somewhere in

---

66 *Press play on Track 15.*

between. Let's say Manningtree if I was on the train and Newmarket if I was driving, defaulting to Silverley if I'd plumped for the B-roads.

In London I may have been just another face in an already star-studded media landscape, but in Norwich I was now a seriously big dog. I was receiving more sexual advances than ever before, many of them from women. Every time I entered a wine bar heads would turn. Or alternatively people would just swivel their stools round so they didn't have to strain their necks.

If I'd been a philanderer, this period in my life would have been a turkey shoot. I could have gone out for a drink in any bar in Norwich and left with at least a dozen middle-aged woman plucked, gutted, and slung over my shoulder. With sex at my place to follow.

Of course the local men-folk didn't like this. Even my old Our Price buddy Paul Stubbs seemed to have his nose put out of joint. He ambled over to me one night as I was picking through some bar snacks.

'What size are your feet, Alan?'

'I'm an 11,' I replied, tossing an olive sky-ward.

'Well I suggest you buy some 12s.'

'Oh yeah? How come?'

'Because you're getting too big for your boots!'

Even accounting for the fact that I never wore boots, this was a good line. And as he ran up and down the wine bar high-fiving a random selection of other jealous males, Stubbs knew it. As I caught the olive – which admittedly had been in the air for a long time – in my mouth, I knew this had been a shot across the bows. But like so many others, it was a warning I chose to ignore.

But my new-found clout in Norfolk was probably most noticeable in my voiceover work. For years I'd played second fiddle to Pete Farley. Now this guy was good. Name any of the major advertising campaigns from '86 through to '91 (Dunfield Carpets, CDA Automotive, Arlo Wholefoods) and Farley was always there or thereabouts. All the rest of us got were the crumbs off his table.

It's not even like we could go foraging into Suffolk for scraps. Because Farley had it sewn up there too. The first of a new breed, he was truly pan-Anglian. Rumour had it that his tentacles even stretched up the fens to Cambridge. The guy was bullet-proof.

Once in every while me and the rest of the boys would meet up for a few pints. As the guest ale flowed, we'd plot how to bring him to his knees. It was nothing sinister (we weren't like that), we just wanted a fair shot at the big jobs. The exception to this – and he'll chuckle when he reads this – was fellow voiceover artist Vic Noden (think 'Asprey Motors – stunning vehicles, stunning prices').

Now Noden would really do a number on Farley. By 9pm he'd have wished every terminal illness under the sun on him. By 10pm, and with us all the worse for wear, he'd have infected the wife too. And by closing time, well, let's just say Farley's kids weren't long for this world either! We'd all be *crying* with laughter.

Except when we'd all bid each other good night, jumped in our cars and driven home, the same conclusion had always been reached. Farley could not be toppled.

And then one day along came *On the Hour*. All of a sudden, Alan Gordon Partridge was box office (in Norwich). No longer a quiet little mouse, now I would roar like a lion.[67]

---

67 Literally in the case of Fairview Ride-On Lawnmowers. 'Fairview, we're kings of the jungle. Rooooaaaarrrrr!!!!'

Gone were the days of doing second-tier work for a few shek-els here and there. Now some of the biggest names in corpo-rate Norfolk were wangling four-figure deals in my face like a large willy. And believe me, it felt good.

The other day I pulled out my 1992 diary. I dusted it down, buffed it off and allowed myself a peek inside at the compa-nies I'd lent my voice to. It read like a *Who's Who* of the companies I'd done work for in '92.

Work literally *rolled* in that year – most of it enjoyable. There was the odd engagement that I found unsettling, but you take the rough with the smooth. One spring evening, for example, I provided commentary over the PA for a private greyhound racing event for a group of local businessmen, at a track I'm not able to name. I was well paid and given unlimited buffet access but only realised at the last minute that the dogs were chasing an actual rabbit. And by then, I'd already committed to doing the commentary.

I fulfilled the commitment to the best of my abilities, consoling myself at the end of each race with the knowledge that I was being given a small window into what it would have been like in medieval times to be hung, drawn and quartered.

Yes, it was a busy time for me. To manage my affairs and also because I deserved one, I took on a personal assistant, a local spinster who lived with her mother. She'd worked in a very junior capacity at Radio Broadland in Great Yarmouth during my six months there, and while I wasn't exactly blown away by her ability or attitude, I noticed that she was affordable.

But it wasn't just in my VO work that things were changing. I was receiving the kind of countywide exposure that few of the Norfolk alumni had ever experienced. Okay, I wasn't yet in Delia Smith's league but I was certainly in Bernard Matthews territory. And when you're being spoken of in the same breath as the country's leading farmyard-to-table strategist, how could you *not* become a monster?

As the months rolled by, keeping my feet on the ground was becoming ever harder. I remember picking up the post from the mat one day and just standing there, stunned. I'd opened an innocuous-looking envelope to find – and I'm shaking just to think about it – a Burton's Gold Card. The grand-daddy of all high-street store cards, it not only came with a complimentary shoe horn, but also entitled the bearer to free alterations on every suit purchased.

Yet something wasn't adding up. I hadn't even come close to hitting the £500 annual spending threshold required to 'go gold'. And they knew it. I just couldn't get my head around it. It couldn't be real. It was probably just an admin error or a cruel wheeze dreamt up by some of the lads at Radio Norwich. But the more I looked at it, the more I realised it was the real deal. No, there was no getting away from it. Someone *very* senior at BHQ (Burton Headquarters) had decided that, just to curry favour with Alan Partridge, it was worth breaking one of the most non-negotiable rules in UK retailing.

I felt my legs start to buckle beneath me and reached out to steady myself on the bannister. I had dreamt of this moment for years. I tried to call out to Carol and the kids, but my voice failed. All that came out was a strangled whisper: 'Guys, I've gone gold.'

And with that, I lost consciousness.

***

I remember boarding a Norwich-to-London train one Friday morning in late 1991 when something extraordinary happened. On the platform I'd come across a young man who'd just returned from fighting in Gulf War One. He'd lost both his legs after being on the receiving end of a road-side bomb and (probably quite rightly) had been decorated with every award for bravery. As the train came in we got aboard and sat down next to one another. Naturally I couldn't wait to start quizzing him about the almost comical mismatch between the domestically-built T-72 tanks used by the Iraqis and the far superior M1 Abrams and Challenger 1s under the command of the Americans and British respectively. (I'd even heard impressive reports about the Kuwait M-84AB.) But I would never get the chance.

I'd only been sat down a matter of seconds when a hush descended over the carriage. People were looking my way. Suddenly, like a scene from a very good movie, one passenger started clapping. Then another and another until, soon, the entire carriage had joined in the applause. Some people were shouting the word 'hero' or 'thank you'. It was as if all my years of selfless commitment to the Norfolk community were being recognised in this one spontaneous outpouring of emotion. Not by the mealy-mouthed critics or the slippery commissioners but by the most important people of all – the normal, everyday man on the street/train. I just sat there motionless, allowing myself to be sprayed in the face and body with a high-pressure jet of public appreciation. Never before have I felt so humbled.

If there was one disappointing aspect to this, it was that the young soldier next to me was the only person not to applaud. I know he'd lost both his legs, but you don't clap with your feet. I thought about taking it up with him but thought better of it. No, I said to myself, be the bigger man, let it slide. He may have publicly humiliated you, but look at it this way – if you ever needed to go head-to-head with him in an impromptu limb audit, there would only be one winner. And with that thought, the train pulled away.

***

It was a full week later that I realised my mistake. They'd been clapping for the military amputee. Every man jack of them. And there I'd been, drunk on the ale of celebrity, arrogantly assuming that their thanks and praise had been heaped at me.

I felt ashamed. In an act of contrition, I grounded myself for a week and denied myself access to the BBC club. If I could have given my legs to that soldier, after being killed in a car accident perhaps, I definitely would have done.

In the end, I just got my assistant to leave a box of chocolates on a cenotaph. I was going to leave a card with it, but I thought it would look a bit too much like the Milk Tray man – which would have rubbed salt in their wounds, given their mobility issues.

I felt so stupid because, without exception, those guys out there – whether they're disabling landmines, driving tanks or photographing inmates – are *all* heroes.

9.

THE MOVE TO TV

***

AND THEN CAME THE news that the programme was to be transferred to BBC television.[68] Our editor Steven Eastwood had found out at noon and busily set about sharing the good news. But these, don't forget, were the days before mobile phones. And I wasn't in the office. I was in Ealing. I'd heard that BP had done a pretty awesome job on the refurb of one of their garages, so I'd driven over to take a look.

I was not disappointed. Things got off to a flying start before I'd even turned my engine off. *What* a forecourt. Crisp new signage, beautifully re-laid tarmac, they'd even installed the new generation of pumps I'd read so much about. With 20%

---

68 *Press play on Track 16.*

more nozzle pressure, the petrol just flew into the tank. Apparently as you filled up you could actually feel the power of the gush through the handle.

And the shop! It was like a newsagents, a supermarket and a Halfords all rolled into one. For the hungry driver in particular, the pickings were rich. My eyes darted across the chill cabinets. Microwave pasties, reheat-and-eat pies, packaged sandwiches – the choice of perishables was truly humbling. As I stood there drinking in the whole incredible experience, one thing was abundantly clear to me: I was witnessing the start of a whole new era of petrol station excellence. And so it turned out to be[69].[70]

To some of you it might seem weird that I was so damn buzzed up by a petrol station. But all I can say is that I must have sensed something in the air. And sure enough, when I got back to the office, Eastwood told me about our impending transfer from wireless to goggle-box.

'Alan, the show's moving to TV!'

'OMG,' I spluttered, inadvertently inventing the now-popular acronym.

'We found out this morning but you weren't around,' he went on. 'I'd have phoned you but mobile phones haven't yet reached mainstream adoption,' his shrug seemed to add.

---

69 The next quantum leap forward was to come in 2003 when – breaking the mould once again – the guys at Beyond Petroleum launched their fabulous Wild Bean cafés. Quite simply, shit hot.

70 Little did I know that some years later I would be spending a lot of time in one of these petrol stations as a certain Geordie chum saw me through the many stages of a pretty hefty mental meltdown. But that's for later. And please don't skip ahead. Just stay patient, keep reading and you'll get there.

I didn't mind, though, because there was only one thought in my mind – my career was about to go megastrophic.

Soon enough, launch day arrived. And right from the off, things just clicked. They say a chain is only as strong as its weakest link. Yet from Christopher Morris (anchor) to Rosie May (environment) to Ted Maul (replacing Kev Smear as roving reporter) to Peter O'Hanraha-hanrahan (economics editor) to yours truly (sport) there simply was no weak link.

In fact, the consensus was that the show – renamed *The Day Today* – worked even better on telly. Viewers said they preferred it, because now they could see us, whereas before they had to make up what we looked like in their heads. By way of example, a lot of folks said they expected me to have far nicer eyes.

I also insisted on doing my studio reports with the word 'sport' in massive letters behind me (see picture section). Some people thought this was ego. In fact it was a savvy move designed to keep the deaf on-side.

The Day Today was a plum job, though, and I knew it. Okay, I wasn't especially chummy with my colleagues but that was alright by me. I wasn't invited to Rosie May's birthday drinks, Peter O'Hanraha-hanrahan's summer BBQ or the funeral of Ted Maul's little girl (though to be fair, neither was anyone else). But who cares/cared? Not me! You don't have to be best buddies with your work-mates to enjoy your job. And I certainly wasn't (best buddies), but certainly did (enjoy job).

More worrying was the risk of my job being given to some-one else. Occasionally certain young BBC starlets (Ryder, Irvine, Bonnet) would start circling, keen for a piece of my sports beat. But I was fiercely protective of my patch. I was like a lady swan guarding her cygnets. If anyone came too close, I would rear up, spread my wings and chase them across the park. And if they happened to be accompanied by the family dog, then I'm sorry but that dog was going down.

I still believe I was right to be defensive – and, on occasion, orally threatening – because for a sports journalist in particular, the early 90s was a time of plenty. Whether reporting for radio or TV, the country was awash and a-slosh with sporting giants. Never mind interviewing them, it's an honour just to say the names of these sporting greats. I'd often sit at home, saying them aloud, letting their names drench my teeth and gums like a good-quality fluoride mouthwash.[71]

In athletics there was Linford Christie, Sally Gunnell and the not unattractive Fatima Whitbread. On the track we were witness to the derring-do of Nigel Mansell, in the ring the very hard punches of Frank Bruno and out at the crease the swashbuckling style of Ian Botham, known to friends and colleagues simply as 'Beef'.

And I, Partridge was lucky enough to meet them all. Just the other night I sat down in front of my roaring gas fire, poured myself a glass of bitter and totted up all the sports stars I've met over the years. The grand total: 116. Not bad for a young lad from Norwich. Not bad at all.

If pushed, though, I'd have to say my favourite was Sally Gunnell.[72] Not only did she insist on competing with a full face of make-up and a big, ballsy squirt of perfume, but she was also ruddy good company.

---

71 I remember around this time bumping into former *Grandstand* presenter Frank Bough at a fancy dress party in Shepherd's Bush (long story). I commented that the early 90s really was a golden age for British sport. Frank simply took the ball gag out of his mouth and said, 'You're not wrong, Alan' before dropping on to all fours and being led away.
72 *Press play on Track 17.*

Top: The place of my birth, The Queen Elizabeth Hospital, King's Lynn. In an era before MRSA, cleanliness was maintained by a combination of soap and aggressive, largely buxom matrons. NHS car parks were free, too, although those days are now a distant memory. It's not too bad if you're just bobbing in to drop off some grapes or beer for a loved one. But for expectant fathers it can be cripplingly expensive, especially if the birth is being slowed down by your wife having an unusually long cervix. (It seems wrong that wealthy dads whose spouses have shorter birth canals and more elastic vaginas should pay less.) The council say they're trying to encourage people to use public transport but I think that's horseshit.

Above: Norfolk, 1956. I'd just crawled into this group photo and taken centre stage – nothing changes! I remember being irritated that the girl behind me had put her hands on my shoulder when I was perfectly capable of sitting upright on my own. I don't know what any of their names are, though some have suggested that the girl is Anne Frank. However, for a number of reasons this seems unlikely.

Above: A semi-detached house in Edgbaston, Birmingham, much like the one my childhood nemesis Steven McCombe lives in. We never saw eye-to-eye but I've moved past that now because I prefer to let bygones be bygones. It's not, as some have suggested, because I earn a lot more money than he does. It doesn't matter to me in the slightest that McCombe wouldn't know the top tax band if it broke into his house and attacked him while he slept. Nor that the engine in my car has double the cubic capacity of his. FYI, I also drive with more skill (e.g. can go round roundabouts using only one hand).

Opposite top: One of the many places where I attended Scout camp. I remember how we'd all sit around the campfire singing 'Ging Gang Goolie' until the sun came up, or until our 10pm bedtime, whichever came sooner. Then we'd all snuggle up in our sleeping bags to tell ghost stories or see who could shine a torch into their mouth for longest. I never got involved with this, wrongly assuming it carried a significant cancer risk. It was while camping at this exact site that I first mastered the sheepshank. People say knot-tying is a useless skill but try telling that to my bin bags!

Opposite bottom: On the day this was taken, my parents had been called into school by the headmaster because he was concerned my posture had homosexual overtones. He'd been alerted by my tendency to turn in my right knee and my preference for slip-on shoes. Also note that my father had insisted I tuck my tie into my shorts. In terms of psychological abuse, this was just the tip of the iceberg.

Above left: Me, reporting on *The Day Today*, where my beat was sport (plus the Paralympics). I used to warm my voice up beforehand by singing the national anthem to the tune of *Live and Let Die*. Not easy, but it can be done.

Above right: There are few men alive who can pull off a haircut that's longer at the back and sides than it is on the top. I am one of those men. On windy days I would go outside and run into the wind, just to feel it billowing behind me like a superhero's cape. I was very wary of having it cut off. I didn't want to become a broadcasting version of the guy from Samson and Jemima. But I'm glad to report that when I did get sheared the impact on my career was minimal. For old times' sake I kept the cuttings. They're in a Waitrose Bag for Life in my shed. There's probably enough to stuff a loose pillow or a compact lumbar-support cushion.

Opposite: As soon as I heard that Roger Moore had agreed to appear on *Knowing Me Knowing You*, I rushed outside and ordered a subordinate to take a photo of me standing against a wall with my thumb up. In this shot the cold indifference of the brick contrasts beautifully with the wild elation that swirls inside me. In Western cultures an upturned thumb is a sign of contentment. In Middle Eastern cultures it translates as something very different. Had you seen me doing this in Tehran it would have meant I wished to molest Roger anally. Nothing could have been further from the truth.

Above: Superman had Kryptonite, I had Tony Hayers. Here he is, standing behind me before the filming of *Knowing Me Knowing Yule*, during which I punched his lights out with a dead turkey. It's hard to describe the pleasure I felt as the free-range meat crashed into the cheek of the mealy-mouthed commissioning editor. But I'll have a go ... Let me see. It was like the combined ecstasy of sneezing while driving over a humpback bridge. That's how good it felt when I punched Hayers's lights out with a dead turkey. Afterwards, it occurred to me that you could have a turkey-glove boxing event in *It's a Knockout*. I looked into it but came up against a wall of bureaucratic red tape regarding the contestants' potential contraction of salmonella. I offered to have all the 'gloves' cooked in an oven beforehand but this failed to satisfy them, which proved that the salmonella excuse was just a ruse. It all boiled down to that insidious new cult/fad of 'animal rights'. No one ever mentions *human* rights.

Top: Me, Sue Lewis, a stable lad and a horse (second left). There were concerns that it might get spooked by the noise from Glen Ponder's band and run into the audience. We knew there were going to be school kids in the front row, and Health and Safety estimated that if things went wrong, up to 20 children could be trampled before the horse could be lassoed and destroyed. In the event, however, the beast behaved impeccably. It was a credit to itself.

Above left: Singing an Abba medley with lovely-shouldered American *chanteuse* Gina Langland. Many people felt that despite having no formal training, I actually out-sung her, certainly in terms of volume. I've always been able to hold a tune, though. As a child I'd sing in the shower, often when it wasn't turned on. I just liked the acoustics in the bathroom.

Above right: Me, giving an inspirational address to a roomful of teenagers at an event to promote careers in the Norfolk media. I'd arrived wearing a tie but quickly switched to a cravat in order to blend in better with the 16–18-year-olds. I would have gone open-necked but there was a pretty chunky pimple on my chest, the result of forgetting to shower after I'd got home from squash.

Above left: Paddington Green Police Station, the UK's highest-security police station and the scene of my incarceration on 21–22 October 1994 following the sad, bad death of chatshow guest Forbes McAllister. In a desperate attempt to be released I pointed out to the policeman that I had laid on hot food for my colleagues as part of my show's wrap party. Unless I turned up at the Pitcher & Piano to pay for the grub up front, they would be deprived of around eight dozen mini Kievs. I'll never forget the police officer's riposte. He simply said, 'Sounds like they've been spared a fate WORSE than death.' Well, I laughed my head off and for a moment clean forgot that I was on a manslaughter charge. DI Lance and I became lifelong friends after that, and he is to be technical adviser on my Norwich-based detective series *Swallow* (should it happen).

Above right: Highgate Cemetery, the final resting place of Karl Marx, Jeremy Beadle and Forbes McAllister. For the first three years on the anniversary of his death I would go to visit him. I'd wait until his wife had left his graveside (usually biding my time tucked away behind the massive stone head of Mr Marx). Then I'd go up and say a few words. Nothing too profound. Just an apology. And then, more often than not, there would be an awkward silence. After a while I'd puncture the silence with chit-chat, normally about the news, the weather or whatever reality TV programme was on at the time. I haven't been back since July 2001, however, due to the fact that I had begun to find the visits boring. Also, hiding behind that giant communist head gave me the heebie jeebies!!

In 1991 I was sent out to Tokyo to cover the Athletics World Championships. Sally was taking part in the 400m hurdles (for women). We all watched as she quite literally overcame all the obstacles put in her way to romp home to a creditable second place. Yes, Gunnell had silvered.

Within minutes she'd put on high heels and a new pair of dungarees and joined a bunch of her fellow athletes at a local bar. It would have taken her longer, but she already had make-up on, you could probably smell her perfume in Hiroshima, and as she'd only actually been running for 53.16 seconds (a new British record by the way) it seemed crazy to shower – a wet wipe administered to the main danger zones had been deemed more than adequate.

Yet no sooner had the shin-dig hit its stride than Sally's chums and buddies seemed to drift away. Gunnell may have run *her* race but the rest of them were yet to compete. Their loss however was very much AP's gain (my gain). And as Sally wasn't ready to head home, we moved on to a restaurant serving authentic Japanese nosh.

Of course, these days young professionals hotfoot it to Pret a Manger every lunchtime to gobble down box after box of sushi. But back then, things were different. Back then, our tastes were simpler and less foreign. As a result Sal and myself were pretty miffed as we browsed the menu. What *was* all this stuff?

Others might have given up and headed off to a Western fast food joint, but not us. Our attitude was very much 'when in Rome …', so when the waiter came round we went for it and ordered a couple of bowls of rice.

For the next three hours we chatted away like there was no tomorrow. Sally may only have managed silver, but in a Chatathlon our conversation would easily have brought home the gold. We seemed to cover every topic under the sun. Favourite film, best cheese, biggest regret, smallest regret, euthanasia. But little did we realise, as our ace natter entered its fourth hour, that our cultural ignorance was about to be our undoing.

The problem was a little thing called 'sake'. We'd been knocking back glass after glass of the stuff, assuming it was nothing more dangerous than indigenous pop. Yet as we left the restaurant we soon realised that we were catastrophically ming-monged. Sally was so gone she thought her silver medal was currency. And I was so gone that I later mistook Sally for Kriss Akabusi (look him up).

But what a laugh we had as we staggered along the street like silly idiots. I dared her to hop all the way back to the hotel (she did). She dared me to pick up a bin and smash in the window of a nearby shop (I didn't). We checked out a few more bars and even stopped in at a local karaoke place, duetting on UB40's 'Rat in Mi Kitchen'. And, at last, at long long last, when we finally made it back to our digs we couldn't believe our eyes – it was nearly quarter to eleven. What a night!

***

It was in my first few months at the BBC that I received one of the finest pieces of advice in Britain. I was over at TV Centre preparing to interview a bantamweight boxer (I forget his name and ethnicity) when I saw a man coming out of the disabled toilet – it was none other than the late, great Des Lynam.[73]

---

73 Lynam may have been unencumbered by disability, but he was also a senior figure in the BBC of the 90s. As such, he was contractually entitled to use these roomier facilities whenever he wished.

Clocking me, he wandered over, doing up his belt and seeing to his fly.

'Heard you on the radio last night, Alan.'

'Crumbs,' I spluttered. 'Thanks.'

'I liked what you did.'

'Crumbs,' I spluttered again, in much the same way as I had done previously. 'Thanks.'

'But a word of advice on your broadcasting voice.'

I stiffened up like a cock; a cock that was afraid of being attacked by a fox. What was he about to say? Gladdeningly, I didn't have to wait long for the answer, because it was a conversation in real time.

'Your broadcasting voice is solid enough, but it's too nasal. If you ever want to make the leap to TV ...'

'I do, Des, I do,' I thought to myself, but didn't say out loud.

'... then you want to pull the nasality up by about a quarter. And Alan?'

'Yes, Lynam,' I said, for some reason selecting to use his surname rather than his first name.

'Trust me on this one.'

And with that, he was gone, as gone as gone can be.

That night I barely slept. Thoughts were tumbling around my head like the trainers in the washing machine I referred to both on page 3 and page 64. Des was right. How could I not have spotted this before?

My mind drifted back to my earliest broadcasts on hospital radio. I had indeed beefed up the nasal quality of my voice, thinking it lent it a timbre that was trustworthy, authoritative and basically quite nice. It sounds crazy when I think back to it, but I was so convinced of this that I used to deliberately try to catch a cold. The all-too-common viral infection of the upper respiratory tract was an excellent way to cause profound blockages of the soft palate which in extreme cases can make you sound like Melvyn Bragg before he had that operation. As such, it was perfect for my needs.

Many was the day I'd ride the public bus system of Norwich, seeking out any passengers with the snivels. I'd move over to them and casually strike up a conversation. I'd talk about the stuff of everyday life – the weather, last night's TV, the design of the new Opel Kadett which, staggeringly, had a transaxle that allowed the clutch to be replaced without removing the transmission unit. I didn't care really, just as long as I was close to them.

And when they finally reached their stop, I would always, *always* insist on a handshake – or better still, a long, lingering, long embrace – to up my chances of contamination.

Once I was so desperate I even doused myself in pepper. I stood next to a man with a nose throbbing like a Belisha beacon and waited for him to sneeze. As he threw his head back I inched even closer, only moving away again when I knew I'd been covered in a fine sheen of infected nasal drizzle.

Yet now, almost four years later, I saw the folly of my ways. My voice had become *too* nasal, *too* serious. If I was to fulfil my ambitions of being a top-quality TV broadcaster I needed a cadence that was versatile. I needed a voice that could flit like a carefree moth from the heavyweight to the powder-puff.

I spent the entire night stood in front of my bathroom mirror doing everything in my power to quash exactly 25% of my vocal nasality. Of course with radio being an entirely aural medium, the mirror had no part to play. I could just as easily have stood in front of a wall. (But, truth be told, I had spotted a pimple developing on my neck – roughly three inches south of my left ear lobe – and was keen both to track its growth and plot its destruction.)

By daybreak I had finally cracked it. Although, as a result of ten hours of unbroken speaking, I had also lost my voice. Ironically, the three weeks I subsequently had to take off work very nearly cost me my job. But I clung on, I survived, and returned as the broadcaster I am today. I now had a voice that could take on any chat-based challenge; that could swoop and glide from genre to genre. It was the voice that I still use today – high-brow yet inclusive, candid yet mysterious, loud yet quiet. In short, it was the voice of I, Partridge.

As for the neck pimple, it expanded for a further 48 hours before I was able to take it down using a hot pin.

10.

MY OWN SHOW

***

MY STAR WAS RISING, like the bubbles in the glasses of champagne I would have been enjoying if I liked the taste of champagne. I was being recognised in hotel bars, train station WH Smithses and the local branch of Do It All.

It was a pleasantly warming sensation at first, before a stern lecture-to-self in my bathroom mirror (bought from Do It All funnily enough!) made me wise up. 'These people don't care about you,' I said. 'You mean nothing to them. They'd sooner earn an extra £1,000 a year than worry about whether you're going to be the next presenter of *Sportsnight*.'

And that realisation – that these people would stab me and spit on my jolting corpse – probably did colour my approach to the general public.

Don't get me wrong, I didn't become a recluse. But I steeled myself against hangers-on and well-wishers, typically meeting their so-called compliments with a snort or a stony silence.

In the BBC things were different. I worked on a style of glad-handing that I felt sure would ingratiate myself to more important people and earn me a reputation of being a charming TV personality. It had worked for Dale Winton, who could switch from air-kissing a commissioning editor to screaming hot spittle into the face of a researcher in about three seconds. But he was inhaling a lot of nail varnish remover around that time, I'm told.

Back to me. I was becoming known for my no-nonsense interview style, and my never-say-die attitude, certainly in my opinion and I'm sure in the opinions of a great many others.

Sometimes that meant being ruthless, a trait I demonstrated when grabbing the first interview with javelinner Steve Backley after a quite lovely throw at Crystal Palace. Seeing ITV's Jim Rosenthal jostling for position, I sidled up behind him, muttered 'Hello Jim' and, as he turned to respond, he fell/ was pushed off the media rostrum. He landed on a stack of hurdles, suffering cuts and bruises as well as some seriously duffed-up pride. Well, Gary Newbon went spastic.[74] The two of them were the Tweedle Dum and Tweedle Doo of ITV Sport – great friends on and off camera – and our feud was real and long-standing.

Newbon tore his jacket off, then his shirt, pounding at his belly and tits and shouting 'Come on then! Come on!' It was incredibly unseemly and I know Gary was kept away from athletics events for a good while after that.

---

74 Note: at the time this word was deemed acceptable. How times change!

I secured the interview and asked Backley some searching questions about his training regime, skin-tight sportswear and marital status. The piece went out that night. You could see Newbon in the background, facing away from camera but slumped on a folding chair (by then in tears), but needless to say I had the last laugh.

I hated ITV back then – and that loathing spurred me on to be the man on the scene whenever a sports star or their attractive spouse had anything to say. I had an easy way with people, and much like Piers Morgan today, was able to flit effortlessly from the high-brow to the utterly juvenile, from the serious to the inconsequential in a heartbeat. Unlike Morgan, I can also flit back the other way, whereas he is often stranded in thick alley for the remainder of the conversation. You can actually see his eyes swivelling as he struggles to break free of the tabloid moorings. Still, he's a good interviewer and a solid guy.

But I was a bloody good interviewer and a bloody solid guy.[75] And I began to wonder if I was fulfilling my potential. My son was teaching me about quadratic equations at the time and although I convinced him that they were genuinely irrelevant in real life, it convinced me that I should look for a fresh challenge. Like so:

Alan asking sports questions = a bloody good sports interview.

Which means, if you divide both by 'sport':

Alan asking questions = a bloody good interview.

---

75 *Press play on Track 18.*

It went something like that anyway. Fernando's had algebra in them, but his maths homework wasn't important back then. That might sound cruel but my focus was almost exclusively on my continued career progression.[76]

At a BBC party that autumn, I introduced myself to a commissioning editor by the name of Adam Walters. I remember the moment well.

'You're Adam Walters, aren't you?' I said.

'Yes,' he replied.

Walters was being talked of as the next big thing in BBC commissioning, something I found hard to understand (and still do) given that the role of a commissioner is basically to put a tick or a cross in a box. Who knows? Maybe he had neat handwriting. Or maybe he had friends in high places.

Either way, Adam was a good person to know. So I found out where he played squash and would make sure I happened to be having my shower and talc there at the same time as he/him.

Quaffing a juice afterwards one day, I suggested that I come in to talk about the idea of a chat show, in which I, the chat show host, would chat to guests on the show. He was intrigued at what was a really fresh idea and an appointment was duly arranged for that afternoon.

I ran home, excess talc spilling from the bottom of my trouser legs. I popped on my newest blazer, brushed my teeth, waited six hours, brushed them again and called a cab. As I zoomed towards Shepherd's Bush, I opened the window, imagining my face on the billboards that massively spruce up Holland Park and that make Shepherd's Bush roundabout a

---

76 Fernando confronted me about this many years later. And after initially telling him to get stuffed, I broke down and admitted to a momentary lapse of parental judgment.

pleasure to circumnavigate. It would be called 'Alan's Show', I'd decided, and would be absolutely ace.

I bounded into the foyer, announced that I was there to see Adam and waited. And waited. The receptionist couldn't find any record of Mr Walters. 'Are you sure he works for BBC TV?' Then everything went quiet.

Mouth dry, head spinning, and suddenly keen for a poo, I staggered from Television Centre. Steadying myself against an old woman who was there for the BBC Tour, I took another step into the street and bellowed at the sky.

'They want me back on the radio!!!'

You see, Walters was a *radio* commissioner. Of course. *Of course.* I should have known. He had that lifeless, grey, dead-eyed quality that they all have at Broadcasting House. I called a cab and, with a heavy heart, went for a meeting with Adam Walters. Of Radio 4.

It wasn't the best meeting I've ever had. Almost on auto-pilot, I ran through all the famous people I knew (who, I said, I could definitely get) and Walters seemed duly impressed. I was in a seriously bad mood, no doubt, but Adam's compliments and the excellent selection of biscuits there soon cheered me up. He all but offered me a show there and then. Paydirt!

People ask me if I found that daunting. They don't know Alan Partridge. If anything was making me apprehensive it was that a light-hearted comment – in which I joked that I owned my own production company and would make the show myself in exchange for a hefty development and production fee – was somehow taken at face value.[77]

---

77 Some people have subsequently accused me of lying that I owned a production company. It wasn't a lie. It was a joke that was taken seriously. And if they can't see that they're idiots.

So the next morning I created a production company by putting posters up around Norwich and giving work experience to family friends. And lo, Peartree Productions was born.

Alan's Show – this was a working title – began production on 9 August 1992. Peartree Productions was a thrilling place to work, dynamic and young – indeed, many of the staff should technically have been at school. We really felt we were making something important. And so it proved.

We worked out a format – I would ask questions, the guests would answer, as if in conversation – and after a few trial runs I had it down pat. Unable to afford celebrity bookers, we relied on two researchers, Lisa and Jason, to approach agents. And on the whole, they did a good job. (Lisa's personality could be an issue. I suspected her of smoking cannabis and, as her employer, rifled through her bag to be sure. Nothing, but she went berserk. Her attitude really, really stank sometimes.)

The date of the first show was approaching. But we hit a snag! The BBC had decided that *Alan's Show* 'wouldn't work as a name' on the grounds that people might not know who 'Alan' was. I said, 'I dunno where you've got that idea from!' And I invited them to my local Do It All as a fame-proving exercise (they declined). Alas, we needed a new name.

A team meeting was hastily called and we embarked on 'brainstorming', an American business technique in which ideas are graded depending on how loudly they're shouted. As the team screamed at each other, I noticed that my favourite CD, *Abba Gold*, was on the stereo and a song came on that I felt would be perfect.[78] I sat and listened as the debate raged on among my colleagues before shouting, 'Shut up, you wallies! Shut up and listen to the music!!'

---

78 *Press play on Track 19.*

That got them. We sat in silence as the refrains of the song, 'The Winner Takes It All', blasted from the office Alba. It seemed so right, with its title reflecting my sporting heritage while announcing myself as a triumph in the cut-throat world of broadcasting. As I sang along, eyes closed, I imagined it playing to the applause of a studio audience.

In the end, the group persuaded me that it didn't set a particularly inclusive or humble tone, but another track,[79] 'Knowing Me, Knowing You' – which is centred on the theme of people 'knowing' each other – seemed to fit the bill.

We put a call in to Abba's people and waited for the good news. But all we got was a snub. Abba, it seemed, wanted to receive a special payment, or 'royalty', if their song was broadcast.

This was insane, I reasoned. The man on Norwich market who sells towels plays this CD every week. Does *he* have to pay a 'royalty'? Does a single mum have to pay a 'royalty' if she blares it from her Fiesta car stereo? We were being victimised.

I later discovered that royalty payments were an extremely common – but no less sickening – requirement of music broadcasting. So we had the song re-recorded by the Jeff Lovell Orchestra.[80] This version retained all of the poetry and drama of the original, but Jeff, himself on guitar, added much more treble to the mix and with extra cymbal work managed to add a sheen of accessibility and, dare I say it, stardust to an already magnificent song. We had our musical motif.[81]

---

79 *Press play on Track 20.*
80 Free of charge. This was a big break for Jeff and the gang. In fact, they later won a contract to play on a cruise ship to Santander off the back of me.
81 Some people mistakenly believed the track was recorded by the Geoff Love Orchestra. Wrong! If I had a pound for everyone who made that mistake, I'd be pig rich.

Aha!

What is that? What is Aha? Well, it's a duosyllabic exclamation that has spilled from my chops and given pleasure to millions across the globe. Some would say it has come to define me. But how was it formed? I'll tell you the truth.

We'd not even rehearsed it. I'll say that again (or you could just re-read the first one and skip this next one.) We'd not even rehearsed it. I came out on stage for that first show, sweating freely and visibly from my face, neck, pits, back and pants. 'Knowing me, knowing you,' sang the Jeff Lovell girls.[82] And as the track reached its conclusion, they sang it again.

My eyes filled with a burning white light and Abba drenched my brain. 'Ahaaaaa!!!!' I boomed. It just came out. WALLOP! The audience didn't know what to say. Me, I took it in my stride, literally shaking at how right, how ruddy *correct*, it had felt. Throughout that show, I said it a few more times. And I opened all subsequent shows with the same shout. And you know what, it became something of a calling card, voted years later 84th in Channel 4's 100 Best Catchphrases.

And if people to this day shout it out at me, in the street, or when I'm trying to pay for my shopping, or if I ring up a call centre to renew car insurance, or in a doctor's waiting room if I'm having trouble digesting food, it doesn't bother me. I'm fine with it. I like it. It makes me feel good and glad. Why wouldn't it? So if people think it does bother me or that they're getting one over on me, or that it might be a good way of riling me, they could literally not be further from the truth. I do not give a fucking *shit* either way.

---

82 I say, girls. One was in her forties and recorded her vocal with a ten-year-old son eating sandwiches by her side.

No, if anything, I embraced it. In fact, the phrase has become so synonymous with Brand Partridge that I later took steps to claim some kind of entitlement to it, flying to Gothenberg to negotiate directly with Björn and Benjamin's lawyers for rights to shout (but not say) the word 'Aha' 50 times a year in perpetuity for the rest of my life or until 2015, whichever comes sooner.

But that's by the bye, the first show was a great success. Brainbox author Lawrence Camley was a ruddy good sport, Ally Tenant (a TV mind quack) was interesting, although perhaps too smutty for an audience reared on shipping news and dramas about farms. As with all feminists she combined a hatred of being sexualised with a fixation that everything is to do with sex. I mean, do you like having it off or not?? Hello???

Afterwards I went to congratulate Adam Walters but he was tied up in a meeting, sitting still while the BBC's Controller of Editorial Policy, John Wilson, paced and shouted incoherently.

Every show thereafter was a great success. 'Don't read the reviews,' said Martin Bell one day in a corridor. 'Don't have to, mate!' I shouted back, a spring in my step. Each show seemed more informative, entertaining and superb than the last, although I felt the guests could have been better behaved. Controversial lawyer Nick Ford was an especially crass interviewee, not attempting to hide his homosexuality at all as far as I could tell.

We garnered pleasing column inches for what was a poorly marketed Radio 4 show, aided in no small part by the resignation of government minister Sandra Peaks in our third show. She'd been siphoning government grants into her husband's construction firm and paying twin 17-year-old rent boys to engage in sexual acts. Although our conversation was somewhat fractious, Sandra and I remain very, very good friends and I regret my line of questioning deeply. The so-called controversies were nobody's business but Sandra and Clive's.

The show was being talked about – not just in DIY super-stores or trumped-up newsagents but in media circles. We enjoyed further publicity from the death (figuratively speaking!) of comedian Bernie Rosen in week five and the death (actual) of Tory peer Lord Morgan of Glossop in our final show.

But I don't think anyone was too upset. Lord Morgan's family began legal action and asked some searching questions about our indemnity insurance, but I don't think anyone seri-ously believed we'd been responsible. Can you imagine? Cause of death: chat!!![83] I don't think so!!

No, far from it being a downbeat end to the series, I was in high spirits. Our final show had seen a guest appearance from Tony Hayers, then acting commissioning director for BBC TV and a man who frankly made Adam Walters look like a pathetic radio idiot. Tony and I hadn't met before but, knowing he was important, I'd kept an eye on him and admired him from afar, most notably in the BBC canteen from behind a newspaper.

Walters had made it clear that Radio 4 wanted a second series. 'Join the fucking queue, mate,' I said with my eyes.

After the final show, with Tony heading for the car, I ran up behind him, shouting to be heard over the noise as Lord Morgan's body was lifted into the ambulance. 'Tony,' I said. 'Are you going to put this baby on the goggle-box or what?'

I was pleased he'd come to the last show of the series because by this point my new look was really taking shape. My

---

83 I'm laughing as I write this.

clothes were, and would remain, somewhere in the sweet spot between smart and smart casual, but it was my hair that had taken the quantum leap forward. Chat show hosts normally keep things pretty trim up top. I however liked to think outside the square. So I'd grown it. It was now thick, full and if I tipped my head right back, shoulder-length (see picture section). If the day was an even number, I'd wash it. And if it wasn't I'd just shake it loose and brush through a little olive oil. It worked for me then and I know it works for Jonathan Ross now, though he's replaced the olive oil with Fry Light cooking spray.

As this thought had been so long, I decided to repeat my question. 'Tony,' I said. 'Are you going to put this baby on the goggle-box or what?'

'We'll see,' he said, which at first I thought was a worryingly non-committal hand-off. But then I thought about it,[84] about his specific choice of words. 'See', he'd said. Not 'hear', 'see'. He was talking in visual terms. This I felt sure was him saying, in code,[85] your show will be *seen* on the television. I punched the air and whooped before lowering my voice out of respect for Lord Morgan's nearby relatives.

The next day I walked into Peartree Productions and doubled everyone's pay. Then sacked Lisa.

---

84 *Press play on Track 21.*
85 Would make a good chapter in *The Da Vinci Code.*

11.

RADIO'S LOSS

***

A TV CHAT SHOW is different from a radio one. Hair must be better kempt, the studio must be de-drabbed, a house band is required. And other things like cameras and monitors differ as well.

These weren't my concern, though. I was the talent. And the world would know my name.

Hayers had us scheduled for a 9pm BBC2 slot. I'm often asked if that miffed me. The natural home for a broadcaster like me would surely have been BBC1, 7pm. The chat show landscape of the time was barren and desolate like the moon or Malta, and ITV's *Aspel & Company* – the only serious rival for the chat show crown – had been put to sleep. (As an act of kindness, trust me. *Terrible* show.)

BBC1 was crying out for *KMKY,* and the decision not to place it there was a loony one. But miff me? No. I looked at the bigger picture. If ever a TV channel needed helping out of a hole it was BBC2, 1993/1994. And I was the man to give it a shot in the arm.

Don't get me wrong, I wasn't an avid watcher of the channel, being neither a young urban male or book-bothering clever-clogs. But I did watch *Top Gear,* and I knew damn well that its fortunes represented an accurate bellwether for BBC2 as a whole.

In 1993–4, *Top Gear* – and by extension BBC2 – stank the place out. Tiff Needell's voice was cracking every other word, like an early-day Michael McIntyre. Clarkson was a point away from a driving ban so was test-driving cars like they were hearses, and Quentin Wilson ...

Never the most upbeat of motoring journalists, something was up with Quents. Don't get me wrong, he'd been a bit weird for a while: the cadence of his sentences had started to get on everyone's tits, and he was walking round all uppity and pretending to like art. More privately, he'd bought a series of vintage Bentleys but didn't know how to drive them, secretly preferring his Toyota Avensis. But he'd even cut down his mileage in that.

No, there was more to it than that. I followed him to the bogs at the Motor Show in '93 and asked him straight out what was up. He wasn't able to meet my eyes but shook his head sadly. 'I've fallen out of love with them,' he said. 'I just can't stand them.'

'What, who?' I said, asking two questions for the price of one.

And with a heavy hand, he gestured out towards the Birmingham NEC. At the cars. All of the cars. He'd had his fill. And at that he broke down. We held each other, crying, for what seemed like ages. And from that moment onwards, I knew that he was shot. *Top Gear* was shot. BBC2 was shot. I made a big decision that day. I would forget about BBC1 and be BBC2's White Knight,[86] riding to the rescue, the salvation of the listing TV station.

Having agreed to be the face of the channel for the foreseeable future (and agreed to drive Quentin around for an hour every Saturday so that he and cars could 'start again'), I noticed that the atmosphere around TV Centre was different. There was literally a spring in everyone's step. Ironically-bespectacled producers peeped out from behind laptops and rubbed their eyes as if greeting a new day. Production managers whistled as they worked. The nervous women who do typing and whatnot seemed less mousey than normal. It was a new dawn.

Having salvaged BBC2, I set about making the best show that had ever been on it. *Knowing Me Knowing You* would be broadcast from a studio 25% larger than *Aspel & Company*'s and make use of a house band (a trait subsequently appropriated by US talk shows such as Letterman and Conan O'Barian).

Finding the band was easy. I'd seen local musician Glen Ponder rock the joint at a Norwich wine bar months before. Dressed in tails and armed only with a baton, he was the conductor to what was essentially a pub band – a needlessly high-brow touch that I felt would fit well with the tone of my show.

And finally, after months of slog (made more complicated by Lisa's vindictive employment tribunal), we were ready. I was to become a star.

---

86 Not racist.

12.
GLEN PONDER, MUSICIAN[87]

***

SAY WHAT YOU LIKE about Glen Ponder – and I have, frequently – but he was a virtuoso conductor of lounge music, possibly the most talented easy-listening batonsman of his era. He and his loyal band of minstrels (musicians) were a fixture on the Norwich music scene, effortlessly able to switch between the rival demands of a wine bar, a hotel lobby or a shopping mall forecourt. He was *that* versatile. As soon as I saw him and his band in action, I knew they *must* be given a big break. By me.

Glen had just finished an awe-inspiring during-dinner set at Café Symphony in Norwich (now, at long last, a Nando's) when I decided to broach it. I followed him to his bus stop.

---

87 *Press play on Track 22.*

'Mr Ponder,' I shouted as I approached.

'Let's have it then, fucker!' he said, wheeling round and baring his fists and clenching his teeth. I pretended not to notice and ploughed on.

'Great set back there, man,' I said, using the word 'man' so he knew I was familiar with modern music. 'Magnificent tracks.'

He looked at me in order to size me up and gauge my intentions. His breathing was shallow and his eyes were wild. I had to say something.

'Are you okay?' I said in a quiet soothing voice, as if I was a Conductor Whisperer. He was instantly becalmed.

'Sorry about that,' he said, now at ease. 'I thought you were a mugger.'

Glen, it turned out, was responsible for collecting up the coins that were tossed at the band, carrying them home and piggy-banking them. As such, he was often targeted by youths, vagrants and Scots.

Clearly, I was none of these things and we were able to strike up a conversation.

'Wanna be a star?' I asked, casually, pretending to inspect my fingernails. He just looked at me.

'I'm Alan Partridge,' I said, but he looked at me even more blankly. 'From Radio 4's *Knowing Me Knowing You*,' I added. Still nothing. Then I added *The Day Today* and *On the Hour*, fruitlessly. I listed several other pieces of my work, but it wasn't until I mentioned *Scoutabout* that the penny dropped. Flippin' *Scoutabout*.

Undeterred, I suggested that he and his band sign up with me. He agreed there and then, before we'd even discussed terms or mentioned money – which I found both refreshing and a bit desperate. But I remembered a piece of advice I'd been given by Bernard Matthews – 'It's when they're tired, desperate and hungry that they're at their most compliant' – and I suddenly knew that this could work out very well indeed.

Of course, it didn't. I made Glen and his group Brandysnaps[88] my house band and, while not expecting an unending gush of gratitude, I was anticipating a little bit of respect. What I got from Glen, alongside rank amateurism and off-kilter comic timing, was literally a slap in the face[89] – and that hurt me. It hurt me a lot.[90]

Full disclosure. My first choice for house band had been the Jeff Lovell Orchestra, the outfit who had re-recorded the theme to *Knowing Me Knowing You* for my Radio 4 show, but Jeff was something of a recluse, having badly disfigured his hands saving an oboe from a van fire. He was also perhaps a little ill-suited to the top-of-the-show comic banter that the role required, having lost his sense of humour in a van fire.

That said, I still had high hopes for Glen and his band.[91] But from the get-go, I realised I'd made an error. A week before the show, I'd ordered Glen to get a haircut and he had reluctantly obliged, losing his waist-length corkscrew curls in favour of a shorter, smarter style. But, like an adolescent Samson, it was as if the loss of his locks created a lackadaisical attitude to the basics of live TV: rehearsal, attitude, deference, obeying instruction from the exec producer.[92]

This resulted in a number of mis-steps in the live broadcasts – unexpected cymbal crashes, Glen mumbling and an

---

88 Current name: Vajazzle.
89 Not literally.
90 Not literally.
91 Current name: Popsox. (I'm writing this footnote on a different day to footnote 88.)
92 I was the exec producer.

all-pervading surliness from the band – which really put me off my stride. My professionalism was such that I didn't betray even a flicker of displeasure on camera, until I was sadly left with literally no choice other than to dismiss him live on air in our fifth show.

Let me just lay to rest, here and now, a baseless accusation. Some have suggested that my relationship with Glen soured when I learnt he was gay. For crying out loud, if I really couldn't bear to consort with homosexuals, do you really think I'd have pursued a career in television? At the BBC of all places?? Be real. I have no issue with gaymen. I'm a firm friend of Dale Winton, for example, one of the gayest men in Europe. (Dale and I spent a lovely weekend hanging out at the Earls Court boat show and he was delightful company – and knows a lot about rigid inflatable boats.)

(I also once shared a stage at a charity dinner with Elton John [see picture section]. Then again he did used to be married to a woman. I know he's with David Furnish now but I've long suspected that relationship is just a cover for his heterosexuality.)

No, Glen's sexuality was not a factor – at least not for me. My assistant was a different story. She had enjoyed Glen's company tremendously, and would probably have classed him as a friend. But her attitude towards him changed like that[93] when she learnt he was gay. Why? Well, she was and is a devout Baptist and, for all their handshaking and tambourine-bashing and shouty singing, many of them are staggeringly hard-hearted when it comes to 'sins of the flesh'. My assistant was typical of this world-view, somehow managing to reconcile the twin passions of home baking and homo-bashing.

---

93 I just did another click. A loud one.

But back to the sacking. Glen consulted his lawyer, citing unfair dismissal. His argument, that 'insubordination' is a disciplinary issue only in the military and therefore not grounds for dismissal in the private sector, saw him (temporarily) reinstated pending a tribunal, in time for the final episode of the series.

We muddled through that, a little frostily. But what followed was a regrettable period in which we began to sue and counter-sue each other on a juvenile, tit-for-tat basis. It was vindictive, uncalled for, and cripplingly expensive.

After several years, Glen and I managed to patch up our differences. We shared the common ground of both despising our respective lawyers and would often laugh about how much we were spending on their unnecessary legal advice. (Glen lost his flat as a result and lived in a YMCA for six months.)[94]

I dropped my legal actions against him some time ago, but he apologetically intends to pursue his against me, because his bandmates are currently suing him for unpaid earnings and he needs the money.

And so it is that he forges ahead with his live shows, long past the point that he derives any enjoyment from them. Indeed, with severely arthritic fingers, every swish of the baton is agony for him. I still go and watch from time to time and afterwards we go out for a Nando's together (you know which one!).[95]

(I enjoy the taste of chicken and chips enormously, and am only slightly put off by Nando's bewildering ordering system in which customers must pay for food at the counter, set the

---

94 And I apologise to Glen for my 'kid in a sweet shop' comments around this time.

95 The one that used to be Café Symphony. I mentioned it earlier?

table themselves and then wait for the waiter to bring the meal over. Interestingly,[96] Glen and I have developed an unspoken but quietly effective NES – Nando's Efficiency System – in which we ensure that not a second is wasted. We secure a table and then, with coats draped over the backs of our chairs, we separate. My role is to grab a menu and secure a place in the queue. From there, I loudly read out the food options so that Glen can hear. He, meanwhile, is scurrying to the far side of the restaurant to grab cutlery, napkins and condiments, but all the while he is listening to me and shouting back his order. I place it and pay. We usually end up back at the table at roughly the same time and then enjoy our chicken dinners, while chuckling at the many people who are still waiting for theirs despite having arrived way before us.)

Of course things take on a different hue if you dine solo. Last time I went to Nando's I was Glen-less. I placed my order but forgot about the cutlery. My food arrived and I had neither knife, fork or spoon. Admittedly, in a chicken-and-chips scenario the spoon is less important, but I could sure have done with a knife and fork – the former to cut with, the latter to maintain carcass stability.

Cursing the absence of my partner-in-chicken I went over to get the required eating tools, walking as fast as I could without breaking into a run. Just my luck – they were awaiting a refill on both the knives and the forks! Spoons, on the other hand? Dozens of them. I had no choice. With a lateral shake of the head and a vertical raise of the eyebrow, I return to my table. I've made the effort to find cutlery, I'm darn well going to use it. And I have to say it worked out okay. I shovelled the chips into my mouth as if I was eating pudding, and as for the

---

96 It is.

chicken – it was just a question of trying to drag the meat off the bone by using the spoon as a paw.

And what of me and Ponder? Well I don't talk much about our rekindled friendship. My assistant still harbours an openly bigoted dislike of Glen and his husband (whose name I don't know). But I enjoy it, and I'm proud to be friends with the greatest bossa-nova maestro this country has ever produced.

13.

LIFT OFF, SHOW-WISE

***

'GOOD MORNING, PEARTREE!' I bellow as I enter the offices of my prod co (production company).

'Good morning, Alan!' reply my staff.

'How are we today?' I continue, genuinely wanting to know.

'Great/not bad/back's still playing up/very well/fine/bit tired as my neighbour decided to do the fucking hoovering at two o'clock in the fucking morning,' reply my staff.

By now Peartree Productions was a well-oiled machine. We had some great people, working at optimum level.

Jason had been promoted to an assistant producer and had a newfound confidence since his psoriasis had cleared up. I had taken on George Dwyer as creative director. He had worked as PR man for the Russian Circus[97] and had some daring, out-there ideas, few of which made it through compliance. He's been living in the Wormwood area of west London for ten years.

Jill on reception was good to have around the place, clinging on to the last of her good looks and happy to buy choc treats for us all every Friday. Rupert Summers, who had experience of live TV from manning the telephones on ITV Telethon '88, would produce the show.

But it was Lewis Hurst, a theatrical agent who had invested some money in the company, who really pulled the strings. A bearlike homosexual, he was well-connected and well-to-do in a way that puts some people[98] massively on edge. But it was Lewis who had put in a call to Roger Moore and secured him as a guest in our first show. I was so pleased I insisted he join me round the back of the office block to take a photographic record of my feelings (see picture section).

It was also he, with a trademark tuft of jet-black nasal hair hanging down from each nostril, who had rushed into my office one day to tell me that celebrated *chanteuse* Gina Langland had agreed to appear in show three.[99]

But there were quite a few others in the company too who I'm unable to name. I've not forgotten them, having not known what they were called in the first place. My management style

---

97 Not the State Circus, another one.

98 But not me.

99 Better still, she would join me in singing an Abba medley live on air (see picture section). And what a medley it was! It was so in-tune it was almost out-of-tune!

Behind the scenes, though, it hadn't been quite so easy. On the night Gina had chosen to wear one of those dresses that stops before the armpits. She looked amazing in it but odour-wise it was an error. So while my eyes were happy, my nose was anything but. I'd spotted the potential

was that of an estranged father. At times caring, at times distant and with little to no interest in the individuals under my charge. And believe me, it just works.

The show began and was an unmitigated success. Viewing figures collapsed as the series went on, but only because it was getting lighter in the evenings and more people were out rambling or sitting in beer gardens.

The fan mail came in by the sack-load. Jason suggested I save it until the end of the series so that I could maintain concentration, which I did.[100]

There were one or two hiccups, but that's the nature of live television and I honestly don't think people noticed. Again, some of the guests were a little surly, but that has to come down to the booker and at the end of the series Jason was duly dismissed. (He went on to make his name producing a certain Orwellian house-based reality show that demeans us all.)

Tony Hayers gave us a few notes after the first show, and repeated the same ones after the second, third and fourth, but crucially didn't after the fifth or sixth, which suggests he was deeply satisfied with the trajectory of the series. We also bore in mind that he was only in the role to cover Georgia Harrison's maternity leave, so we didn't need to keep him onside for the long-term.

---

whiff prob in our dress rehearsal and had quietly asked my people to take the microphone I was going to use for our duet and spray it with after-shave or, failing that, some of that lovely air-freshener from the loos. And it really did the trick. Whenever I got a second to turn away from the audience I was able to raise the microphone upwards and give it a good, deep sniff. It was basically an improvised nose sorbet.

100 The sacks of letters were sadly destroyed in a fire before I could peruse them.

Success came very naturally to me. I'd go into a steakhouse or swimming pool and people would turn and exchange knowing glances. I was suddenly hot, appearing on *Through the Keyhole* and *Points of View*. I was also a guest on Clive Anderson's chat show (see picture section), embarrassing my host by revealing to the audience that he had started out as a humble barista. (I remember he resorted to feigning bewilderment at one point when I yelled at him, 'Now get me a mocha, baldy!')

I could get tables[101] at a moment's notice. I was stopped on the street by people telling me how 'unbelievable' my show was. I was hot and it felt goooooooood.

And then, live on air in the sixth and final episode of my chat show, I shot a man through the heart with a gun.

---

101 Restaurant or snooker.

14.
THE DEATH OF
FORBES McALLISTER

*****

CANTANKEROUS BON VIVEUR FORBES McAllister had brought
with him two of Lord Byron's duelling pistols, purchased in
auction from under the considerable nose of Michael Winner.
As I politely inspected them mid-interview, I discharged one
and the bullet penetrated and destroyed Forbes's heart. As
with so many gunshot wounds to the heart, it proved fatal.

I won't have been the first British chat show host to kill a
man on air, and I won't be the last. But I make no excuse for
what happened. I accept complete responsibility and you'll
not find me making mealy-mouthed excuses for what was a
truly tragic event.

What I will say is this. Forbes McAllister had led a long and
full life, but with a diet rich in cholesterol and alcoholic booze,

it's very probable that his health was failing. We can only speculate as to how badly his health would have deteriorated or how painfully drawn out his eventual death would have been – because I ended his life in episode six of my chat show.

Forbes, who may or may not have had a violent temper, was to be the final guest on my show. I remember in the green room before the show that he had incredibly sweaty hands. It's rare that I notice another's man palm-piss because my own inner-hands tend to work up a torrent of clamminess straight after towelling, one of the many reasons why I often greet new acquaintances with a curt nod or a wave. But I thought, 'Jesus Christ, now they're wet.'

This should have rung an alarm bell, because although I didn't know it at the time, our perspiration would soon create a lethal lubricative effect, which when combined with studio lights and a hair-trigger pistol would blast a man's chest into kingdom come. (Note that this in no way tallies with the findings of the coroner. These are my findings, not the Crown's.)

The show had been quite a strong one. It was certainly a little fruity. Of the six people on the sofa, 50% were gay. (Two lesbians and a gayman – although the gayman, Scott Maclean, was only ten at the time and probably unaware of his sexual trajectory.)[102]

Not on the sofa, but undeniably on the show were Joe Beasley and Cheeky Monkey. Having Joe appear was my one big regret in this episode.[103] I'd seen him at Bournemouth

----

102 Scott has continued acting, but now stars exclusively in gay pornography. Fortuitously, he has grown into the spitting image of Richard Gere, so has made a lucrative series of films that pay sodomical homage to Gere's back catalogue: *Gays of Heaven*, *Pretty Man* and *An Orifice and a Gentlehand*.
103 Or rather: one of two. Don't forget that I killed a man. Keep reading!! LOL.

Hoseasons way back in 1979, before so-called 'alternative' so-called 'comedy' had been foisted upon the world. Joe was streets ahead of his time, writing his own material and bringing a fresh perspective to the art of stand-up comedy. Unlike 'alternative' 'comedians', Joe's act – classy ventriloquism mixed with snappy one-liners – was mercifully unencumbered by the need to provide 'social commentary', unless he represented the Tories and the monkey whose rectum he forced his hand up represented coal miners or something.[104]

At Hoseasons, he'd raised the roof. I saw members of the audience doubled over, desperately trying not to wet themselves. Afterwards, Joe modestly suggested this was more to do with their age than his act, but I know good comedy when I see it. So I promised him I'd remember his name and give him a TV break as soon as I could. I honoured that promise on 21 October 1994.

I don't feel that Joe prepared properly for the show, and his act suffered as a result. I happen to believe that his joke about a Swedish Fred Flintstone[105] is a quite beautiful piece of writing, but he struggled to remember its precise mechanics and it slithered out of his mouth like a bad oyster. I stepped in to put him out of his misery[106] after about 90 seconds.

It had been an experience best forgotten but shamefully, in the years that followed, Joe did his best to trade on his disastrous TV appearance – he even attempted (unsuccessfully) to claim legal ownership of the sobriquet 'troubled TV funnyman' when the whole Barrymore thing blew up. Lesson learnt, Alan! I've never given anyone a break since then. It's just not

---

104 I'm not going to waste time thinking about this.
105 Abba-dabba-doo!
106 I didn't *kill* him! Or rather: I didn't kill *him*.

worth it. Joe never bothered to apologise, not even through the medium of the monkey.

But ignore that. This chapter is about Forbes McAllister. And I'd hate for my guests' unprofessionalism or sexual peccadillos to detract from the solemn death of a good[107] man.

To be fair to myself for a change, Forbes had been a pretty awkward guest and had brought the pistols on to the show himself and had very sweaty hands and was making sudden movements and saying some pretty off-putting things about bagpipers.

But, as I say, no excuses. At the show's denouement – trust Mr Professional here to time the slaying so it gave the show a neat conclusion! – Forbes gave me his sweat-drenched guns to inspect and shocked me with a loud bark of 'Be careful with that!' One thing led to another, and a bullet led to his heart.

I covered him with a plastic replica of my face and did my best to close the show. The two lesbians, Wanda Harvey and Bridie McMahon, went a bit hysterical. They'd been told to stick around on the sofa until the credits rolled, but when Forbes's remains slumped in their general direction, they bolted – in a pretty craven attempt to spoil the series sign-off. For that, I've never forgiven them.

It was a bit of a blur after that. My producer Rupert Summers lost his head and said a few mean things to me. I let that go. He was in shock and needed help not censure.

The police arrived and with Forbes bleeding over the sofas, which we'd actually only hired,[108] I signed off series one.

---

107 You have to say that.
108 One deposit: gone.

Then I looked over to where a policeman was putting the pistols carefully into transparent freezer bags. Those flippin' guns, I thought. I hated them just then. In the intervening years, I have received a great many letters from gunsmiths who have said that the greatest professional sadness a gunmaker endures lies in spending hours perfecting the release mechanism of a flintlock pistol, only for a collector to display it ornamentally. This was exactly what Forbes had in mind for them. I had at least prevented that. (I always think that like a dangerous dog sinking its teeth into the waddling rump of a fat postman, a pistol must experience the bittersweet bliss of fulfilled destiny at the moment of discharge – before quite rightly being destroyed.)

At least, my gunmaking friends seem to suggest, Lord Byron's beautiful and ballistically awesome pistols were allowed to perform the task for which they were painstakingly created – killing a man.

This was reality TV before the term was invented – real and raw and red in tooth and claw. Peter Bazalgette of Endemol fame is sometimes wrongly credited with the invention of reality TV.[109] In fact, it was Alan Partridge.

I've been asked many, many times what happened next. When the cameras stopped rolling and the audience filed out, what happened to muggins here? Well, I'll now do my best to describe it.

---

109 It's a little known fact that Peter's grandfather Joseph designed the London sewer network. Some people have very unkindly suggested Peter has simply taken what his granddad did literally and continued it metaphorically, delivering an unending torrent of human filth and waste into our homes. But I'm not one of those people. I think he's quite good and has made a reasonable contribution.

For added drama, I'll be slipping into the present tense, but I don't want that to suggest in any way that this took place anything other than a long, long time ago.[110]

***

'Why did you do it? Huh? Why the eff did you do it, Partridge?'

A bad-breathed copper shouts in my face and I turn my head away from what I think is the odour of Walker's Smoky Bacon – which I usually quite enjoy.

'What's your motive, Alan?' says a woman detective constable. 'Whatcha kill the victim for?'

I'm in a dark, dank room deep in the nick, handcuffed like a common criminal. A strip light flickers and buzzes as a rat scuttles across the floor.[111] The woman detective constable screams in frustration and slaps me across the face.[112] My eye closes up but I look back at her defiantly.[113]

The interrogation goes on for ages. 'Please,' I hear myself say. 'I've told you all I know. Can I please just go home? I'm doing a store opening at ten for World of Leather.'

'The only thing you'll be in tomorrow is a World of Trouble,' says the copper, a line that even at the time I thought was pretty good for someone who probably didn't get any A-levels.

Truth is, there is no store opening. With negotiations for a second series of *KMKY* going well, I have two other meetings the next morning that could shape my career. A current affairs show for a soon-to-be-launched TV channel from the mind of Kelvin McKenzie (alongside Derek Jameson), and a quiz show

---

110 *Press play on Track 23.*
111 Legal disclaimer: Not all of these things definitely happened.
112 See above.
113 See above.

for Maltese television that was based on *Blockbusters*. Both meetings are slated to take place in the same branch of Harry Ramsdens. I need to be there.

The interrogators don't let up, though. The torment lasts for hours before I'm thrown into a cold cell, and pick myself up from the straw[114] and filth.

Through a hatch comes a tray of food. I paw at it listlessly until I notice that it contains chicken nuggets. And what chicken nuggets! These boast all the smoky zing of McCain Southern coating with the tenderest cuts of white meat. The beans are lukewarm but not overcooked[115] and a generous dollop of smash adds a buttery finish that sets the plate off beautifully. To drink, a mug of steaming tea. A really, really good meal.

My solicitor arrives. By his own admission, he's better equipped to handle employment tribunals than homicide but it's a pleasure to see him. He's a massive fan of the show and insists that until the last five minutes it had been 'very good'.

I suffer the indignity of giving fingerprints – a relatively straightforward task that took longer than it should have because my hands were by now very, very sweaty and it was hard to produce a clear print.

Once released in the glaring sunlight of the sun, I'm hauled into the BBC for crisis talks, without a care for my other meetings. Hayers is quiet and it's really hard to work out how he feels the series has gone. A health and safety officer has a lot to say, which feels like bolting the stable door after the horse has legged it in a hail of gunfire.

---

114 Now I *do* remember there being straw.
115 Few things are more depressing than beans that have been over-boiled and stirred until the structural integrity of the beans have broken down into a kind of pulse mush.

As the exec producer, it turns out I have ultimate responsibility, which seems unfair to me – and I say so. We craft a press release and then I try to arrange a meeting with Hayers to discuss 'not just a second series, but other potential projects'. Everyone pipes up with 'For fuck's *sake*, Alan,' as if my career should die just because Forbes has.

Then I go home. People are quick to claim the credit when things go well, but journalists' calls to the BBC were met with an officious: 'Alan Partridge is not and never has been an employee of the BBC. He is a private contractor and all such contracts are under constant review.'

The shooting of Forbes McAllister was, without question, the pivotal moment in my life. I often think it's like that film *The Sliding Doors* with Gwenyth Paltrow. But instead of tube doors shutting, it was a bullet fired directly into a celebrity's heart. Not deliberately, or even recklessly. (Even after all these years, I feel compelled to add that caveat …)

You know, there were two victims that day. Me, because of everything I went through. But Forbes McAllister is also a victim in a way, because of course he died.

15.
SPLITTING
FROM CAROL

***

TRUTH BE TOLD, I knew it was probably curtains for me and Carol in 1989, when I asked her to act more demurely at a Radio Norwich summer roadshow and she responded by downing her glass of wine and getting another one. You don't piss about with a guy's career like that.

We lasted another six years – six years which for my money were among the happiest times of my life – and while I'm certainly not angling for a reconciliation with a woman like Carol, stranger things have happened. I believe there are few things that can't be sorted out over a coffee and a cuddle and I'm not saying I want her to at all but if she ever did have the guts to pick up the phone and admit she was wrong and was leaving her new lover and would I consider giving it another go, I'd be polite enough to give the idea proper consideration – on the strict proviso that the possessions of mine that I surrendered during the divorce were returned to me and that the sexual intercourse with other men was knocked on the head.

I first got wind of Carol's infidelity when she came home from the gym wearing a pair of black Asics cycling shorts after having gone out wearing a blue Adidas pair. Also, the Asics pair were for men.[116]

Suddenly things that had seemed innocent – the snazzy new hair do, the packet of condoms in her glove box, reported sightings of her in nightclubs with a man – started to collect in my craw. What was she up to?

I began to keep a diary. I publish it below only to demonstrate how in the right I was.

21 Aug 1995 – Carol's acting suspiciously again. Can't explain why but if you could see it you'd agree.

24 Aug 1995 – Carol's bought a new dress. No sign of it on any bank statements. A gift from a lover? [EDIT] Just realised she could have used cash.

30 Aug 1995 – Carol smells of a new aftershave – L'Homme I think. But I'm still using a giant bottle of Pagan Man [it was an ex-display model off a ferry]. Enough evidence to confront?

31 Aug 1995 – Didn't confront.

---

116 *Press play on Track 24.*

6 Sept 1995 – Carol's brother turns up and tells me she's seeing[117] another man. Reluctantly discredit his testimony on the grounds that he's a former alcoholic and current weed junkie.

21 Sept 1995 – Carol now staying at the gym two nights a week in order to be first on the cross trainer. Suspect that's a lie. Put in a call (false voice) to all local hotels to check she's not staying there.

4 Oct 1995 – Park up outside the gym and watch Carol enter. She stays until 8am the next day. Thank God. Thank God. She is staying at the gym.

26 Oct 1995 – Carol 40% less randy than this time last year. Menopause or sourcing sex from alternative supplier?

8 Nov 1995 – Found men's pants in the back of the Micra. Gotcha!

8 Nov 1995 – Actually what if this is a Gotcha? Edmonds can be one sick bastard, and I do have the profile to be the subject of a BBC1, Saturday night prank. Hmmm.

9 Nov 1995 – Realised they were my pants. Relieved/ disappointed.

15 Nov 1995 – Had a succession of calls to the house. Whenever I answer the caller hangs up. Even when I impersonate Carol.

---

117 He says 'banging' actually but I mean, honestly.

1 Dec 1995 – Heard Carol on the phone saying: 'That was great sex last night.' Oh this is so confusing!

[I spent several sleepless hours that night constructing rational explanations for this sentence. Perhaps she'd caught the tail end of a blue movie on Channel 4 and was chatting to a girl-friend about it? Maybe she'd said 'sects' in a reference to some pseudo-religious team version of step aerobics? Perhaps it was someone's name – Jim Greatsex? Perhaps she was trying to say Great Six in a Scottish accent. Come sunrise, I'd convinced myself of all these things.]

8 Dec 1995 – Struggling to find a spare moment to confront Carol. She's always at the ruddy gym.

15 Dec 1995 – Got drunk and tried it on with Sue Cook. She was so understanding – though witheringly emphatic in her rebuttal.

21 Dec 1995 – Had a long chat with Bill Oddie. An experienced birder,[118] he's lent me his binoculars and given me some great advice on how to remain still for long periods of time and go completely undetected in undergrowth and shrubbery. It's surprising how many of these techniques can be used to track an enemy or errant spouse.

---

118 Some people wrongly refer to birdwatchers as 'twitchers', a phrase emphatically rejected by the birding community – presumably because they think it paints birdwatchers as hunched weirdos beset by debilitating tics, which isn't always the case. I'm assured that only a small minority of them suffer from these kind of spasms.

*22 Dec 1995 – Called in sick to Peartree. Told Carol I was off
to the office then set up a vantage point opposite the house.
Binoculared her entering the premises with a man then
shutting the bedroom curtains.*

*22 Dec 1995 – Decided to stop keeping a diary now. I'm not
an idiot.*

Yes, it seems the French-smelling sex provider was Carol's
fitness instructor. Far from being French, he was actually from
Luton. His only Frenchness was his cowardly duplicitousness
and the kissing he did with my wife.[119]

***

I was waiting for Carol when she got back from the gym that
evening. She breezed into the kitchen, as I sat at the kitchen
table with a bottle of wine. I hadn't drunk from or opened it
– drinking during the day makes me nauseous – but I think
the effect worked.

'Been enjoying yourself? I said, but with loads of emphasis
so it was clear that 'enjoying' might have a double
meaning.

'Mmm-hmm,' she said, like she didn't have a bloody clue.

'Have a nice time at the "gym"?' I said, making inverted
commas around the word 'gym' with my fingers.

'Yes,' she said. Her knowledge of mimed punctuation was
pitiful.

---

119 i.e., 'French kissing' – a technique in which two mouths dock at the
lip, creating a closed arena for intermittent insertions and exploratory
recces of the tongue interspersed with quicker prods, darts, scoops and
jabs.

'Have a good workout?' I said, slotting my right forefinger in and out of a hole I'd made between the thumb and forefinger of my left hand.[120]

'Yes,' she said. Not a flicker. Who doesn't understand the finger-sex-mime for goodness sake? I lost it, throwing my empty wine glass crashing to the floor but it landed on the carpet of the hall in one piece.

'Careful,' she said, suddenly irritated. 'You nearly broke that.'

'What, *like you broke my heart?*'

Silence. I was particularly pleased with this line because it's the sort of thing I'd usually think of long, long afterwards and then admonish myself for not having come up with at the time.

'I know, Carol. *I know.*'

But then she turned to face me and looked so sad that I started to cry on her behalf. And then on my behalf. And then I didn't know whose behalf I was crying on because I was making a right mess. I had a cold at the same time so it was like a mucal tsunami.

She picked up the wine glass and handed it to me so I could have another go and this time I clattered it on to the lino where the stem snapped. Still not the smithereen effect I wanted but better than before. 'Thanks,' I said.

Then she led me to out to the garden and explained that she'd been having an affair with her gym instructor.

I asked all the obvious questions. Since when? Why him? How can you be attracted to a man who basically wears

---

120 Known in the international diving community as the OK sign – the left hand bit, I mean. For god's sake, don't do the sex mime to indicate you're able to breathe.

leotards? She told me all about him, including his name – which I'm not going to publish here in case, like Abba, it somehow entitles him to royalties.[121]

Eventually, after lots of crying (me), shouting (me), and sighing (both), we went back inside – we'd realised that the next-door neighbours were having pre-Xmas drinks and could hear everything. 'Enjoying this are you?' I shouted through the hedge. 'You like a bit of grief with your mulled wine??' I thought afterwards.

I explained to Carol that I'd forgive her. We'd try again in the morning, perhaps go and talk to Sue Cook about it, but she was shaking her head. I began frantically pitching shows at her – desperately outlining my portfolio of programme ideas in the hope of convincing her that we could be happy and rich. But she just kept shaking her head.

The doorbell went. Bill Oddie was standing there. I opened the door to him and was just saying, 'This isn't a good time, Bill' when he saw Carol. He could see I'd been crying and was clearly doing the mental maths. No one spoke for a while and then Carol gathered up her things, brushed past us and headed back to the Micra. She turned the ignition and a blast of 'The Winner Takes It All' came through the speakers before she could switch it off. I began to cry and she looked at me through the windscreen and reversed, very proficiently, on to the road.

We watched her go until she'd disappeared round the corner. At which point, we stopped watching. I noticed Oddie was just standing there. 'Not a good time, Bill.'

'Yeah, I know,' he said. 'I just wanted my binoculars back.'

***

---

121 Must get up to speed on this royalty thing.

I want to be fair to Carol. Yes, she's mind-blowingly selfish. Yes, she takes grumpiness to a staggering new level. Yes, she's manifestly not as clever as me. But she does have good points. On French holidays, she took to right-hand driving with real panache. She also makes relatively decent meatballs.

That pretty much covers it.

Carol left me 14 months after the last of my TV chat shows. I wasn't in a good place (the back garden usually) and she'd found it difficult to offer the right[122] support.

But I can't speak for Carol. Nor would I want to. Only she knows why she wanted our marriage to end, so she's very kindly outlined – in her own words – what went wrong. Over to you, Car.

'I loved Alan and probably didn't fully appreciate what I had. He was working hard to provide for me and the kids and I probably took that for granted.

'He was away from home more than I'd have liked but I acknowledge that Peartree Productions needed him and he had a career on the telly. You can't do that if you're swanning around at home, for crying out loud.

'He'd be working long hours trying to resuscitate his production company, his mind forever racing with new ideas and formats. Every now and then, in front of guests, I'd laugh at the sheer inventiveness of them.

'But yes, Alan's career hiccup hit me hard. I'd invested a great deal of hope in Alan being a fixture on mainstream TV for years and years to come. God knows, he deserved it and was (is!) a damn sight more of a talent than the likes of Tony Robinson or Andy Marr.

---

122 Any.

'When his show hit a few snags and he was hung out to dry by the BBC, I began to realise that my dreams of being on the arm of a BBC mainstay were fading. I mean, he'd come back stronger – that was never in any real doubt – but I was impatient and wanted all the rewards that he'd promised me.

'Hurt, upset and I guess a bit too moody about the whole thing, I took to visiting the gym. I'd suggested that Alan come too, but after every unreturned phone call to the BBC he'd dig an angry hole in the garden and so any spare energy went on that. Besides, he was already in pretty good shape.

'At the gym, I met a personal trainer. He was young, physically in peak condition – no arguments about that, fair do's, some people have a lot of time on their hands – and didn't stretch me intellectually, which did my confidence the world of good.

'In a clear contravention of my marital vows, I began sleeping with the guy. God knows how Alan feels about that. I never stopped to ask his permission or run the idea by him. This carried on for an indeterminate amount of time.

'I then split with Alan, who hadn't been having an affair. Not because he couldn't. He could. He was a well-regarded TV personality. You think he was short of offers? Dream on. But he exercised self-restraint. What can I say – that's Al.

'Alan wasn't perfect. There were a couple of minor niggles which I won't bore you with now. It wasn't anything significant, and it was certainly not in the bedroom department, a room where to be honest he played a blinder.

'So, that's my story. It's the tale of stubbornness, broken promises, broken dreams and – I have to admit – my own

shortcomings as a spouse. I'll now hand you back to
Alan. [123]

Thanks, Carol. Appreciate that.

Carol scotched ideas of a reconciliation and said we were splitting up for good in 1996, and I – of course – demanded sole custody of the children. Fernando wasn't keen as he was living in Cambridge midway through the final year of a politics degree, while Denise was living in Ipswich with an art collective. I consulted a lawyer nonetheless and he advised me not to pursue it. The law *always* takes the side of the woman.

---

123 These are Carol's actual words in the sense that I ghost-jotted them and faxed them to her I don't know how many times for her to sign off. She had ample opportunity to make amendments but declined to do so – ergo, she's happy with it.

16.

YULE BE SORRY!

***

THE DAY AFTER I confronted her, Carol had said to me she wanted to clear her head so moved out just before Christmas. I sat on the edge of the bath, sobbing and eating a pork pie until the pie was gone – at which point I felt a heck of a lot better.[124]

Don't get me wrong, the prospect of spending Christmas in unbroken solitude didn't fill me with cheer, but it actually turned out to be alright. Brilliant even. I've subsequently done the same (out of choice) on four other occasions.

The benefits once you think about them are obvious. You're free to break the rules. That year I had a glass of beer at 10am.

---

124 *Press play on Track 25.*

Imagine that! A glass of beer and a piece of toast on Christmas morn. I didn't finish it – it was horrible – but I chortled as I thought of what the 'ball and chain' would have said. Stupid cow.

Then there's the almost overwhelming sense of liberation that comes with wearing a dressing gown (nude beneath) without having to anxiously reknot the string every few minutes. The gown flops open and reveals your goolies? Big deal! No one's there! It just feels good. After a few more glasses of beer, I put on a CD of Christmas songs and marched up and down my landing to 'Stop the Cavalry' by Jona Lewie.[125] After a few minutes of brisk promenading, my gown spread apart, like the curtain of an old proscenium arch theatre to reveal a one-man show by John Thomas. I let it.

There were other reasons why Christmas alone was enjoyable too but I can't remember them at the moment.

Besides, bugger all that, I had a TV show to make!

I had been given a chance of redemption – a Christmas special of *KMKY* which had been agreed as part of the initial series commission. And with the internal inquiry into the regrettable death of Forbes McAllister still ongoing, I had yet to be deemed culpable of anything.

The upshot: the BBC was duty bound to honour my contract and broadcast *Knowing Me Knowing Yule*. Not that this was the only consideration. I'd argued strongly that we must respect the memory of Forbes and plough on. We owed it to him to treat his death with the tact and decorum it deserved. Besides, I'm confident the Beeb would have wanted an hour-long special from me anyway. I'd proved myself over the course of

---

125 A *brilliant* marching song, up there with 'Road to Nowhere' by Talking Heads and 'Portsmouth' by Mike Oldfield.

Knowing Me Knowing You to be someone who makes television as unmissable as Forbes McAllister's aorta.

So, for all my domestic problems, I had to push on. Carol had left on Christmas Eve 1995. *Knowing Me Knowing Yule* was to be broadcast five days later. Bring it on, as American peace-keeping soldiers scream when given backchat by unarmed natives.

The knowledge I could switch from the bony chest of my wife to the fleshy welcoming bosom of the British viewing public provided sweet, sweet, sweet succour.

Emotionally, I'd invested a great deal in the success of the show. And *nothing* was going to go wrong.[126] I spent Christmas Day alone, practising my musical number again and again and again until I my throat swelled up and I couldn't fit Christmas pudding down it.

The show was conceived by me as a kind of televised mulled-wine-and-mince-pies party that would take place in an exact studio mock-up of my house.[127] There'd be guests milling around, food being cooked, an air of festive cheer and three lovelies dressed as Mother Christmas. (Bit misleading that. They were basically models dressed in Santa outfits, on stand-by to hand out mulled wine and mince pies.[128] It's wrong to call them 'mothers'. There's no way any of them had been through pregnancy or suckled young. You could tell that from their bodies.)

And yes, we did have some last-minute gremlins. We had an eleventh-hour panic sourcing wheelchair ramps for

---

126 But brace yourself for the fact that it does.

127 An idea subsequently stolen, wholesale, by *Jimmy Hill's Sunday Supplement.*

128 Not beef mince.

[CHECK]-aplegic former golfer Gordon Heron, while star guest Raquel Welch cancelled three hours before we went live. Far from knocking me off course this provided a much-needed emotional outlet, as I was able to spend 30 minutes venting down the phone to her. I spewed all my bile into Raquel's delicate ear, sometimes confusing her name with that of my ex-wife, sometimes not. Referring to her appearance in *One Million Years BC*, I called her a historically inaccurate sexy bikini sex woman, spitting that dinosaurs had long since been extinct before the arrival of admittedly sexy hunter-gatherer cavemen's girlfriends that she'd played.

Still! We still had a great show lined up. The now permanent chief commissioning editor for BBC TV Tony Hayers was going to come and chat, we had bell ringers, the world's biggest Christmas cracker, TV chef Peter Willis,[129] a sexy trio of models I called Christmas Crackers and Mick Hucknall had agreed to perform because he was, in his words, 'trying to bang one of them'.

An appealing line-up certainly. And yes, there were a few glitches, but most of them occurred in the final four minutes of the show, and so I'm still satisfied that we produced a piece of high-quality television.

Admittedly, I left the studio a little shaken and with a hurt hand – but my spirits were up. As I'd walked on set that day I

---

129 Now the Michelin-starred chef-proprietor of Just Willis, but at the time suffering his own psychological meltdown which manifested itself in him appearing as transvestite Fanny Thomas. This is a period of his life about which he is deeply, deeply embarrassed, and if you meet the guy for god's sake don't bring it up. Much like Tom Robinson, he's now sorted himself out and has a couple of kids. He's left his homosexual days behind him and now does nothing more gay than shop for antique furniture. Good on you, Fanny! Oops! I mean *Peter*! ;-)

had no inkling whatsoever as to what a seminal moment this was. It would be my last show on BBC television.

I won't dwell on what happened other than to say our attempt to enter the *Guinness Book of Records* by pulling the world's biggest ever cracker went wrong due to the unbelievably shoddy workmanship of its makers, White City Pyrotechnics.[130]

That upset me to a disproportionate degree. One thing led to another and I ended up punching a golfing cripple in the face after he'd made an off-colour joke at my expense, and then responding to Tony Hayers's have-a-go intervention by belting him a couple of times too. But the rest of the show was nothing like that.

In retrospect, I'd taken my eye off the ball and allowed certain boundaries of acceptable behaviour to become blurred. I know – of course I know – that punching a wheelchair-bound former golfer in the face with a turkey-encased fist was wrong, just as twatting a BBC executive, twice, is inadvisable.[131] But I was operating on about four hours' sleep since Christmas Eve and I had set myself and the show unrealistically high standards.

But let's not get hysterical. Some people assume it's *always* wrong to smash a cripple in the face. But is it? Let me paint a hypothesis: what if the cripple, like the Jackal from 'Day of the' fame, actually had a false leg and was using a hollowed prosthetic limb to hide a specially adapted American bolt action Savage 120 rifle. What then? Is he still off-limits, fist-

---

130 The company no longer exists, but its owners James Judd and Tony Dee have set up Greenacres, a chain of care homes for the elderly which I *urge* you not to use – even if it's the only one in your area and your parents have become a real handful, toilet-wise.

131 Although *god knows* they need thumping now and then.

wise? I'm not saying Gordon Heron was an assassin necessarily. But you can see the point I'm making.

What if Osama bin Laden had been in a wheelchair when crack US forces entered his compound and, with no concern for their safety, bravely shot him in the head and neck? Similarly, a Zimmer frame could easily be four tommy guns in disguise with fake rubber feet on the bottom which the bullet could pass through once the Zimmer was aimed horizontally. What if he had one of them? Yes, there'd be an outcry from disabled pressure groups but would his killing have been *wrong*? It's not black and white. I'm just saying, sometimes – *sometimes* – not to hit a man in a wheelchair is an abrogation of responsibility as member of the public or the US military.

Besides, the realisation mid-broadcast that certain participants were attempting to sabotage the show had got on my wick so, yes, I responded. I make no apology for that. I was like a wounded animal. If you step up to me, you better brace your ass for a genuine smackdown. They stepped, I smacked. Down.

I couldn't face going home. So after unwinding with a few halves of bitter, I spent the night with Glen Ponder. The next day I felt much happier.

Some of the next day's reviews focused far too much on the final few minutes – and those that didn't each contained the phrase 'self-serving' or 'vanity project'. I found these comments deeply offensive. People[132] had *asked* to know more about my background and to find out who the real Alan was – if there's something vain or self-serving about spending £29,000[133] creating an exact replica of the inside of my home

---

132 A class of schoolchildren aged 8–9 years old.
133 In real terms, less than a woodwork teacher would have got in the 70s.

so that people gain a better understanding of me and my life, then guilty!!

Hayers, who required emergency dental treatment which I was happy to pay for, was needlessly off with me in the days after the show. He was angry that I'd invited him on to the show as a guest to, as he called it, ambush him into recommissioning *KMKY*. Nothing could have been further from my mind.

He was also angry that I'd punched him in the face.

I left messages with his PA to say I'd booked us in at a Pizza Express so I could buy him lunch to say sorry. I didn't hear back so I thought I'd better go anyway on the off-chance a message hadn't been relayed to me. He wasn't there, but fine. I wanted a pizza and tiramisu anyway, so it wasn't as if I was going especially for that. That would be *sad* and I'm not/ wasn't.

It wasn't a big deal, to be honest, because I'd already started thinking that I didn't want to be on BBC TV any more so it was fine.

Three weeks later I received a letter from Raquel Welch's lawyer instructing me not to contact her ever again. And that was fine too.

17.

RETURN TO NORWICH

***

IF THE BBC THOUGHT I was going to sit around waiting for them to mull over a second series or have yet more 'meetings' or conclude a criminal investigation into a man's death, they had another thing coming.

If a shark stops moving, he perishes. If I stop broadcasting on the TV or radio, well I don't know what happens because I've never let it come to pass. Probably not death but something pretty unpleasant – like glandular fever or the mumps!

I needed to work, so I approached Nick Peacock, then head of Radio Norwich, at a charity gypsy fight. Nick's a larger-than-life[134] character but I saw him as a heck of an

---

134 Fat.

admirable guy. He was beset by hygiene issues[135] but his indomitable spirit and enormous wealth had enabled him to achieve a marriage.

It's true what the Bible says, I mused to myself on their wedding day: beauty really is only skin deep. I mean, Carol Smillie is beautiful but blanks me every time she sees me and has a habit of tutting when I speak. Meanwhile, Anne Diamond is one of the nicest people I've met.

So I was pleased that even Nick could find someone. It reminded me of the relationship between Catherine Zeta-Jones (incredibly beautiful) and Michael Douglas (looks like a grey crow).

Anyway, Nick was helming Radio Norwich and had always been a pretty solid guy. So in between bouts, Nick and I found a quiet corner of the warehouse and I broached the subject of returning to Radio Norwich, in a role over and above and away from my erstwhile sports brief.

Sports reporting had been fun – I think I mentioned the evening I spent with Gunnell – but my horizons had broadened. People now looked to me to provide a much fuller 'broadcast experience'.[136] Merely providing award-winning snippets of sporting headlines would have left them short-changed and angry.

No, I'd lanced the all-rounder bubble, and the pus of mainstream acclaim had been all that it emitted – any sport that had been around had scabbed up and dropped off. I said to him, 'Nick, what can I do?'

He said, 'Do what you want.'[137]

---

135 See previous footnote.
136 My phrase.
137 He's my cousin.

Bloody hell, I thought. This is ideal. Nick wants me to do it, the listeners want me to do it, I want to do it.

'Oh, I'm not sure the listeners want you to do it,' he said. (I'd thought it out loud.) 'But tits to all that, I'm sure we can sort something out.'

It was such a refreshing attitude, I agreed to re-[138] sign there and then.[139] Listeners are important, certainly, but automatically placing them on some kind of raised plinth (or 'pedestal') is tiresome. Sometimes people need to put the DJs first.

Nick was ballsy. He'd been in charge of the big revamp of Radio Norwich, which to the naked eye comprised of a new aluminium handrail by the steps, and a slightly bigger sans-serif font on the signage. He said there was much more to it than that and said he'd overseen a major organisational restructure which I wouldn't understand. Try me, I said, and he reeled off some high-falutin corporate speak which I won't bore you with now but which I did understand.

There were plenty of familiar faces still at Radio Norwich and I was confident I'd be welcomed back by the guys there. No one had had a problem with me when I left the station back in 1991.[140] In fact, I'd seen some of them in bars and restaurants in Norwich during my chat show heyday and I'd frequently arrange for a glass of wine and an autographed napkin to be sent over, which I'd then acknowledge with a smile and a nod.[141] That was something I didn't have to do.

---

138 The hyphen here is crucial. Totally different word without it. Totally different.

139 *Press play on Track 26.*

140 I'd stood up in a meeting and said, 'If any of you people have got a problem with me, tell me now.' And no one did, which proves they didn't.

141 I'd seen Gary Davies do this to a group of 10 air hostesses in a Travelodge near Luton in 1990. Next morning, he told me he'd later slept with every single one of them. [CHECK]

But I did because at the end of the day I'm a good guy. As my mother used to say: it's nice to be important but it's more important to be nice. FYI – she was neither.

Don't get me wrong, I knew that there'd be the odd snide comment from people who think that a two-and-a-half-hour radio show five days a week is – I'm laughing as I write this – somehow a step *down* from presenting a half-hour TV talk show once a week (12.5 hours of weekly output, versus 0.5 hours). But there are idiots in all walks of life.

No, I wasn't worried about being welcomed back into the fold. Employees at a London station like LBC or Radio London or London FM might have been a bit sniffy about it, but people in Norwich are warmer-of-heart than their bitter London counterparts with their negative-equity and their stab wounds.

No, I wasn't worried about being welcomed back into the fold.[142] I was fully prepared to be the big man and chat to each employee individually to ensure there were no hard feelings, so I made sure I sidled up to each member of the team – in the kitchenette, outside the lavs, jogging after them in the car park. I was making the effort and it paid off. At the end of each of these conversations, I said: 'Right, point blank. Do you *like* me?' And they all said yes.

It was good to be back. I was pleased that I wasn't making television programmes. I was happy. This was good and I liked it. In short, I was glad to be back working for the radio station I'd been at five years earlier.

Had things changed at Radio Norwich in the time I'd been away? Not a great deal. While a few of the faces were different,

---

142 I know I've used this sentence twice in as many paragraphs but I do want to make the point that no, I wasn't worried about being welcomed back into the fold.

the people who owned them were the same. By that I mean, the intervening years hadn't been kind. For example, the girls on reception had sagged in the jowls a little and while I'd flirted with them in the past,[143] it didn't seem appropriate any more. But apart from the onset of ageing, I was pleased to see that the ethos, the spirit and the playlist of Radio Norwich were all exactly the same.

***

Nick and I fell out shortly afterwards. I'd asked for – and been given – the breakfast show. Done deal, shake of hands, my press release written. So when, just a couple of days before launch, I bumped into the incumbent brek-jock – a journeyman DJ called Dave Clifton – outside Oddbins, I commiserated in that hollow, plastic way that passes for friendship in the media.

'Bad break, mate,' I chirped. 'Good luck in what remains of your career.'

Dave frowned as he loaded his cans into the boot of his car, and claimed he wasn't going anywhere, mate. I told him I'd been given the breakfast show and he sniggered in a way that made me want to thump him in the guts.

'Depends what time you eat breakfast,' he laughed and drove away, wine bottles clinking in the boot like the laughter of a glass-throated child.

Nick (his skin now cloaked in a bumpy rash as a result of work-related stress and a wholly inadequate hygiene routine) had reneged on his deal – rendering him dead to me then

---

143 'Is it me or is it hot in here??' (if they were wearing a particularly revealing top) or 'I'm going to have to report you two. You're looking so lovely you're distracting people from their work!' (mock anger).

and always – and had slotted me into the early morning show. Providing classic hits, news, weather and chat from 4.30 to 7am was by no means a bad gig but it wasn't the flagship vehicle I'd been dangled. I confronted Nick in a corridor and told him he was making a massive mistake. 'You're making a massive mistake,' I said.

He mumbled something about upsetting the listeners and scurried off, but I followed him down the corridor. 'The listeners? Remember what you said? "Tits to all that, I'm *sure* we can sort something out! Tits to all that, I'm sure we can sort *something* out! Tits to all that, I'm sure we can *sort* something out! *Tits* to all that, I'm sure we can sort something out!"'

I'd followed him to studio 2, bamboozling him by placing the emphasis on a different word each time, and continued bellowing it for a while before I realised that Emily Boyce was in there doing the weather. She covered the microphone and said 'Do you mind?'

Realising my error, I gasped a sexual swearword. Although still hoarse with anger, I must admit I was deeply embarrassed by that. But I'm pleased to say Emily and I became firm friends and I never dropped the Fuck-bomb over her bulletins again.

Nick and I are no longer close – in fact I was delighted when I learnt that he wasn't invited to Fernando's wedding.[144] He left the station with a stress-related illness and I'm glad. I'm told that he's lost a lot of weight, but at a rate that made you think twice about complimenting him on it because it was more likely to have been the consequence of a serious illness. Again, glad.

Up With the Partridge – again, the name *Alan's Show* was vetoed by people who think they know my own output better

---

144 I wasn't either.

than I do – proved to be nowhere near as depressing as expected.

To be fair, the demographic was a real melting pot: farmers, taxi drivers, new mums at their wits' end, fishermen, late-night returning ravers, and the disturbed people for whom darkness brought only despair. That gave the show a really spontaneous feel.

On my insistence, we conducted audience research, using a survey that I designed, which turned out to be chock-full of insights and learnings. In fact, the findings directly shaped my show. With the majority of Norfolk owning or having access to a telephone, it seemed utter folly not to build the show around a phone-in feature. Similarly, we learnt that a daily feature in which we asked aviation fans to call in with sightings of RAF training exercises was causing distress to the families of servicemen and consternation among RAF top brass who argued that it had serious security implications. I thought that was a bit precious. But after 18 months, Scramble! was quietly dropped. This was agile, responsive radio and I was its pioneer.

I began to fall in love with broadcasting all over again. And in a funny, kooky, zany kinda way I think it fell in love with me again too.

***

I may have been back at the exact same station, in the exact same building, at the exact same desk (the ergonomics needed work), but I was in no doubt that I was on a steep upward career trajectory.

Helming my own show, with neither the limitations of a sports-only remit nor the self-serving irritation of studio guests, was a challenge as new and fresh as an egg salad. This time, I set the agenda. It was me and my personality and, as

I've been blessed with a superb personality, it translated into shit-hot radio.

For the first time, I was also at the controls when it came to selecting music. I knew that soundtracking my listeners' early mornings was a major responsibility – music is a powerful emotional catalyst, and research suggests that people are at their most irritable between five and six in the morning. I was playing with fire. If my listeners were anything like me, hearing a sub-par song on the radio before breakfast could see them slamming cupboard doors in the kitchen, scrubbing themselves down with bodywash a bit too aggressively, or shouting at the assistant on the carphone. And I was buggered if my music was going to damage cupboard hinges, torso skin, or carphone cradles – all of which I value enormously.

The knowledge that I was the conductor of my listener's mood saw me gemming up on what 'quality music' meant. I'd spend hours in HMVs, Virgin Megastores and second-hand record shops staffed by greasy-haired 40-year-olds dressed as 20-year-olds, listening to contemporary music of every genre – Britrock, heavy maiden, gang rap, brakebeat. And I came to a startling but unshakeable conclusion: no genuinely good music has been created since 1988.

The relief was, as Americans say, freaking awesome. The death of music on or before the release of *Arthur 2: On the Rocks* meant I was freed from the obligation of keeping up to date with contemporary music trends. Instead, I could continually revisit music that embodied an era of Thatcher, Hot Hatches and men who looked like girls – Bowie, Strange, Le Bon, Ant (not of 'and Dec' fame).

I also knew I couldn't just play music and read out the song title and artist – I wasn't Mark Goodier for goodness sake. I needed to speak good as well. Having learnt a lot from my time in London and on TV, I knew if I was going to become the very best disc jockey there was, I couldn't rest on these considerable laurels. After all, Caesar didn't rest on his, he wore them on his head. Same with Hadrian. Would he have built his fantastic wall had he been sat on the aforementioned decorative headwear? I think not!

I wasn't nervous. Some people thought I was nervous but I wasn't nervous. Nervous? Of what?! So no, not nervous. I just knew I had to put the graft in.

And what graft! I'd shadow my colleagues, sitting in on other shows to pick up tips, learn techniques or take ideas wholesale – on one occasion staying at the studios for two days straight until I began to hallucinate during the traffic report of my third show without sleep and jumped into a bank of monitors to avoid a motorbike.

I roped my assistant in as well, instructing her to scour long-wave radio for far-flung stations, and then tape entire shows – pausing whenever a record was played and then unpausing on the song outro – so that she could present me at the end of each week with an audio dossier of continental broadcast trends.

Invariably, I didn't have the time to listen to them – of course I didn't – but I know she enjoyed being involved, even if she could only tune into most LW stations by standing on a box and holding the radio out of an upstairs window.

In summary, then, I was becoming a better all-round broadcaster day by day. This bit could even be cut into a montage and set to music[145] like the training sequence in a *Rocky* or *Karate Kid* movie, albeit with less physical exertion.

---

145 *Press play on Track 27.*

18.

LINTON TRAVEL TAVERN

***

NOT A LOT OF people know this, but in 1997 I spent 183 nights in a Travel Tavern. To the best of my knowledge this remains the fourth longest period of unbroken residency in a British hotel by any non-OAP.

Carol and her non-Gallic sex-chum had by now returned to my marital home, so I needed to get out. Awaiting news of a second series from the BBC while simultaneously needing to fulfil commitments to Radio Norwich, meant that Linton Travel Tavern seemed an obvious choice.

It was situated in the sweet spot between London and Norwich, the perineum between the two metropoles at the Eastern rump of England. To say that it was *exactly* equidistant between the two wouldn't be quite true – that honour belongs to JCC Wholesale Butchers on the industrial estate behind Mount Pleasant Road. (And no, they won't offer wholesale rates to passing members of the public.)

Now when you go long-term in a comfortable mid-range hotel, choice of room is paramount. This isn't just a spot to lay your head for a couple of nights. This, my friends, is your house. So when I ended up with Room 28 I could not have been happier. Far enough from the centre of the corridor not to get piddled off by the incessant clickety-clack of the lift shaft, yet close enough to the fire exit to make it out alive if Al-Qaeda embarked on a repeat performance of their still-yet-to-happen American atrocity, albeit on a slightly smaller scale. Yes, if things went belly-up, it really was a beaut. And that's before you'd looked out of the window ...

'Oh my god!' I yelled at the top of my voice the first time I'd stopped to take in the vista. For a kick-off, no other room in the hotel could match it for unimpeded views of the A11. At any time of the day or night I could pull back my curtains and give you an accurate update on the traffic situation in either direction.[146] Of course for a road-user such as myself this was manna from heaven. Never again would I be at the mercy of tailbacks. If I saw the traffic was slow moving I'd set off early. If not, at the normal time. It's hard to put a price on that kind of up-to-the-minute intelligence. As it happened the traffic was never an issue for me (my show started at 4.30am), but that's hardly the point.

One of the most special things about going native in a Travel Tavern was how well-designed the rooms were. Everything you needed was so close at hand. It was like all the

---

146 On a clear day, and provided I'd got rid of any smudges on my binoculars, I could even see the M11.

best bits of living in a deluxe house but without the constant, endless hassle of having to move between rooms.

Think about it. Within that one bedroom you had a dining room (the bed), a lounge (the bed), a study (the desk), a meeting room (the bed and the desk), and even a gym (the gap between the bed and the wall). With a nightly routine consisting of press-ups, squat thrusts and shadow boxing, I don't think I've ever been so fit, certainly not while staying in a hotel anyway.[147]

In my last year living with Carol, Anglian Water had (against my will) moved us from a flat rate on to a water meter. To be honest I think they took one look at how clean I liked to keep my car and just saw dollar signs. On the other hand they were moving everyone in the county on to water meters so perhaps it wasn't a pre-mediated act of anti-Alanism. I guess we'll never, ever know. When you've been at the top and people perceive you to be not at the top any more, they often try to kick you when you're down.

I mention this because one of the other big boons of hotel life was the fact that water was free. I could use as much as I pleased. And believe me, I pleased. I'd often fill the bath, get in, then put the shower on too. It was like swimming in the sea

---

147 It's just occurred to me that in the previous chapter, when I said I spent the night with Glen Ponder, I should make clear I meant I went to sleep at his flat. I did not have sexual relations with him. Thought I'd cut in now and mention it while it's occurred to me. Believe me, there was no physical contact and the light remained as on as my clothes, save for my socks which I always remove to let my toes breathe because I have an intermittent athlete's foot. So, as I say, no funny business at all. The only time I've touched a man as I slept was on an Outward Bound course to Snowdonia when I hugged a man in a sleeping bag, but that was only for warmth. Richard doesn't have a gay bone in his body and is as manly as they come. He now runs a nightclub in Brighton called Beef.

during a tropical downpour. I called it my 'Caribbean soak'. Bliss.

If I was feeling like a challenge, I'd kick out the plug, turn the taps on and see if I could maintain the exact water level. It was like balancing the clutch in an old Mini Metro. Although tricky at first, by the time I checked out I could find the bath's biting point within three minutes. Satisfying? Just a bit.

Then there was the food in this place. Goodness me. Why not treat yourself to three restaurant meals a day? I know I did. Although on some occasions I was just too busy in my room – waylaid on an important business call, prepping the next day's show, watching *Emmerdale* – to go down for dinner. In which case I was able to improvise. Don't forget that every room had a kettle. That instantly opened the door to everything from cup-a-soups to Pot Noodles. Combine the kettle with the refrigerated mini-bar and – wallop – you've got yourself jelly.

But if kettle cuisine wasn't good enough for you, there were other in-room options too. At one point I smuggled in a microwave, though annoyingly the game was up within a week. A passing member of staff had been alerted by its unusually loud ding (a common failing of many of the newer Sanyos). I normally muffled the sound by wrapping it in my duvet and lying on top but on this occasion I'd forgotten, distracted by a cracking pile-up on the A11 eastbound (guesstimated fatalities: four, excluding livestock).

I tried to claim I wasn't using the microwave to prepare food. But they refused to believe that I only had it there to speed-dry hand-washed undies. You win some, you lose some.

One meal I'd always dine out for (out of my room, not out of the hotel) was breakfast. It was an all-you-can-eat affair, which was magnificent, but that wasn't the only draw. Every so often they'd have a chef out front making omelettes to order. Now I've always been pro-egg, but even by my standards this woman was good. She could turn out an omelette that wouldn't have disgraced itself on the tables of The Ritz, Little Chef, any of those places.

You had to get there early for Omelette Tuesdays, though, because after a while the quality pretty much fell off a cliff. Linda, the chef, was quite old and to be honest after cooking about twenty I think it all got a bit much for her. If you got there any time after seven thirty, the passion had just gone from her eyes. It was an incredibly sad sight.

A member of staff once told me that things had started to go wrong a few years ago when the fad for free-range foods came in. Linda just wasn't into it. Apparently when it came to eggs she had some sort of ideological objection to paying more than 6p a unit. Like I say, very, very sad.[148]

***

One person stands out from my eight-month Travel Tavern residency.[149] A chap by the name of Michael. He was employed there in what, as far as I could make out, was an unspecified capacity. I did see him behind reception once, but know for a fact that he wasn't allowed to handle money.

He was employed by a woman I referred to as 'Susan', which was her name. I'm not sure exactly how old she was, but she was good-looking for her age. In the early days I'd toyed with the idea of starting a relationship with her. Yet the more I thought about it, the more doubts I had. As a customer, I was

---

148 She'd been raised on a diet of powdered egg, so any real egg – even battery – seemed to her an unnecessary eggstravagence (my word).
149 *Press play on Track 28.*

in part paying her wages. And that more or less made me her boss. No, a sexual relationship with this woman would have been quite wrong. I did feel sorry for her, though, as I could tell she ached for me. But what can you do? I've barely seen her since I un-resided myself from Linton, although I did have a brief chat with her last year in her new role as Facilities Manager for the Norwich Metropole.

'Hi there, Susan. You're looking well,' I began.

'Thanks, Alan. How can I help?' she replied, three hours later (we were chatting via email – the 'you're looking well' thing was just me taking a chance).

'I wanted to ask about half-day rates for your conference room, please,' I responded, instantly – we were still on email but my assistant had my phone set up so it beeped when anything dropped into my inbox. 'PS Do you still ache for me?' I had half a mind to add, but probably in a slightly smaller font so as not to embarrass the poor woman.

A lot of the other staff were pretty joyless, which I thought was a shame because it really was a quality establishment – everything was premier but the price, as Dawn French's former squeeze would say. That lack of passion was typified by a pair of the hotel's younger employees. One was a guy called Ben, the other was a girl who often had her hair in a bun. My abiding memory of them is that they were having a relationship. Either that or they were brother and sister, I forget which.

Like I say, though, the one that stood out was Michael. By the time I left Linton I'd 'converted' him. He was no longer just an employee paid to do my bidding. He was now a friend, who did my bidding. I was dead glad to have a new buddy, but it was also nice to be able to prove wrong all those people who say that it's impossible to make a life-long friend out of a hotel employee.

His background was in the army. He'd served in Northern Ireland and Gibraltar. (He'd been in Cyprus too, but I think that was just on holiday.) So perhaps it's not surprising that he was a firearm enthusiast.

Whereas Michael thought we should all be allowed to own a lethal weapon, I didn't. In fact I am proud to live in a country where it's pretty tough to get a licence for a firearm. The last thing we want is to end up like the USA, where buying a gun is as easy as buying a bagel, and probably as cheap as well, though I'd have to check that. That said, the more I talked to him about it – whether at the Travel Tavern, in his largely unfurnished terraced home or at Laser Quest – the more I began to see chinks of logic in his argument.

I'm certainly not saying he won me over. He didn't. I remain as firmly opposed to gun ownership as ever. But stick this in your pipe and smoke it: what if a burglar breaks into your home when your children are lying in bed at night? Should you just offer to show him the way to the family silver/your collection of semi-antique tie pins? Given the kind of crippling mortgages that this country's homeowners are struggling with, surely they should be able to repel an intruder with a shotgun? No one wants people killed. But even the most liberal person out there would agree that you should be able to at least get them in the kneecaps. That's common sense. Just aim low, the law should say.

Or even worse than burglars, what if you've got foxes that keep coming into your garden? It wouldn't be so bad if they stayed on the lawn, but last night, and forgive the language here, they were fucking all over the herb garden. It's got to stop.

They're actually very randy animals, and that's okay, we've all got needs. But for Christ's sake keep off the flowerbeds. Never before had I been so irked by vulpine intimacy. I was so mad last night that I was considering fighting fire with fire. If I'd had a consenting adult with me (female) I'd have gone to their den and had sex in it. And that's despite the very real danger of coming away with a dirty back.[150]

Of course, that was all just in the heat of the moment. I soon calmed down and realised that a more measured approach was just to stay calm (after all, these were just wild animals following their instincts) and put poison down.

A lot of people criticised Michael for his love of guns. But at least he loved something. And I think we could all learn from that. After all, surely it's better to love something than nothing, even if it means a few intruders get paralysed from the waist down, or the neck down if it's dark and you can't see where you're shooting?

By the way I don't know why I've been referring to Michael in the past tense. He's not dead. I don't think he is anyway – he just texted me.

***

150 I shared that thought with TV comedian Alan Carr and told him he could have it for free. He laughed. The guy's a breath of fresh air. Some people unkindly say the deaths of Inman, Harty and Grayson have put talented entertainers like Carr back into some kind of closet. I hope not. I've long lobbied the BBC for the reintroduction of a primetime TV homosexual.

And yet some people have accused me of intolerance or homophobia, a word that didn't exist before 1980 – if you'd have used the term before then, people would have thought you were referring to a science fiction disease. Uh-huh. Not me. Although call me old-fashioned, but in my day public toilets were for pissing and shitting.

It seems that now that it's not a criminal offence, it's fine for TV homosexuals to be 'active'. Is that a good thing? I'll remain above the fray. That's for you, the reader, to decide.

Although if pushed, I'd say if the 'activity' remains in a private dwelling or hotel, is genuinely consensual and the age disparity is under a decade, let them broadcast.

It's a strange truism that people tend to feel sorry for a man whose house is a Travel Tavern. But for AGP (Alan Gordon Partridge) things were pretty ruddy swell. This was one of the most creatively fecund periods of my entire life. I was absolutely fizzing. I was like an Alka-Seltzer. Or a Berocca. Or to be honest just a bog-standard soluble aspirin – they've all got baking soda in. I remember once bringing this metaphor to life in a meeting with a senior executive from Fenway Plastics. I was on a short-list of two to front a corporate video. Seeing that he was wavering, I went for broke. I went right up to him, bared my gums and made a very loud fizzing noise in his face. It backfired. Not least because my mouth was still littered with bits of recently consumed banana.

It wasn't just corporate stuff keeping me choc-a-block busy. I also had projects on the boil with 24 broadcasters around the world. How many of the UK's other blue riband presenters could say that? And although the exact level of commitment from these channels was hard to gauge, they had at least taken my calls.

I was also injecting seed capital into a number of exciting business ventures. In the days before *Dragons' Den*, this was Partridge's Nest. Local entrepreneurs would come and meet me in my room. I'd lie on my bed eating grapes like an emperor and quietly listen to their pitches. I could tell they were nervous – after all, get through this and they were staring down the barrel of an investment in the high three figures – but I remained stony-faced. Again, like an emperor.

When they were done I'd put down my transparent bag of fruit and begin my questioning. Within minutes I would almost always have found their flaw. And I'd tell them too. 'Your business isn't scalable.' 'Your sales projections are gubbins.' 'I don't like your face.' Occasionally, though, very occasionally, someone would leave the Partridge's Nest having struck gold (up to a ceiling of £999).

In late 1997 I was ball-deep in a project that looked set to revolutionise the business travel market. A local man (don't recall his name, think it was either Jim or Tom, so I'll call him Jom) had come to me with the idea of ripping out the back seats of tens of thousands of company cars. If this had just been mindless vandalism against cars I would have laid him out there and then. Seriously, I'd have knocked his teeth out. But it wasn't, it was much more than that. It was an ingenious way to save businesses millions of pounds (or billions of pence) a year.

Why spend all that dosh paying for travelling employees to stay in expensive motorway hotels when you could just replace their back seats with beds?[151]

But it got better. The discarded back seats could be re-purposed as cut-price sofas for low-income families. You were helping the poor *and* creating a secondary revenue stream (revenue river more like!). I was so blown away by Jom's pitch I don't think I ate a single grape.

Right there and then I wrote him a cheque for £300. I would have gone higher, much higher. I would have pumped that man so full of seed capital it would have been coming out of his bum (up to a ceiling of £999), but I couldn't because it was the end of the month and I still had a few standing orders to come out.

There was just one hurdle to overcome: the rather delicate subject of (say it quietly) waste disposal. There was no question that travelling employees could park up in a service

---

151 I suggested the name 'Motel' as it was half motor car, half hotel but Jom wasn't keen.

station and get a genuinely great night's sleep in the comfort of their own cars, but how to deal with a call of nature in the middle of the night?

Now I knew for a fact that truck drivers just climbed down and did it on the tarmac. In the morning the cleaners would find neat little piles of it next to where the lorries had been. I was once lucky enough to have dinner with the general manager of Newport Pagnell Services (M1). I couldn't believe how unfazed he was by it. I think his exact words were 'that's just the way they are'.

I'm reliably informed that lorry driver clean-up costs are budgeted for by every service station in the UK. Apparently it gets its own line in the business plan. They'd rather it didn't happen but what can you do? If you try to stamp it out, they just go elsewhere. Don't believe me? Ask Bob Grainger up at Keele (M6). He learnt the hard way. You avoid them depositing their previous meal on-site but you also miss out on them buying their next. Apply a simple cost-benefit analysis: the margin on a service station breakfast is £5.95; clean-up costs are a pound a dump. If they boycott your services, you're looking at a total net loss of £4.95. Ergo, let them go.

The problem for Jom and me was that service stations turned a blind eye for people with HGV licences but that's where they drew the line. At a crisis meeting in early November, we battled to find a solution. The closest we came was the idea of installing caravan portaloos in the boot. We wanted to see if we could hook the flush up with the car's exhaust so that the human waste took the same exit as the CO_2, but deep down I think we both knew it wasn't going to happen. I demanded my £300 back that very afternoon. When it transpired that he didn't have the money because he'd spent it on mattresses, I took the mattresses instead, 15 in all. I've still got them actually. They're in a lock-up in Beccles. But you know what? That's business. If you can't stand the heat, don't cook.

19.

ME v HAYERS

***

I'D FELT SO AT home in BBC TV Centre I resented not being able to come and go as I pleased. Watching the building from a parked car for an hour every Tuesday filled me with a profound sense of sadness and anger, which I could quell only by reminding myself that a second series was still highly likely to be ordered.[152]

This was just a few short months after the slightly mitigated success of *Knowing Me Knowing Yule*. I was well aware that I'd upset Tony Hayers in a personal capacity by punching him in the face with a raw turkey – not kosher, I suspect – but was

---

152 *Press play on Track 29.*

confident that he'd be grown-up enough not to let it cloud his professional judgment.

As far as I'm concerned, I'd honoured my side of the bargain. Fact was/is, I'd been contracted to provide 6 x 28-minute shows, plus a 58-minute special – and I had delivered them.

I missed being in and around the Death Star, as Jeremy Clarkson calls BBC TV Centre. But as a friend of *Grandstand* back-up presenter Steve Rider, I could pitch up in reception whenever I liked and he'd come down and sign me in. Having accessed the building, I could stalk the corridors and have a coffee in the BBC café whenever I pleased. I was determined not to be forgotten, and reasoned that one way to stay right in people's consciousness and appear important was to perform laps of the building's circular corridors while pretending to be on the phone.

After a while, Steve called.

'Alan. I suggest you stop hanging around the place because people might find it disconcerting,' he said.

'Really?'

'I'm only thinking of your career. You know what they say – "Never feed a hungry dog".'

'No, I think it's "Dogs aren't just for Christmas".' I thought for a moment. 'You don't have dogs do you, Steve?'

Steve may not have been too hot on well-known phrases and sayings, but he was blessed with the kind of genuinely great wisdom you only find in men with side-parted hair. In short, he was right. He was always right. After the break-up of my marriage, similarly, he advised me not to eat my lunchtime sandwiches every day in the car park of Carol's gym. I knew deep down I shouldn't be sat there, but sometimes you need to hear it in the silky tone of Steve Rider for the penny to drop.

I thanked him – 'Thanks, Steve' – and hung up.[153]

On his counsel, I kept away from TV Centre and kept a low profile for a couple more months. I had plenty to be getting on with: restructuring Peartree Productions so that the printer was nearer my desk and the researchers sat facing *into* the room; keeping myself in good shape; re-watching every second of *KMKY* to identify areas for improvement (weren't that many); and finding a new place to eat my lunchtime sandwiches. I was also winning plaudits for my successful return to radio with *Up With the Partridge* on Radio Norwich. But I was of course waiting for the call from Hayers that said: 'Alan, we're on.'

I'd recently moved into the Travel Tavern and was enjoying the quite excellent facilities there. Anyone who's stayed in one of the 22 properties in the Travel Tavern franchise will know that those guys 'get' what the weary businessman wants. He wants to recharge his batteries without the namby-pamby fussing of so-called luxury hotels – concierges, extra pillows, free slippers, room service after 10pm. Believe me, my batteries were as charged as a Pentagram Infinity 2600 mAh rechargeable cell battery. Still the best batteries money can buy.

It was quality hospitality from top to bottom, and yes, I liked being there, but as the weeks wore on I became concerned

---

153 As I say, he's a good guy. He'd become chummy with me after a falling out with Des Lynam several years before at a *Grandstand* bonding retreat. Des couldn't help but correct what he saw as speech defects in fellow sports presenters – he'd picked up on my Norfolk nasality in the early 90s, for example. Unlike me, Steve had reacted badly to being told he had a tendency to pronounce 'this afternoon' as 'the zarfternoon' – but the fact is, he does and Des was bang right to point it out. Steve's not spoken to him since – and I'm the beneficiary. I am, Steve admits, his fall-back friend and I am happy with that.

about the radio silence from the BBC. I'd been fobbed off with the excuse that they needed to conclude the inquiry into the death of Forbes McAllister before they could talk about recommissioning me. But even after it was completed – I was effectively absolved, bar the petty conclusion that I was guilty of 'unlicensed use of a firearm' – the recommissioning process felt like it lacked momentum. That's not to say they weren't keen; I'm sure they can't all have been *that* thick. But they were dragging their heels in the way that only a groaning bureaucracy populated by Oxbridge graduates can.

Hayers in particular seemed to have forgotten what his job was. I knew what it was: it was to say 'yes' to quality TV shows. But he was too busy twiddling his thumbs, or getting someone else to twiddle them for him!

Let me tell you something. For a man who works five days a week in the BBC, Hayers was incredibly hard to get hold of. If he wasn't at the chiropodist or at his daughter's graduation, he was on holiday in the Gambia or in a broken lift. I mean, he was never *ever* at his desk.

I knew that scaling back my schedule of cold-calling might look like I'd lost some of my hunger and I didn't want to give that impression at all, so I kept trying. At the same time, I didn't want to sound like a broken record because I'm not. So I displayed my creative side in my correspondence. I'd send him a teddy with a note saying 'Alan can BEARly wait to get started on series 2', or a honey-roast ham with the message, 'When can we MEAT?'

I was on the verge of stopping because this approach was costing me a fortune and I was running out of puns. But then the call came. 'Tony wants to meet.'

I was a bit disappointed by this, because I didn't see the need for a meeting. Why wouldn't he just bike over contracts for the next series? I thought that was a bit off actually (still do) but, ever the professional, I just said: 'Fine.'

'He's booked a table in the BBC restaurant, Friday at 1.'

I knew for a fact this establishment served 'modern European' whereas I'd hoped we could meet at a TGI Friday because I wanted something with chips. So I politely declined, but then reconsidered and called back very quickly to accept.

Victory at last. I phoned down to hotel reception and told them I'd be moving out at the end of the week and then asked my assistant to find me a house that befitted a prime-time TV personality. She found one.[154]

I then phoned arrogant breakfast DJ Dave Clifton and laughed into the receiver for ages. It was important that I wasn't triumphalist about being recommissioned but equally it was essential that I got one over on Dave Clifton. This felt like a happy medium.

***

Two days later I was buying a five-bedroomed house to live in. I didn't expect Carol to come back to me but, knowing that she was living in a four-bedroomed residence, it was out of the question that I would live somewhere inferior when I was to be one of the faces of BBC television for the next decade.

As I was inspecting the facilities, the BBC called. Unable to wait until Friday, they brought the meeting forward. I had one hour to deodorise and get to TV Centre. Tough call. Ingeniously, I ended up doubling up on the two tasks by getting my assistant to hold the wheel on the A140 while I reached into my shirt and swabbed my pits generously with a roll-on.

---

154 Antagonistic talkshow host Trisha now lives there.

I felt, looked and smelt fresh and was in high spirits, electing to forego a conversation role-play in favour of a singalong to *The Very* Very *Best of Tears for Fears*. (Their album was actually called *The Very Best of Tears for Fears* but I didn't like 'The Way You Are' or 'Woman in Chains' and had taped it on to a C90 minus these two tracks, then renamed it to create a compilation that really was the crème de la cream of their output.)

Hayers came down to the restaurant door as I was deep in conversation with Steve Rider (I'd called Steve on the way and asked him to meet me there and engage me in 'high-level chat' to impress Hayers.)[155]

'... and I'll get Barry Sheene to bloomin' well explain himself when I next interview him,' I concluded as Hayers approached. In my peripheral vision, I could see he was as impressed as anyone would be by my casual mention of a former motorcycle world champ who was by now half-metal.

We sat down and Hayers began to make small talk.

'My Lunn Poly brochure arrived this morning so I've just been looking at holidays,' he started.

I could tell something was wrong – he was nervous, shifty. I ordered food and wine for us both – a nice German wine, some Italian food and UK water – as he tried to manufacture some chit-chat. This is *so* BBC, I thought. (Try meeting someone in the BBC and taking the lift with them – I guarantee they'll make some comment about the lift being slow or full. They are *inane*.)

'Portugal is supposed to be nice,' he stuttered.

'Cut the sweet shit, twinkle toes,' I said, like a latter-day Jack Regan. If I smoked I'd have stubbed it out at that moment.

---

155 Thanks again, Steve.

Instead, I set down my knife and fork and swallowed my Italian food. It was clear one of us was going to have to take charge and that someone was going to be me. 'Let's talk about the next series. I want a yes or no.'

His big face went pale and he averted his eyes. 'It's a no,' he said. Nearby diners who'd been secretly eavesdropping on our summit gasped and stared. I'm fairly sure one let a roast potato fall out of his mouth. 'Whaaaat?' they all thought.

I was more sanguine. Don't get me wrong, it was a hammer blow. But I'd expected it and didn't really have my heart set on working with Auntie anyway. The BBC is nothing if not risk averse and I was seen as a bit of a maverick. In fact, some of them called me Maverick behind my back I think.

No, I'd foreseen my career would be with other broadcasters anyway, so I really wasn't arsed.

I felt a bit sorry for Hayers then. Shadowy powers had clearly forced his hand, and he was snivellingly torn between losing a major piece of talent and upsetting his idiotic paymasters.

'Have you got any other ideas, though?'

I snorted. Did I really want to entrust my portfolio of projects to this shoddy outfit? I don't think so. But he practically begged me (it was a bit unseemly actually, people were watching) so I went ahead and listed them. Norwich-based crime drama *Swallow*, *Knowing ME Knowing You* (a factual show looking at the disease), *Inner City Sumo* and *Monkey Tennis*.[156] But as I reeled off format after format – each more daring

---

156 His loss. *Monkey Tennis* was later snapped up by TV stations in Laos and Taiwan and ran for two successful years – after which the format reached the end of its natural life and the monkeys were quickly and humanely destroyed.

than the last – I could see he was retreating into his cowardly, safety-first shell. All genuinely original ideas, all snubbed.

I did have another ace up my sleeve: *Motorway Rambles* – a travelogue of me walking the hard shoulders of British highways, with special permission from the British Transport Police – but it had been co-devised by Bill Oddie and he'd made me promise I wouldn't pitch it if he wasn't there. Fair enough.

The meeting was over. I had things to be doing that afternoon anyway, so I thanked Hayers, and stood up.

'But … but … we've not even had the cheese course,' he said.

I looked him square in the face and, without breaking his gaze, I struck the handle of the knife that was resting on the cheese board. The wooden edge acted as a pivot, the blade as a springboard, firing a cube of cheese up into the air. I caught it and wrapped it in a napkin, which I slotted into my pocket.

'While I'm on the subject of cheese,' I said, as the waiter hovered nearby, 'it's an open secret in the BBC that you *smell* like cheese.'

The waiter caught my eye. 'Ha! I've been *dying* to say that,' he thought.

Well, Hayers didn't know what to say. I didn't care. I'd had enough and the meeting merely confirmed my long-held desire to continue my career well away from the BBC.

I wasn't going to let a coward like him pay for the meal, so I took out a hundred-pound note and slotted it down the waiter's cleavage. And he did have a cleavage.

A noise snapped behind me, like the sound of a piece of flesh hitting a nearby piece of flesh. It was a handclap. It was followed by another from the far corner of the room. Then another. And another. And as I turned to face them, the diners broke into rich applause. It was as if they were saying: 'So long, Alan. The bigwigs might not appreciate you, but by God, we do.'

Thanks, guys, I thought. It means a bunch. Then I very calmly, very slowly, very proudly walked through the lunchtime diners and away into the night. It felt good.

20.

PROOF THAT THE
PUBLIC LOVED ME

***

READERS, PLEASE DON YOUR Kevlar body armour and retreat
from the blast zone, taking care to position yourself behind a
wall or stationary vehicle, because I am about to blow the lid
on one of the most explosive incidents in my entire life.
Women and children should remain indoors, keep away from
the windows and await further instructions.

For extra dramatic impact I will now shift into the present
tense.[157] It's a technique my editor at HarperCollins feels
worked particularly well in the chapter where I described my
own birth. And while he feels it worked less well in the
section on being interrogated by the police after shooting a

---

157 *Press play on Track 30.*

man, he does think it's worth having another go. So here goes.

A small pink tongue emerges from a man's mouth. It hesitates, as if blinded by the light, then darts left and right, greedily scouring the lips for any crumbs of moisture. It finds nothing, so starts again, this time more slowly, gliding over every crease and crevice like some sort of very thorough snake. Still nothing. It bows its head as if to say 'no drink today then', before slithering slowly back into the darkness.

Pan back to reveal that the tongue is mine (as is the mouth). We can tell by the look on my face that something's wrong. It's probably the eyes that give it away. The pupils have gone all dinky. I'm clearly stressed to buggery. A single bead of sweat trickles down my back like a rescue party sent to fetch help. But there is no help where it's headed. There's only my bottom.

I listen out for any noise. I haven't got my hopes up but boy I'd love to hear the roar of an approaching 999 car. Sadly, the only sound to be heard is the slight squelch emanating from my sweat-savaged undies. Unsure of what to do next, I decide to sum up where I am and what is happening to me, just so it's clear. The time is 4pm on 8 May 1997 and I'm being held captive in the home of deranged super-fan Jed Maxwell, I think to myself.

The day had begun so promisingly. I, Partridge was to conduct 'An Afternoon with Alan Partridge' at the Linton Travel Tavern. With Sue Cook as my ravishing special guest, it was to be a chance for me to re-connect with some of my most loyal fans. Yes they could call in and talk to me on my radio show every morning, but it wasn't quite the same. They could never be 1000% sure that they weren't just listening to someone doing a very good impression of my voice. For example

Phil Cool, Rory Bremner or local impressionist James Galbraith (to my mind, the pick of the three – his Desmond Tutu is so good he almost doesn't need to black up).

I'd toyed with the idea of doing an arena gig but quickly ruled it out. My fans (and any members of the hotel's staff who'd excitedly asked to sit in – and not just to bulk out the numbers) deserved better than that. They deserved something more intimate. Not in a sexual sense you understand, though with Sue Cook in the room you couldn't blame a chap for keeping his fingers crossed!! Seriously, you really couldn't. I think she's fit.

The format was to be looser than my TV show, firmer than my radio work. A fun chat with Sue about her life, loves and *Crimewatch* career, followed by an open Q&A with myself. And no topic would be off-limits, with the honourable exception of the recent hit on Jill Dando.

But there was another reason why I was fizzing with excitement like the sodium bicarbonate-rich soluble tablets mentioned in the last chapter. That morning I'd breakfasted with two senior execs from Irish TV channel RTE.[158] As a combination of fruit juice, fried food and hot coffee settled in our contented tummies, we began to get to know one another.

The art of befriending a fellow human was one I had come to perfect by this stage in my life. I could go from total stranger to close buddy in under two weeks. Just ask Peter Sissons.

---

158 I've got a lot of time for Ireland. Its economy was known as the Celtic Tiger, which I loved. Then, of course, it hit the wall, much like that sleeping dog on YouTube. Very funny. Just type in 'sleeping dog runs into wall'. If you don't watch it about ten times back-to-back, there's something wrong with you. I also like sneezing panda, keyboard cat, dramatic chipmunk, skateboarding dog, otters holding hands and 'Don't Taze Me, Bro'.

Meanwhile, the statuses of acquaintance, business partner or lover could all be achieved, on a good day and with a fair wind, inside 90 minutes. Even with the Irish. In fact, especially with the Irish. (Equally, if I'm forced to turn whistleblower, I can go from cherished friend and godfather to your eldest son, to the kind of guy you try to physically attack at a BBC BBQ, in less than an hour. Again, just ask Peter Sissons. Sorry Pete, no choice, mate.)

And so it was that by the end of our pleasantly greasy breakfast, myself and the RTE execs had hit it off in what I can only describe as 'a big way'. Better still, they had agreed to attend AAWAP (An Afternoon with Alan Partridge). We shook hands. 'If this goes well, Alan, we'd be prepared to take the format (minus Sue Cook) and put it directly on to primetime telly on the Emerald Isle. And don't worry about having to relocate to Ireland. You could just come over one day a week to record the show. Obviously we'd sort out your flights for you. Or, if you wanted to get the ferry we'd pay for your petrol for the run up to Holyhead and sort you out a cabin. And if you do buy any snacks on-board just keep your receipts and we'll get you reimbursed within 28 days,' their handshake seemed to say. I was deeply encouraged.

But then, disaster: I received word that Sue Cook had bailed on me. Incandescent with rage, I slammed my fist down on the reception desk. Such was the ferocity of the blow that it left a noticeable dent in the granite. I know their handshake had *seemed* to suggest that Sue wasn't a deal-breaker but it was too late, my confidence was shot to ribbons, pieces and buggery. Oh Cooky, I thought to myself, you are as unreliable as you are fit – i.e., very.

Sure enough, the show was a disaster. Some months later Michael, the kindly ex-Forces Travel Tavern employee, had attempted to put things in perspective. After all, I hadn't shot any of my guests dead. Neither had anyone been punched in the face with a turkeyed hand. And in a way he was right, but in the heat of the moment I couldn't see it like that. To my mind I'd just done a show that sucked some pretty big bum hole.

Worse still, the Irish televisual twosome had left. I gave chase and intercepted them in the foyer. Never before had they looked so Irish. I've no idea what that meant, but I do remember thinking it. Somehow I managed to smooth their ruffled emerald feathers, at which point they asked if they could come back to my house to talk further. I could hardly say no. In Ireland, due to a shortage of office facilities, it's quite normal to have a strategic business meeting in another man's lounge. The problem of course was that I had nowhere to take them. Only months earlier I had been comprehensively de-housed by Carol.

It was now that Maxwell had entered the story. To save my blushes, he had offered me the use of his bungalow. He would pose as my flat-mate/bungalow buddy and all would be well. Except when we reached his home, all wasn't well.

The first problem came in his choice of art. Over my mantelpiece there's a painting of a country church with a herd of geese wandering past. Over Maxwell's there was a painting of a topless female biker, her hair flailing in the wind, her nipples standing to attention like a couple of boob soldiers.

Yet all that would have been fine – after all, breasts are just sacks of fat at the end of the day – if it hadn't been for the *other* room in Maxwell's home. Maintaining the ruse that this was actually my house was proving pretty tense, so I'd gone to the toilet to piddle out some stress. Except I didn't know where the toilet was and when I'd pushed open the nearest door and entered the room – whoops! – I'd stumbled into this terrifying shrine to yours truly. And it's at this point that I'll return you to the powerful immediacy of my present-tense writing.

Fear ripples through me like the raspberry in a raspberry ripple ice-cream. I look around me. From floor to ceiling the walls are *covered* in pictures of Alan Gordon Partridge. This is one of the weirdest rooms I've ever been in, and that includes Bill Oddie's blast-proof underground bird chamber.

Immediately I figure out that Maxwell isn't a good Samaritan, he's a dangerously obsessed super-fan. But the RTE executives behind me see it differently, viewing it as evidence that I'm an East Anglian egomaniac. They flee before you can say 'Gerry Adams'.

I scan the walls. Some of his pictures have come from magazines and newspapers, but to my horror others have been captured with a telephoto lens. I'm now incredibly nervous and give voice to this in the form of a very loud gulp. Yet at the same time I can't help but notice that Maxwell's photos are actually very good, especially because many have been taken while crouching behind bins, squirrelled away in bushes or – Jesus of Nazareth! – hidden inside my shed.

I particularly like one shot of me stepping out of the shower, circa 1994. Don't worry, reader, you can't see my privates. In fact, Maxwell has cleverly used the cactus on the window-sill as a kind of photographic loin cloth. But what it does capture is a certain muscularity. This was the year, don't forget, when I had set myself the goal of being able to do a one-armed press-up. And while I was destined never to succeed, all the gym work had left me with a body that would not have looked out of place in a magazine for men who like to look at other men.[159]

Yet what really draws me to this photo, what really speaks to me, is its portrayal of my hidden vulnerability. Sure there's the raw, animal power of my physique, but there is also an essential fragility to my personality. And that's communicated with real poignancy by the fact that there's nothing more than a spiky Mexican plant shielding the world from my freshly washed penis and balls.

Yes, I like Maxwell's work very much indeed. But there's no time to dwell on this. 'I've got something to show you, Alan.' Blocking the doorway, Maxwell removes his shirt and utters a sentence I will never forget. 'I've had a scale drawing of your face tattooed on my stomach.'

For a split second I think maybe it's one of those transfers you used to get free with bubble gum. But no, it's too big, too complex to simply be an old-fashioned lick-and-peel. It really *is* a tattoo. Though one thing it *isn't*, is to scale. Even with fear muddying my senses, I refuse to accept that my face is as big as a torso.

The next thing I know, Maxwell has donned a plastic Alan Partridge face mask. Although not official Partridge merchandise, these masks are nevertheless a lot of fun. Still available from *www.maskplanet.com/partridgeface* at £9.99 for ten (excluding postage), they're ideal for parties of all kinds. All I ask is that they not be used for Halloween. Have a bit of respect.

---

159 Each to his own and all that, but the idea of a man looking at my rock-hard buttocks and salivating makes me want to run home and deadlock the doors. And please don't infer from that that I'm a homophobe. I'm not and haven't been since I attended The Boat Show with Dale Winton, Paul O'Grady and Noel Edmonds – he's not gay but you get the picture.

It's now that things take a worrying turn for the worse. In what I fear may be the first stage of some form of ritualistic sacrifice, Maxwell begins to chant a terrifying noise. Avian in nature, I think perhaps it's bird song, a crow maybe. To my relief it turns out that he's just shouting my well-known TV catch-phrase ('Aha! Aha! Aha!'), but the panic has galvanised me. I need to get out of here.

My only concern is that he may be preparing to use a weapon. If it comes to hand-to-hand combat I have every confidence that I can take him down. As a teen I'd been schooled in the ways of Judo. I chose not to progress to the very top belts as I knew I was becoming capable of badly hurting someone with the sheer proficiency of my self-defence techniques. The thought of breaking my opponent's arm, or ensuring that his shoulders remained in contact with the mat for a count of three, only to discover 20 years later that he had become, say, head of Norfolk's biggest Range Rover dealership, made my blood run cold.

Fair enough I'm not karate world champ Jackie Chan, but nevertheless there's a certain sense of invincibility that comes with knowing that 30 years ago you were awarded a green belt in Judo.[160] My guess – Maxwell will pick up on this and stand aside.

My guess is wrong. Maxwell twists my arm and fixes me in a headlock. Clever. He knows that one wrong move from me and my head will be ripped clean off. I have to act fast. Quick as a flash, I elbow him in the nuts, nodding as I hear the

---

160 It's a strange feeling that only people with high-level self-defence capabilities can ever really experience. I once discussed this with some sumo wrestlers who I interviewed with a translator, and they completely agreed.

satisfying thud of bone on gland. I've just turned his testicles into a couple of bollock pancakes. And it feels good. 'Would you like lemon juice with them, sir?' I roar, inside my head.

Fear still ripples through me like it does in that flavour of ice-cream I mentioned earlier, but my will to survive is strong. No, Maxwell, Alan Partridge isn't ready to die just yet. Despite the fact that my wife has left me and my kids rarely take my calls, I have a wife and kids to live for. At this point he's still doubled up. I charge over and – bang, bang – head-butt him twice in the back. He screeches like an alley cat. 'Looks like I got the kidneys then!' I roar, still inside my head.

I quickly consider my next attack. Time for a bunch of fives, methinks. Looking around I see Maxwell catching his breath. Then, like an animal rearing up on to its hind legs, or like a human standing up, he stands up. I send a command to my brain. Instantly the fingers of my right hand start to curl inwards. Within seconds a fist has been formed. I launch it directly at my assailant's eye. 'Delivery for Mr Maxwell!' I roar, this time remembering to say it out loud.

'Really – what is it?' his furrowed brow seems to ask.

'A knuckle sandwich!' my fist replies.

Somehow recovering from the force of the blow, Maxwell picks up a chair and swings it at my brain. I duck, thwarting him with the sheer speed of my knee bend. Now on my haunches, I have an idea. Tucking my head into my chest I launch into a ferocious forward roll. It skittles the insane super-fan in the blink of an eye.

For several minutes we thrash around on the floor like Tarzan and that crocodile (I'm Tarzan, he's the croc). If I'm honest the rolling around does little to advance the fight and causes neither of us any injuries. We get back to our feet. Maxwell now has me by the throat. We both know we are entering the endgame. He thinks he's got me, I can see it on his ugly mug, but he's not counted on one thing – POW! – I floor him with a classic one-inch punch. Textbook stuff, a real gut-buster.[161]

With Maxwell fighting for air, I see my chance and make haste for the exit. But before I can reach my car, he's giving chase. In his hand is some sort of weapon. I don't get a chance to look properly but my hunch is that it is either a gun or the brush from a dustpan and brush. In a split second I've reached my car, slid across the bonnet and got inside. I crank the ignition. The gentle throb of the Rover's British-made two-litre engine is as comforting as a nice big hug from Mummy (would have been, were she still alive). Before Maxwell can reach me I wind down the window and holler something witty. It may have intimated that he was mentally and physically disabled, I forget now.

As I put the pedal to the metal he's tearing after me. Yet for the first time since I entered his house, I'm starting to feel confident – the Rover 800 can out-accelerate most cars in its class, never mind a sprinting nut-case. But as I ease her into third, a wry smile dancing across my increasingly moist lips, I spot something awful. I'm driving down a dead end! I slam on the brakes and can't believe it when the car comes to a halt without careering through the fence. Then again, I had bought British.

---

161 I'm shocked by my own strength. I feel like those women who lift cars to free their trapped children. I've always thought it's odd how little press attention these stories generate. Maybe they are just urban myths, but I'm very interested in the argument of my friend Michael. He believes the truth is that the government deliberately keep a lid on these stories because they don't want housewives to know how strong they really are. Food for thought certainly.

By now Maxwell is almost upon me. I bolt from the car, swivel on my heels and begin to sprint, leaping over a five-foot stile like it isn't there. I hurtle across a farmer's field, my legs eating up the ground, my arms pumping like the pistons of a big Victorian steam engine. It doesn't even matter that I'm wearing a shirt, tie and blazer, nor that instead of running spikes I have on faux-leather shoes bought from a supermarket.

Within minutes I have sprinted for what is surely about four miles. More to the point, Maxwell has given up. And who could blame him? I've just blown my previous personal best for fleeing across fields right out of the water.

I just manage to stagger to a public phone box. I call my assistant and tell her to (a) collect my car and (b) deal with Maxwell personally. Hanging up, I slump against the side of the phone box and slide into a heap on the floor, the calling cards of a hundred local whores raining down on me like big drops of prostitute rain. I begin to weep. I have cheated death. I am free.

And today? I am stronger, wiser and happy. People assume the episode must have profoundly affected me but I can honestly say it's not something I ever think about. Move on. (You may now remove your Kevlar body armour.)

21.

HAYERS: DEAD

***

SUE COOK'S VOICE WAS shaking. Ordinarily, it'd be hard to tell whether it was through emotion or because the pubs had yet to open, but this was 3pm so I knew it was the former.

It was five months after the now totally forgotten Maxwell incident and I'd just been MCing over the public address system at the Swaffham Country Fayre, one of the red-letter dates on the Norfolk agricultural calendar but smaller than the Norfolk Show. I didn't care about that. I was and am a positive person – an arialator-half-full kinda guy.

FYI – this was agriculture with the emphasis very much on 'culture'. Face-painting and craft stalls were the order of the day, and an accordion player was on site, playing television theme tunes to delighted passers-by. I was happy to be there and soak all this up – it was proof positive that 'culture' isn't confined to London. In fact, the only time I've ever seen an accordion in the Big Smoke was one strapped to a Romany woman[162] outside a tube station. I enjoyed the fayre, although I left early because people were hassling me to return to TV.

No sooner was I back at the TravTav, than Sue phoned.[163] She'd been phoning for an hour. Something must be wrong. But something wasn't wrong. Something was right.

'Tony Hayers is dead,' she said. 'Tony Hayers. Dead.'

This was the sort of thing Sue did for a laugh all the time, but on this occasion I knew she was genuine. Hayers was dead.

---

162 I actually have the utmost respect for elderly Romany women, after one of them read my fortune in a beer garden with incredible accuracy. I'd honestly never met this woman before but she reeled off intimate details of my life that left me dumbfounded. She listed five things that rang true as a bell.

i) She said I was concerned about travel. CORRECT. I'd just put in an expenses claim for a non-work-related train journey (back to my car after an over-ambitious ramble) and was panicking that I'd be exposed.

ii) She said someone close to me with the letter e in their name had had health concerns. CORRECT. My daughter DEnisE (my capitals) had had been suffering from migraines and was sent to see a specialist, although it turned out to just be stress-related illness from over-work.

iii) She said I had been unlucky in love. CORRECT. Carol and others.

iv) She said I would be given good news by a man wearing blue. CORRECT. Not three days later, I would told by a British Gas engineer that my combi boiler repair was covered by the original warranty.

v) She said I should be wary of 'the Birdman'. CORRECT x THREE. In the months that followed I was shouted at by Bill Oddie (looks at birds), crippled golfer Gordon Heron (name of a bird) and Jim Rosenthal (looks like a bird).

Some people will say there's nothing psychic about this – that these could apply to anyone, that they're vague, or that every now and then she's bound to get lucky. Alright, if it was just one or two maybe. But FIVE of them? Get real.

163 *Press play on Track 31.*

I bowed my head for a full minute to spare a thought for his loved ones. A tear tumbled down my cheek as I pitied his younglings.[164] Only then did I begin to smile. Whatever your views on human death, this was a good thing to happen. The world, the medium of TV and more specifically my mental wellbeing were all improved by the death of Tony Hayers, 41.

I mined Sue for the key pieces of info. He'd fallen off a roof, trying to fix a TV aerial. My first reaction: the interference probably had nothing to do with the aerial; more likely caused by wide-band impulsive noise generated by nearby heating thermostat. That's *basic*. I chuckled to myself – he was even clueless about television at home. Can't say I'm surprised!

My second: who's taking over? I closed my eyes and waited for the answer. Not that I was desperate. I had plenty of ideas and was in demand for broadcasting work elsewhere. Hamilton's Water Breaks had pencilled me as understudy for their next corporate video; I was in the early, early, early stages of repurposing *Up With the Partridge* for TV; and the pilot script for *Swallow* had received admiring glances whenever I left it poking out of my bag. But as the nation's broadcaster, the BBC was probably my more natural home. Whether I would deign to return depended on the identity of Hayer's successor.

Sue grunted with pleasure. 'They've only gone and give it Chris Feather,' she said. Then she had to go because the 3.50 was starting and she had a bet on.

This was the dream scenario. Before his liver transplant, Chris Feather had been a rising star at the BBC – blessed with

---

164 But at four and six, their memories of him would at best be vague and, on the plus side for them, his death would lead to a welcome cash injection because of the life insurance that people in his position all too predictably take out – don't tell me that doesn't sweeten the pill.

the common touch and not a clever clogs. You wouldn't find Chris in an ivory tower unless the Ivory Tower is the name of a pub! Our paths had crossed in local radio, when he'd been a fledgling producer, and I'd been impressed by his way with people and his knowledge of ELO. (It was he who had alerted me to the fact that Roy Wood could play the bassoon.)

For his part, Chris had been blown away by my tenacity, my restless creativity and the fact that the camera/microphone loved me. He pledged that we'd work together in TV. I still have a beer mat on which he scrawled that very promise.

Yes, he drank too much and, yes, he was slovenly and coasted through several years of his career and wasn't a student of the genre in the way that I was.[165] Chris was more of a casual observer. But he was the best man for the job and I'm not *just* saying that because he liked me.

It was only polite that I got in touch to offer my congratulations. But that could wait. First I had to be there for Jane Hayers. I barely knew her and she'd not exactly covered herself in glory by marrying an idiot like Tony, but widows are needy people and I was going to do everything in my power to support her. So I sent her a travel clock wrapped in black tissue paper and in a black box – not the ones from aircraft.[166] The card was fashioned from black card. Inside in silver Pentel, I'd simply written, 'You are really sad' and I'd made the 'o' of the word 'you' into a smiley face. (I'd thought

---

165 I still am. Rare is the day I settle down for an evening in front of the *Million Pound Drop* or *The Cube* with Phil Schofield, without access to a notebook and fountain pen. I scribble notes on production techniques and format. 'Too much make-up on Bradbury', 'Impeccable, Tarrant. Impeccable' or 'Invent quiz show with world record prize'.

166 Which are actually painted red. Try finding a black cuboid on a sea bed. It'd take you all bloody day!

about doing a sad face but I wanted it to be a celebration of his life.) I posted it to her and only then realised I'd forgotten to sign it.

On the day of the funeral, I was one of the first to arrive. To my surprise Chris Feather was there too. Clearly, this wasn't the forum to discuss my employment at the BBC so we acknowledged each other with a nod and I set about comforting Jane.

Jane was bearing up well but as I approached I could see the suffering in and around her eyes. I held her and we cried together. She was happy with the travel clock, but was still upset at being widowed. Understandable. I hadn't been expecting a mail-order clock to cancel out the grief, I'm not suggesting that.

As she wept, I continued to hug her. But *in no way* was it sensual. Well, certainly not on my part – I can't speak for her and I guess she was in a bad place. Grief manifests itself in strange ways. Besides, I've always thought people can be too quick to judge widows who strike up affairs soon after their loved one has died. Cut them some slack! It's no reflection on the dead guy – it's just that, sometimes, the sweet succour of sex can help speed up the grieving process.

***

It was a day later and, after a respectful period of mourning for a man whose death I was over the moon about, I was in the office of the new head of programmes for BBC Television. Mister Christopher Feather Esquire.

Chris was in good spirits, alert and of sound mind. He had drawn up a contract that would tie me to BBC TV on a £200,000-a-year deal. I broadly agreed with its terms and signed my approval on the dotted line.

I wouldn't say I was particularly ecstatic. It was no less that I deserved, which meant it was one positive that cancelled out the negative of Hayers's snubbing me. But not a second positive that would have pushed my happiness level higher than average.

Chris took the pen.

'This might seem like it was drawn up on a whim, but I know exactly what I'm doing,' he said, clearly and alertly. He winced as he gripped the pen.

'I trapped my hand in a door earlier so my hand hurts and my signature might end up looking a bit weird, but I should still be able to sign this.'

He did so slightly gingerly but in a very lucid and legally binding way. I shook his good hand and left.

22.

HOMESLESSNESSNESS

***

I BADE MY FAREWELL to the Linton Travel Tavern in the only way I knew: by taking my luggage to the car and paying my outstanding balance with a credit card. I was touched that Duty Manager Susan had taken the trouble to see me off/take my payment.

'There's your receipt, Alan,' she said. I could tell she was keen to chat.

'Six months, eh?' I continued, commenting on the duration of my stay in the hotel. 'That's almost long enough to gestate a baby.' I winced. It was a clumsy choice of words. I'd already established (see page 152) that she ached to have me inside of her. So it followed that she also longed to bear my child.

For several seconds we embraced, or rather our hands did. Finally, with the handshake over I got into my car, made sure it was in neutral, turned the engine on, found the biting point, checked my mirrors, indicated to pull out, released the hand-brake and drove away. I'd also put my seat-belt on.

All in all, it felt good. I was ready to embark on a new chapter of my life, roughly similar to the one before the one before this but better because my fee was higher. Yes, I'd be back at the BBC making television programmes and earning north of £200k per annum as a result.

My intention was to resurrect Peartree Productions but with better, cheaper personnel. It had been wound down but not dissolved. I thought of it as more of a sleeping volcano, dormant for several months but always ready to ejaculate hot TV content into the air and over the surrounding land.

I moved into a penthouse in Regent's Park – not because I liked London or wanted to show them, show them all – but simply because it was practical for me to be close to TV Centre. I still drove back to Norwich for my radio shows.

It was an expensive place to rent, certainly. I don't know the exact figure but it didn't really matter because I was earning north of £200k per annum. It was really big as well, with four good-sized bedrooms and a kitchen that had a coffee maker built into a wall, like a scalding hot vending machine (never used it).

I was happy there, sipping coffee (I'd used the kettle) and looking out over the high-rise London skyline as I dreamt up the perfect guest list for the new series: Sir Clive Sinclair, Loyd Grossman, Charlie Dimmock, one of the Britpoppers, Sebastian Coe. Yes, these were ruddy good days.

***

But these days were as fleeting as a collection of fast birds. Upsettingly for audiences and Alan Partridge alike, I was never given the chance to make my much-wanted TV shows. Because shortly after I had left Chris Feather's office, Chris Feather had died. Right there in his chair.

Yes, within minutes of signing the deal of his life, Chris had breathed his last. I sent a message to his daughter, saying 'I hope it's of some comfort to know that the last thing he did before he died was a truly courageous piece of commissioning.' I know she received it because I got a 'Read Receipt' in my email inbox.

At this point, you're probably thinking 'because'? But what's that got to do with it? How does the death of Chris affect a contract between you and the organisation he worked for? And you'd be absolutely right to think that. It'd be like arguing that the Treaty of Versailles is now null and void because David Lloyd George isn't with us any more.

And, believe me, this was an argument I made very forcefully. A fortnight later, I was in TV Centre with my lawyer (who's more au fait with citizen's advice and whether ramblers can traverse your land than TV contracts – and was pathetic actually). Incandescent with rage, I don't think I've ever screamed at television executives that loud before or since.

And what a weaselly collection of pond-life they were. Chris's successor, Jessica Boyle, was a sigh in human form, every utterance accompanied by a shrug or a rolled eye. For a woman in her position, her posture was a disgrace. Boyle is one of the new breed of BBC TV execs for whom television programmes seem to be a genuine inconvenience.

She was flanked by Kev Butterworth, a once friendly BBC lawyer who might have been a strapping Irishman but is also one of the few men I know who's beaten by his wife. I think it started from a sex game that went wrong 12 years ago. He once said to me, 'If only I could remember the code word' and then began to well up.[167]

The rest were your usual mixture of John Lennon clones and failed CBBC presenters who have ended up in HR. They pretended to make notes as Boyle outlined exactly why she didn't want another chat show from me. But it was all viewing figures and audience appreciation ratings and stats and figures.

'Listen, love' I said, 'if TV was all about numbers, they'd put a keypad under the screen and turn it into a giant Casio calculator!'[168]

This cut no dice with anyone in the room. 'Alan, sorry ...' they all kept saying, but looking at each other rather than at me.

'It's a contract,' I said. 'A *legal document.*'

'The contract, yes ...' Boyle sighed. 'I wouldn't set too much store by that.'

'Is that right? Well, let's see what the Director General has to say about this!' I shouted and stormed out of the room to the end of the corridor.

---

167 He's moved to America now so he won't mind me talking about it, but his wife did used to beat him quite a lot. She's still in the UK but I'm not naming her. Anyway, I think she's reverted to her Polish maiden name. She's a teacher in Nantwich.

According to Jim, she used to beat him with a plastic hosepipe then whirl it round her head so it made a futuristic noise. It may well be that she used to work for the BBC Radiophonic Workshop. (The BBCRW used to manufacture sounds in the pre-synthesiser days. It's an open secret that the Tardis noise was made by a BBC engineer scraping his keys down the fat wires inside a piano. And I'm told the sliding doors on *Blake 7* were made by a clothes brush being swept across the back of a leather jacket.)

168 I'd prepared this in advance.

A minute or two later, I found myself back at the meeting room, having forgotten that the corridor is a circle. Too tired to argue or stomp any more, I collected my satchel and jacket to the sound of embarrassed silence and left.

I knew then and there and then that this was the end of my relationship with BBC television. It was sad in a way. And so, before heading to the car park where my assistant and some sandwiches were waiting for me, I strolled back round the corridor – one last time. Ever the maverick, I went against the grain, meandering *anti-clockwise* through the corridors of laughing liberals. Then I bade the building good day and left.

People have suggested I bottled out of taking the BBC's breach of contract to the highest court in the land. Others say that have heard whispers that there were 'discrepancies' with Chris's page of the contract.

Neither is true. I'd just had enough. I could easily have seen out the contract, made a cool million and given them half a decade of my life. But I had bigger fish to fry. That day, I left the BBC, the BBC didn't leave me.

***

So the BBC had reneged on my new TV deal in a way that shredded any remnants of honour or integrity they may have had. I had racked up substantial debt, and cash flow meant that I defaulted on the rental agreement of my London apartment and was asked to leave. I was homeless.

I'd only just left the Travel Tavern, and even though I could definitely have gone back to a warm welcome, £49 for room and breakfast was now out of my budget. I had nowhere to turn – and forlornly tramped the streets in my Rover 800.

Night was beginning to fall and, with a seriously heavy heart, I was about to drive to the modest bungalow my assistant shared with her racist mother … until I remembered something! A solemn promise, a vow that had been made to me more than three decades before. The words had been intoned by my (*metaphorical*) guardian angel Trevor Lambert. He'd looked into my seven-year-old eyes and made me a rock-solid pledge: 'You can come and stay any time you like.'[169]

***

'Hello?'

It was Sheila who answered the door, now a bit mumsy, like Fran had been. There was a raised inflection at the end of her greeting but these days you don't know if that's because it's a question or because the speaker mistakenly thinks they're cool.

Quite reasonably assuming it was the latter, I replied 'Hello' and kissed her on the cheek. She recoiled a little bit and then tried to shut the door on me. She made a kind of yelping noise, which is when Kenneth appeared. He looked older because he was 35 years older than he used to be.

'Alan?' he said. Again, I wasn't sure about the question/ cool thing. But this time I said, 'Yes it's me.'

He smiled a bit and put his hand on her shoulder to reassure her. (It could be that she had a poor memory for faces and didn't have access to a television set, I thought.) She didn't demur so he said, by way of explanation: 'Alan Partridge!'

'Ahaaaaaaaa!!' I boomed and Sheila bolted down the hall.

I strode in and dropped my hold-all neatly to one side, before walking into the lounge and warmly greeting them all. They looked astonished – but then, it occurred to me, you

---

169 *Press play on Track 32.*

would be. They'd not seen me since I was about 17! I'd not been in the house since I was seven!

Trevor's asthma was now something to behold, and he had some of the most severe breathing difficulties I've ever shared a room with. He was rigged up to breathing apparatus with an oxygen mask strapped over his mouth and nose. The guy was still audible though and, when reminded who I was, politely asked, 'What can we do for you?'

I reminded him of his invitation to come back and stay 'any time'. At first I was embarrassed that he had no memory of it, but then I reasoned that he was old which explained why it might have slipped his mind. If not for that: awkwaaaaaard!!!!

My timing couldn't have been more perfect. A few months earlier and I'd have returned to a pretty empty nest with just Fran looking after her wheezing husband. But as luck would have it, Sheila and Kenneth had moved back into the family home quite recently because Fran had had a stroke and now needed round the clock care. For her part, she seemed a little diffident and didn't say much, but then she was still a long, long, long way off a full recovery.

After a quick cup of tea, I bade them good night and bounded up to my room, lying on the bed with my hands behind my head. (Lying on my back I mean, not my front. I was in a state of relaxation rather than internment.)

Yep, it felt good to be in the home when I'd been at my happiest – and to be back among the family, although Emma no longer lived there (she was dead). Her space was filled, if you like, by Sheila's husband Tim, a pretty nice bloke who had seen my shows and said he quite liked them.

Staying there was just the tonic. My three months at the Lamberts' were just enough to get me back on my feet. I referred to them frequently on *Norfolk Nights*, and my listeners took their trials and tribulations – Kenneth's continued unemployment, Fran's slurred speech – to their hearts.

We each had to make compromises, of course we did. I had to store my property in the garage even though it was cold in there. For their part, the Lamberts knew if I was going to manage a solid morning of show preparation, I needed the kitchen to myself between 9 and 12 – I had to insist on that.

For a while, things went smoothly, but soon Trevor's breathing became a bit *too* loud. It was really off-putting. So I eventually decided to take my notes and Dictaphone to the public library and do my work there.

In fact, I became such a fixture there, I heard one member of staff quietly refer to me as Karl Marx. I don't think so! I'd take his ideas about the redistribution of wealth and shove them where the sun don't shine! The workers own the means of production – I ask you!

I was determined – absolutely adamant – that I wouldn't outstay my welcome at the Lamberts. And so, after 14 weeks, I saddled up and hit the road.

'Thanks for having me,' I said.

'Don't mention it,' Fran Lambert seemed to say with the good side of her face. 'You can come and stay any time you like.'

23.

SWALLOW

***

ON THE TITLE PAGE of my pilot script for Norwich-based detective series *Swallow*, I wrote the words: 'Dedicated to the memory of Stacy Morgan, 7.'

Stacy wasn't dead – she never even existed actually – but I thought it would set a poignant tone for the episode and/or gain enough pity to sway the mind of a commissioner. But I've scrubbed Stacy's name off now and replaced it with that of Pete Gabitas, who did exist and is now dead. He's sorely missed.

I'm often asked if I have a manager or agent and, instead of answering with words, I used to take out a ten pound note, tear a quarter of it off and then scrunch that bit up and throw it in a bin.[170] Never had one. Waste of money!

---

170 I've stopped doing it now.

And, as my career has proved beyond doubt, I've never needed one.

But if anyone came close to filling the role of agent/manager, it would have been Pete Gabitas. The MD of BlueBarn Media, Pete was a big-hearted, big-bellied guy, who liked nothing more than providing cut-price production facilities to the region's most creative minds – and then rounding the day off with a pint or two! We were kindred spirits, each/both sharing a love of Norwich, quality music and hovercrafts.[171]

Does he say the unsayable? You better believe it! He's like Norfolk's very own Jeremy Clarkson, but one who actually believes the stuff he comes out with. He's *whip* smart.

He had his share of enemies, sure, but that comes with the territory when you're hoovering up the lion's share of corporate production and post-production contracts in the North Norfolk region. People were forever trying to topple him off his perch, something I found especially callous when he revealed he was suffering from a serious illness, the little-known 'tall poppy syndrome'.

All healthy competition you might think. Until I tell you that Pete died in a car 'accident' on 1 April 2005. Look to your right and you'll see I've put inverted commas around the word accident. There are many of us who suspect foul play. I'm no conspiracy theorist – although I often regale

---

171 I can't speak for Pete of course, but my early interest in these floating vehicles was sparked by the chase sequence in *Live and Let Die*. Sometimes you forget films, don't you, but this scene has always stayed with me. It's up there with classic scenes such as the Union Jack parachute bit in *The Spy Who Loved Me* and the scene in *Sophie's Choice* when she has to choose which of her children to send to their certain death. As you can see, I *love* movies.

dinner parties blow-by-blow with the arguments advanced by *Capricorn One* and *JFK*[172] – but I am convinced that Pete was murdered.

It was around 11.30pm when his wife's silver Peugeot 306 cabriolet with red interior careered off the road and into a primary school. Yes, he was way over the drink-drive limit – and ordinarily I'd agree that the alcohol could have been a factor. But knowing Pete as I do/did, I can assure you he's a better driver when drunk. So much so that he's often given me a lift home when he's been drunk and I've been sober.

That night, he'd had six pints of lager and half a bottle of wine – pretty much the sweet spot for his driving capability. To the untrained eye, he looked very, very drunk. To the trained eye, my eye, I know that he was fine to drive.

So, having ruled out alcohol as a contributing factor in the crash, you have to ask who wanted Pete dead and how did they do it? I'm in the process of making a YouTube video about the case under the banner of 'Alan Partridge scrutinises ...' (hopefully the first of many).

---

172 I have similarly strong views on the death of Princess Diana (indeed, when she died I wanted to ring up the media and say, 'Happy now??' but I didn't have their number).

To this day, there are so many questions that don't add up. When I hear people refer to it as an 'accident', I shake my head and chuckle at them. Ditto when people say the twin towers were not detonated by the CIA.

By a similar token, I'm proud to say that one of my favourite books is Erich Von Daniken's *Chariots of the Gods* which alleges that Jesus was genuinely an alien. And people may scoff, but I'm yet to meet anyone who can provide a compelling argument that the ascension into heaven was anything other than Christ taking off back to some kind of mothercraft.

Of course, I don't believe *every* word he writes, but Von Daniken himself says 2% is conjecture and 98% is probable fact.

Funnily enough, it's the kind of case that would be perfect for a regional detective like Swallow.[173] Pete was a massive fan of Swallow, perhaps seeing a little of himself in the rule-breaking cynic.

I'll give you the quick pitch now: Swallow is a cool 50. He's works in Norfolk CID. Whereas most regional detectives drive a classic or unusual car, Swallow has saved up to buy a brand new five-door Audi A3 turbo diesel in metallic graphite grey with black fabric interior. He's not interested in satnav, leather seats, or CD stacker systems. That, to Swallow, is just so much bullshit.

His vice? Well, booze has been done, so I thought it would be quite nice if he was bulimic. (I got the idea from seeing John Prescott cleaning himself up in the toilets of the Savoy.)

Fastidious but austere, Swallow always carries a checklist of items: a comb, two biros, Fisherman's Friends (the mint, rather than people), and a faint smell of vomit. Plus an evidence bag which he never uses for evidence, but keeps folded in the right-hand pocket of his donkey jacket in case he has a big meal. Yes, Swallow's always very well turned out, with pressed slacks, black leather tie, buffed-up shoes and a rich brown leather jacket.

His is a restless mind – even in his downtime he has to occupy himself. But rather than immerse himself in chess (been done), Swallow solves Dingbats and other word-related puzzles, including word searches. He likes nothing more than sitting down with a copy of *The Puzzler* in a wicker chair that looks out over the fens and *immersing* himself in puzzles.

He also has a weakness for doing 10,000-piece jigsaws. In case you hadn't noticed, this is a metaphor for solving a case.

---

173 *Press play on Track 33.*

And in the last episode, we'd see him put in the final piece and suddenly seeing that it depicts the face of the local conman. Quite how or why this would work isn't yet scoped out. He's also a keen cook, gardener and birder. He has no middle fingers on one hand, so he can't swear but is permanently doing the heavy metal sign.

I see Swallow as something of an enigma. He has the largest collection of samurai swords in Europe, but no one knows where he got them from. And when not cooking or tending to his gardens or completing jigsaws or finding words or watching rare wetland birds, he plays kendo – the Japanese martial art with body armour and big sticks of bamboo (*shinai*). His sparring partner and friend is Chan, a Chinese widower who owns a laundry next to Wallis Shoes on Exchange Street in Norwich.[174] He's a useful foil to Swallow because, as a laundryman, he doesn't *think* like a police officer.

Throughout the pilot episode, we see Swallow constantly harassing a circus even though left-wing university-educated police chiefs reprimand him for it. But at the end of the pilot episode, his right-wing views are vindicated when he blows the lid on a drug smuggling racket. He works out that drugs are being smuggled in the collective recta of circus elephants when he spots bags of drugs among the grassy balls of dung on the circus floor.

He lives alone. His marriage broke down because his wife was too selfish to recognise his cleverness.

Is he politically correct? Who, Swallow?? No chance. He's old school, and is aware that a disproportionately high amount of crime is committed by the unemployed and asylum seekers

---

174 Don't bother looking for it. It's a Halifax!

so why not stop them and shake them down? The squares at Police HQ can swivel.

In the pilot episode, Swallow suddenly notices there are no black people in Norfolk. Have they been spirited away or were they never there? He has to crack the case.

Also in the pilot episode, he wages a war against the travelling community who almost never have the correct documentation for their vehicles. He frequently impounds them to get them off the road.

The pilot episode follows Swallow as he's assigned a naïve young sidekick, DC Wide-Eye, a stickler for the rules. Together, this odd couple have to come together to find out who's been fly-tipping in a residential area.

It goes without saying that the show will look terrific. The series will be peppered with skyscapes of Norfolk while the opening sequence will be shots of huge deciduous oaks intercut with two masked men playing kendo intercut with a drive-by shooting intercut with two hands playing a jigsaw. The reveal at the end is that the *kenshi* are Swallow and Chan and the jigsaw player is also Swallow.

Incredibly, the rights to *Swallow* are still available for purchase. I can be contacted through the publishers.

24.
OTHER, BETTER
TV WORK

***

PEOPLE WHO WORK IN broadcasting hate to admit this but it's true: the vast majority of TV is unwanted. Audiences sit there, stuffing Doritos into their fat mouths, passively allowing television programmes to wash over them with the odd drib or drab landing in their eyes and ears. Do you honestly think anyone ever *wanted* to watch *Going for Gold* with Henry Kelly?[175] Or set the video for *World in Action*?

It's hardly fulfilling to pour your heart and soul into making TV content only for it to be used as an audio-visual backdrop to a man doing a crossword or a tired mum smacking one or both or all of her children.

---

175 Not even Mrs Kelly.

The same cannot be said for corporate, marketing or public information videos. In watching them, your audience has made a conscious, active decision to view. They've gone out of their way to remove the free DVD from its polythene sheath, to turn off their BlackBerries for a health and safety induction, or to shuffle their way to the recreation room to learn about the dangers of diabetes.

They've made an appointment to view, and that knowledge makes the work utterly thrilling. It was this exciting realm that formed the next stage of my broadcasting career.

I hope this doesn't sound vulgar but the money is effing brilliant. It's borderline grotesque. I was *not* complaining. These people will pay through the nose for a presenter who has the gravitas, humility and time on their hands to front content that will be seen by less than a thousand viewers. I had that humility. And time. And gravitas.

Markedly different from publicly available TV work, this kind of presenting was a real learning curve. And I learnt plenty: you *must* smile when you say the name of the product – even if it's for a genito-urinary complaint. There's no need to speak louder for a geriatric audience.[176] And there's no budget for wardrobe so dress smartly before leaving the house.

Between 1996 and 1998, I became quite indispensable in this specialist strand of broadcasting, having seen off Rob Bonnet and John Stapleton in the land-grab that followed Nick Owen's back injury. Until then, Nick had earned – and this is only my estimate – more than £12 million a year, and while I didn't even approach those kind of numbers, I earned enough to pay for a hire-purchase vehicle and a static home.

---

176 They sort that out in the dub.

Play your cards right (and I do) and this kind of work can provide a deliciously regular source of income. This sort of ready dosh can be handy when you need to pay for life's essentials – groceries, utility bills, the slush fund you set up some years ago to defend yourself against the odd bout of unavoidable legal action.

But I say again – it's not just anyone who can land these kind of jobs. You need to hit a certain level of ability before the really big boys start knocking on your door. You don't seriously think that just anyone can be trusted to record a ten-minute sales video for, I dunno, Beccles-based Startrite Intrusion Detection Systems? I mean these alarms save lives.

Pick the wrong man (Rav from *Crimewatch*, for example) and potential customers will take one listen to his voice and zone out. The net result? People are going to wind up dead. Try sticking that on your CV.

So it makes me proud to say that during those years I have fronted over 60 corporate videos for everything from potato-based processed food products to Latvia.

Of course it wasn't always plain sailing.[177] I was once cow-bombed while stood on a traditional East Anglian narrowboat[178] fronting a piece of sales collateral for the county's leading off-land holiday operators.

It was a sunny afternoon and out on the Norfolk Broads the mercury was nudging 90. On the river-bank beyond, holiday-makers and the unemployed were sunning themselves in 32 degrees of pure British Celsius. It was then that my marketing patter was interrupted by a cow falling on me from a motorway bridge.

---

177 This pun will become more enjoyable as the paragraph progresses.
178 See?

Incredibly, a group of militant APFs (anti-Partridge farmers) had decided that revenge was a dish best served deceased.[179] They had waited for me to cruise beneath them and then tipped the big dead Friesian right on top of me. As I lay there, fighting to catch my breath, trapped under what was essentially a vast leather jacket, I knew I was lucky to still be alive.

It crossed my mind that the animal had simply fallen from the bridge while stopping to look at the view (and what a view – formed when rising sea-levels began to flood medieval peat excavations, the Norfolk Broads, with their reed beds, grazing marshes and wet woodland, offer even the most casual of boaters over 100 miles of stunning navigable waterways). But no. To borrow from the parlance used by the farmers, Partridge had been 'beefed'.

I mention that story because my publishers felt it would make 'a good anecdote for your book', but actually most corporate engagements are far less dangerous. In the year 2000, I was hired to front *Crash, Bang, Wallop*. It neatly brought together three of my biggest passions: cars, car crashes and high-quality sell-through videos.

Had *Police, Camera, Action!* not already been a hit international TV show, it would have been the video that inspired *Police, Camera, Action!* The idea was simple. We would play to one of the most innate of all human traits – rubber-necking.

---

179 The previous week I had got myself caught up in a row with the local farming community over some comments I may or may not have made (I did make them) about intensive farming techniques. For the record I'd like to say once again that these comments were made in the heat of the moment and that I fully and categorically retract many of them. And actually, issues of slander aside (remember the slush fund mentioned above), it made for some scintillating radio.

And I had an idea for a USP: why not show fatalities? Please don't misunderstand, road deaths break my heart. I've lost count of the number of times I've been reduced to tears when slowing down at the site of a pile-up to grab a few snaps on the camera phone. But isn't that the point? By showing unedited footage of RTA fatalities, weren't we shocking drivers into being more careful? The deader they are, the stronger the message. And believe me, the drivers I had in mind could not have been deader.

In the end I was over-ruled, though we did reach a compromise. We would show horrific accidents, but we'd use crash test dummies. I personally oversaw some of these shoots and I cannot tell you how much fun it was. We had families of four – just dummies remember – flying through windscreens left, right and centre. I hadn't laughed so much in years. I wanted to do one with a crash test dog but apparently they don't make them.

We got most of our footage from the Highways Agency and the police, plus the odd one from me following people home from company Christmas parties. I'd do the tailgating and my assistant would hang out of the window with the camcorder. It was simple, safe and almost always ineffective.

Ironically this was the time in my life when I was least at risk of being injured in a car crash myself. Due to an unfortunate Toblerone addiction, I had ballooned[180] (see picture section). I even disabled the driver-side air bag on my Rover. It was simply not needed.

At this time I was also considering switching to an automatic. Like any real man, I much preferred a manual but my new-found bigness meant there were logistical issues to

---

180 I'll get to that! Calm down.

address. The recent expansion of my left thigh had effectively taken my gear stick out of the equation. When I got into the car, the contents of my leg would take four or five seconds just to settle. I'd sit there watching as it advanced like lava. I'd often have the engine running and a CD playing before it had finally come to rest, with the gear stick nowhere to be seen.

It was a great job to do, though, especially if you loved cars. And I, of course, am every inch the car-o-phile. I can't recall the first word I ever spoke but I do remember that it didn't take me long to go polysyllabic. And when I did, into my world came words like combustion, camshaft, Halfords. I didn't need to use them all that much in those early days of play-school and Tufty Club, but they were just there, tucked away in the back pocket, ready. And to a young child still getting to grips with the world, I cannot tell you how reassuring that was.

Growing up, I adored words and loved reading. I could always be found with my head in a good paper. The rag of choice in the Partridge household was the *Daily Express*. And I actually enjoyed it as a nipper. Which does make sense, given my mental age at the time. But one day, things suddenly changed. I was becoming a man, with my own thoughts, my own opinions, my own pubes. I knew I needed something radically different. I rushed straight out and bought the *Daily Mail*.

I sometimes flirt with the *Telegraph* or peep at the *Times*, but it's with the *Mail* that I've stuck ever since. It really is a rock-solid daily. I especially love Richard Littlejohn. He doesn't just shoot from the hip, he fires bazookas from it. Immigrants, travelling tinkers, and especially homosexuals – many of his pieces are so good I rip them out and laminate them. I keep them in my downstairs loo, a simple, wipe-clean tribute to one of the most progressive thinkers in the United Kingdom.

Anyway, sorry, I'm jumping around the years here (I'm like a ruddy Tardis!).[181] My point was that as a youth I'd always read the paper. And I'd see stories about teenagers from broken homes joy-riding cars. Well it would turn me green with envy. Speeding round the council estate in somebody else's car, spaffed off their faces on sniffed glue. It was the stuff of dreams. Apart from the glue. I always imagined that I'd trade my share of the Bostik for a bit longer behind the wheel. Besides, surely it sticks all your nose hairs together?

Of course joy-riding was just a crazy adolescent flight of fancy. In reality I didn't drive a vehicle until I reached the legal age. I'll always remember the morning of my 17th birthday. I was hoping to open the curtains and see a shiny new Triumph Dolomite gift-wrapped on the drive. But I didn't get a car. That's not to say I wasn't pleased with my attaché case. The other kids in my class had to make do with satchels (boring!), whereas I looked quite the young professional, striding around with my nearly-new, jet-black Samsonite. It was a great feeling to arrive fashionably late, then make a show of flicking open the lock and pulling out my PE kit.

Mum was the one that took me out for driving lessons. Dad said he wanted to but couldn't because of his temper. In reality, though, I got taken out very rarely, so I had to improvise. I'd sit on a chair in my bedroom, with a cushion for a steering wheel and upturned school shoes for the clutch, brake and accelerator. I guess these days you'd call it virtual reality. It might sound stupid, but I believe it's as a direct consequence of my hours in the simulator that I was able to pass my test after just three or more attempts.

---

181 For overseas readers not familiar with *Doctor Who*, the Tardis is a very small police station that can travel through time.

But it wasn't just the driving I loved. I had a real reverence for the Highway Code too. Still do. If Gutenburg had known that one day his printing press would allow for the publication of the Highway Code, I'm sure he would have given us a pretty broad smile and an enthusiastic medieval thumbs-up. Because people forget that it doesn't just save lives, it's also a damn good read. More than that, it can help in social situations. I've lost count of the number of times I've broken into an impromptu braking distances quiz to plug an awkward silence at a cocktail party.

I remember once June Whitfield thought the braking distance for a car travelling at 50mph was 28 metres, not 38. Imagine that! Yet while her error quite understandably got one of the biggest laughs of the night, I was still duty-bound to tell her that those ten metres might be a harmless bit of fun at a drinks reception, but out on the open road they could mean the difference between a quiet Sunday drive and a dead baby.

I never heard back from the DVLA, but for the sake of all our children I can only pray they came down on her like a ton of bricks. That said, a ten-car pile-up triggered by the ignorance of June Whitfield would have been manna from heaven for *Crash, Bang, Wallop*.

I worked with the same company on a number of other projects but ultimately our relationship was doomed. It came to my attention that some of their other business interests were not a good match with Brand Partridge.

I'll give you a prime example: wet t-shirt contests. Becoming quietly aroused as you watch a couple of young tits slowly reveal themselves though a piss-wet t-shirt might have been acceptable family fare in the 1950s, but no more. Modern women are very different beasts. And I use the word 'beast' in its most complimentary possible sense.

One can hardly imagine a quintessentially 21st-century lady like Carol Vorderman allowing her lady breasts to become sodden solely for the amusement of the nation's sell-through-video-buying public. Not that it wouldn't be a pleasant sight. The last thing I want to do is cause Mrs Vorderman any offence. I've absolutely no doubt that her chest is every bit as impressive and accurate as her maths.

25.

MARCHING ON: SKIRMISH

***

A HUSH DESCENDED OVER the studio. I took a breath and spoke.

'You have two phosphorous bombs, a confiscated IED, two fin-stabilised mortars and a German MG3 machine gun with a full magazine. The target is a missile silo. What are you opting to play with?'

'Phosphorous bomb, please.'

'I can tell you that the silo is adjacent to a hospital. Play or rearm?'

'Play.'

'He's gone for play, which means this is a high-risk question. Your topic is American sitcoms. Get this wrong and you wipe out the hospital and are back down to £100. Get it right and the dishwasher is yours ...'

Well, any viewer of UK Conquest/serious fans of dishwashers knows what happened next and I won't spoil the excitement for others by revealing it now. Suffice to say that all 208 episodes of military-based quiz *Skirmish* are available on DVD, and they definitely bear rewatching.

The format was absorbing, high-brow but brilliantly simple: players would vie to complete fictional or historical military operations with the fewest casualties, answering general knowledge questions to gain territorial advantage, tot up Gung-ho Points or accrue weaponry. I'd honestly never been this excited about a format since Noel Edmonds sat me down with a pen and paper and explained the winning strategy for *Deal or No Deal.*[182]

The attention to military detail was second to none, with our armed forces consultant Dave Harrier free to work full-time for the show after his dishonourable discharge from the Scots Guards. It lent the show a quite terrifying realism which in turn gave us wonderful moments of drama. Although never aired, the tension on *Celebrity Skirmish* was such that Yvette Fielding soiled herself.

Skirmish, then, was a runaway success, on a good day achieving its target regional digital optional share of 2% of the regional digital available audience, which is eight thousand people.

It was a new stage of my career. A new show, on a new channel and time I felt to experiment with a new look – not least because I was starting to swell grotesquely in weight. So I began to grow a beard, going so far as to invest in a miniature comb and a gentle wax. I'm told that Matthew Kelly uses conditioner on his but that felt stupid to me. I did order a

---

182 You'd kick yourself if you knew!

quality beard trimmer, though – recommended on Eric Clapton's website.

The facial hair didn't last long of course. As well as causing an itch that called for perpetual and frenzied scratching, it wasn't to everyone's taste. Plus, Bill Oddie threw a tantrum when he heard I was growing it and sent me a very, very curt letter.

No matter, I was back on the telly, and things were better than ever. Better than ever? Come off it, Partridge. Yes, better than ever, so shut your mouth. It was better because it was TV without the restrictive, choking, stifling, suffocating bureaucracy and creativity-aborting compliance culture of the BBC.

***

The BBC is like an uncaring sow, lying there fat and impassive as a host of piglets jostle to suck calcium-rich milk from her many jaded teats. (The metaphor probably doesn't need explaining but, on the off chance that this book finds itself in one of those municipal libraries populated by adult learners, let me explain: the piglets are TV presenters, the milk is cash and the teats are job opportunities.)

TV talent chases BBC presenting work as if it's the be-all *and* the end-all. NOT me though. Unlike your average piglet, Alan Partridge had the gumption to look beyond the udders of this particular swine and monetise his talent via other channels.

My Radio Norwich contract forbade me from moonlighting on rival stations, but I was free to engage in other commercial TV work.

I'd had a damn good go at the Hamilton's Water Breaks vid and maintain that my attempt was as good as if not better than the Cliff Thorburn version eventually used. Cliff is a decent guy and a heck of a billiards-player, but his thick Australian accent (he pronounces Norfolk as Norfoke) cheapened the depiction of what were actually really good water breaks.

But appearing in front of the camera again had literally lit a fire in my belly, and I suddenly had a renewed appetite for on-screen work.

I was approached by Matt and Mario from a production company called AAA Productions, a name that was such a brazen attempt to appear first in telephone directories I couldn't help but be impressed. They met me in the meeting room of a Regus office facility which you can hire by the hour, telegraphing the fact that they weren't even based in the building but were a back-bedroom operation masquerading as a properly established company.[183]

They talked me through the idea of *Skirmish*,[184] about their vision for the show, and ITV's keen interest. They even showed me some marketing material they'd mocked up to promote my agreement to present in the show. It was a photoshopped image of me as John Rambo, armed to the nines with high-grade weaponry and question cards. They'd super-imposed that over an actual screenshot of the moment I shot Forbes McAllister, and included a speech bubble of him saying 'Be careful with that.'[185]

Well, I absolutely hooted with laughter. This was an inspired piece of show marketing that was incredibly crass/inventive,[186] and boded well for the quality of the show. I agreed to take the

---

183 I've done the same many, many times.
184 To be honest, they had me at the name 'Skirmish' but I listened politely all the same.
185 His final words.
186 Depending on your point of view.

job there and then, shaking hands and then leaving their hired meeting room, still laughing my head off.[187]

ITV got cold feet[188] in the end and decided not to take the show, even though Matt and Mario assured me the channel had definitely been interested and they'd definitely had a meeting there, even if they couldn't remember who with.

No matter, because new satellite channel UK Conquest were sniffing around like a randy dog who's picked up the musky excellence of another dog's vagina. The channel's ethos – 'guns, girls, guys, grrrr!' – seemed ideally suited to *Skirmish*.

At first, we were to be its flagship show, broadcast on Monday, Wednesday and Friday (the Wednesday and Friday shows were repeats of the Monday one). Alongside me was glamorous assistant Susie Dent, better known as the resident lexicographer from *Countdown*. Susie resigned after the first show, pointing out politely that the actual format hadn't been explained to her.

Although the loss of such a talented bookworm was a major blow, it proved to be the making of us. It probably suited the tone of the hard-nosed show to have someone a bit rougher, and urban DJ Lisa l'Anson brought a Westwood-style glamour to proceedings.

Before long, we'd massively upped our output and – on my insistence – we were making three shows a day, six days a week. This was to be my undoing.[189]

---

187 A fit of giggles that only stopped on my drive home when I realised I was also crying.

188 There's a clever pun in here.

189 *Press play on Track 34.*

26.

MY DRINK AND DRUGS HECK

***

'ARGH. GWAAG. HUUUH.'

These noises, these gurgles and barks and grunts, they're coming from me. They're coming from my mouth. How long have I been making them? I do not know. Where on earth am I? I do not know. Where's my assistant? I do not know.

One thing I did know was that my face was in considerable pain. Sharp-cornered objects were jostling for space in my mouth, spearing my inner cheeks and stabbing the roof of my mouth. Mixed with the taste of blood was an unmistakable cocktail of chocolate and nougat.

I gasped for breath, feeling my life force waning. 'Is this it then, Alan?' I thought. 'Is this where you're finally going to die?'

I gathered my bearings. I was sat in my car, door open, belt on. It was dark, cold. Pitter-patter went the rain, as if bookending my short and ultimately unhappy life (see Chapter One for the left-hand bookend). I was alone, and felt it.

'[My assistant]!' I called out through the semi-masticated confectionery. Where was she? '[My assistant]!' Nothing.

I caught a glimpse of myself in the rear-view mirror – my mouth and chin were stained brown from all the binged chocolate. My eyes peeped out, redly, from a pair of collapsed lids. My face – my lovely face – was now unspeakably bloated, blotchy skin struggling to contain the expanding Alan within. It was as if bread was being baked in my cheeks. Like a good-looking John Merrick, mine was a face that looked really shit. Ravaged by addiction, it was now home to jowls, eyes and chin that were being dragged torso-wards by the weight of their gelatinous content.

Fat, tired, confused, cold, obese, alone, with chilly feet. I had hit rock bottom. I forced another two prisms of chocolate into my already over-subscribed mouth and waited for death to come.

***

The human brain comprises 70% water, which means it's a similar consistency to tofu. Picture that for a second – a blob of tofu the size and shape of a brain. Now imagine taking that piece of tofu, and forcing your thumbs into it hard.[190] It would burst, wouldn't it?

Okay, now imagine those thumbs weren't thumbs but thumb-shaped pieces of bad news. And there weren't two of them, they were about half a dozen. Imagine you were forcing

---

190 You might like to actually do this.

all six pieces of bad news – a divorce, multiple career snubs, accusations from the family of a dead celebrity, estranged kids, borderline homelessness, that kind of thing – into a piece of tofu.

With me? Good. Now imagine that it's not tofu, but a human brain. And they're not pieces of bad news but six human thumbs. That's what happened to me. In 2001, my brain had half a dozen thumbs pushed into it.[191] I was trying to ignore these thumbs by making three television shows a day, six days a week. And like a civilian hospital targeted by a contestant on *Skirmish*, my brain basically exploded.

It makes me laugh when people suggest that I'm exaggerating my psychological distress to cash in on the craze for 'misery lit'. Actually, no, it doesn't make me laugh. It makes me sigh. What I went through was real, and incredibly tough, and would have broken a lesser man like a gingerbread man being thwacked with a meat tenderiser. That it didn't speaks to my fortitude and ability to bounce back.

The naysayers who try to downplay the very real horror of chocolate addiction, or scoff at a naked man crying in the bath, or intimate that I'm some kind of wally can frankly eff off. And the suggestion that I would resort to hyperbole to sensationalise what I went through literally makes me pass out with nausea.

But I'm getting ahead of myself. Let me take you back in time. Come. Come with me, through the fog-clad mists of time to 1987.

We're in the unnecessarily large studio of Our Price radio. And who's this guy? With the strut and the swagger and the spunk? It's a young Alan Partridge, one of the hottest

---

191 Editor – can you check this metaphor? I've lost track a bit.

broadcasters in in-store radio. He sets down his headphones, and heads for the door, high-fiving a succession of pleased staff.

A head pops round the door. 'Hey, great show, Alan,' its mouth said. Alan stops in his tracks. It's Pepsi or Shirlie from Pepsi & Shirlie. 'Wow, thanks,' says Alan, scarcely able to believe that an established pop star has complimented his show. She'd been in-store to promote a doomed solo single, having had a falling out with the other one from Pepsi & Shirlie.

'We're going for a quick drink, if you guys fancy it?' says Pepsi/Shirlie.

'Fancy it?' says Alan. 'Not half!'

Soon after, Alan, fellow DJ Jon Boyd, a couple of producers and Pepsi or Shirlie from Pepsi & Shirlie are sat in the bar of a Marriott hotel, enjoying pints of bitter (the men) and a wine (Pepsi/Shirlie).

Alan surveys the scene, throws his head back and laughs quietly. He's made it. He's really made it. He shakes his head slowly and basks in the euphoric glow of genuine happiness. And then someone nudges him.

'Chocolate?'

It's Pepsi/Shirlie. Alan looks down to see that she's offering him a strange and unusual confectionery. Brown in colour but lightly pebble-dashed with white flecks, it comes in centimetre-wide segments that together form a rounded pentehedron shape.

He wouldn't normally – even then he was prone to a fat back – but he's in a celebratory mood and feels good. It's a party atmosphere. A bit of fun. Sod it, why not? He takes one.

At that moment, his life changes forever.

(I'm going to revert to both the first person and the past tense now, because it's quite tiring to write like that and I've just had a mug of hot milk.)

At that moment, my life changed forever.

The wallop of honey and almond nougat was the first to strike, the nutty sweetness further engorging my throbbing sense of happiness. Then came the hit of rich milk chocolate, its generous sugar content somehow taking me higher, my mind diving and soaring into a new ecstasy. I felt amazing, gold-plated, Vanden Plas.

We finished our drinks and went our separate ways, but that sensation of deliciousness, acceptance and professional success were, on a barely conscious level, now inextricably linked with Toblerones.

Over the years, I developed a taste for the Swiss delicacy. 'Nothing I can't handle,' I'd always say. It was nothing out of the ordinary. I'd sometimes buy one of the small ones while queuing at a supermarket checkout or grab one to enjoy with a sandwich at a petrol station. I knew what I was doing. It was just a fun snack, a choc treat. After all, who doesn't like Toblerone?

I thought nothing of this until, several years later, I was sexually assaulted (I had my pants removed and arse exposed) by hooligans at a live Comic Relief event. With incredible self-ishness, many of the people who'd pledged money to the poor of Africa were only happy to see the cash reach the needy if they could first peer at my naked anus. When I refused, I was gang-debagged.

Badly shaken, I began to drive home. I was deeply embar-rassed by what had happened and felt small, unappreciated and cheap. I wanted to eat a Toblerone. So I stopped into an Esso garage and ate a Toblerone. I felt a lot better and should have begun to wonder if there was some subconscious link between my self-confidence and the consumption of some Toblerone. Should have, but didn't. That's what addiction does – it makes you focus on little beyond the next fix.

Unwilling to confront my demons, I became steadily more keen on the chocolate snack, silently measuring any hardships I encountered in segments of Toblerone. Argument with Carol? Three slabs and I'll be fine. Disparaging remark from passer-by? Two should do it. My assistant is being an idiot? Three, maybe four – but she really is pushing her luck.

But as my personal problems began to mount, so did my intake. After Carol left, I'd sometimes get up in the night and eat a whole Toblerone to myself. And I'm not talking about a small one – I mean a medium-sized one. On another occasion, I remember ruining a colleague's birthday meal by eating a third of a Toblerone before joining them for dinner. Sated by the snack, I was unable to finish the lasagne she'd cooked and only had a small amount of dessert. Selfish, yes – but as a very real addict, I was consumed by my own desires. More and more, I ate.

After the death of newly installed BBC commissioner Chris Feather, and a mean-spirited and unnecessary investigation by the BBC, my second series was snatched from my grasp. My reaction? Banging on the door of a BP garage at 2am, pleading for the hit of Toblerone (and getting it – it was open 24 hours. Also, my friend worked there). I was, by some distance, the most depressed and troubled man in the UK. Probably a lot worse than this sounds.

In retrosight, I guess the BBC snub was the real sickener. Until then, I'd been on a fairly even keel. Sure, I had had my share of ups and downs. That's Partridge. Comes with the territory. But the unjustness of the BBC stopping me being on the television saw me shrink into a dark cranny of fed-upness.

And that's when I really began to behave differently. I'd watch endless repeats of *Birds of a Feather*, a programme which I quite rightly despised. My assistant says I stopped checking her expense claims for some time – which really should not have happened – and all the while, of course, I was eating quite a bit of Toblerone. The self-destruction should by now be leaping off the page.

The upshot was that I gained a lot of weight. I mean, that's science. I'm not denigrating the food – at all. But it's just human physiology. Lethargy plus Toblerone equals obesity. Even the guys at Kraft can't argue with that. I'm not having a pop at them or anything.

All of this made me very unhappy. In my mind, I was living in an old hill croft atop the Cuillin on the Isle of Skye. But I was no 'wee bonnie boat like a bird on the wing' over the sea to Skye.[192]

I was a big bonnie man. And if I was a kind of bird, it would be a turkey about to be incapacitated by one of Bernard Matthews's henchmen for some poor family to celebrate the birth of Jesus Christ.

I sometimes thought the kindest thing would be to put me out of my misery, chop my head off, gut, truss and baste me, then cook me on gas mark 5 or 190C for three hours – check after two hours – and then place me centre table for a Christmas feast. In death at least, I'd be able to feed an extended family of say 20, what with me then weighing in at 230 pounds. Even allowing for shrinkage, I'm going to have

---

192 Not least because if I was to journey to Skye a boat would be unnecessary because of the quite elegant road bridge.

had a cooked weight of the best part of 190lbs – easily enough to feed 20–30 guests with sandwiches lasting through to the Epiphany, aka the 12th day of Christmas.

And so, inexorably fatter and more housebound, I saw myself turning into a third bird of a feather, although others routinely mistook me for Eamonn Holmes. Routinely. Even my voice – once so agile and clear – was, like Eamonn's, now muffled and cramped by throat fat.

And then one day, I lost control. It wasn't a single trigger, but an accumulation of minor incidents. How to explain it? It was as if I was carrying a lot of straw on my back. And people kept adding another piece of straw and another piece until I couldn't carry any more because my back had broken. One piece on its own seems harmless, doesn't it? But when added to loads of other pieces of straw, it adds up – until one piece of straw crosses the divide between 'can carry' and 'can't carry, sorry'. That's how I explain it anyway.[193]

I lost control. I lost control and I ended up driving to Dundee in bare feet.

***

I'd heard of addicts blacking out, but thought it was just one of the things people say to get attention. Yet so complete was my mental collapse, I remember literally nothing of my journey to Scotland. Not a flicker of memory, other than the fact it was A11 to Thetford, continuing to Ipswich on the A146, before a short hop on the A140 saw me join the A47 and later the A17, pretty much until the A1. It was A1 and A1(M) including a quick pit stop at Wetherby Services for petrol, more Toblerones and a face wash. Then on the A66 via Scotch

---

193 © Partridge.

Corner and on to the M6 which, after the Scottish border, became the A74. Then it went M74, M73, M80, M9, A9, M90, and then the A90.

It was only after arriving in Dundee and pulling up in the middle of a municipal football pitch to unwrap another Toblerone that I came around, pretty much at the point where this chapter started. So now I'm going to carry on from the point where I stopped and started talking about tofu. I will do that now.

I didn't feel up to the drive home – not least because I had no shoes and felt daft. So I contacted my assistant, who travelled overnight while I lay across the generously proportioned back seat of the Vectra finishing the last of the Toblerones and using the verdant shrubbery as an improvised toilet as and when. My assistant doesn't own a car and the train was, I felt, too expensive, so she'd taken a National Express coach, clutching my best shoes in a plastic carrier bag.

She told me she'd sat next to the coach's chemical toilet and I was concerned that my shoes might smell of human waste, so I lost my temper at her a little bit, but was mollified when I smelt the shoes and they didn't smell of human waste.

She quickly washed and shod me and then began the drive home with the hosepipe dangling from the exhaust like the tail of a giant mouse.[194] But, for such a bird-like woman, she was far too hard on the clutch, so after a few hundred metres I took over and drove home myself. I gave her a lift as well.

Little was spoken on the way back. She could tell from my body language that referring to 'the open arms of Christianity' was inadvisable, so she listed some of the times when I'd either

---

194 Oh, I should have said – this was for a suicide bid which I didn't get round to.

done something well in my professional life or said something spontaneously witty in company. Afterwards, she used the light from her mobile phone to read aloud from *Prima* magazine but quickly fell asleep.

I got home and had a can of bitter and a sleeping tablet.[195] I subsequently made a number of changes to my life, which resulted in me getting better.[196]

I'd done it. I'd bounced back. The doubters could shut their faces because I'd done it. And so with fewer work commitments, a slimmer physique, fresher breath,[197] less clutter on my desk, and a blanket ban on Toblerones, I felt like a new man.

Quite a turnaround then.[198] Yep, it's a tale of incomprehensible pain and hardship, of bravery and backbone, of me and my success. One that could easily be stretched out into a film or novella – if only because that kind of addiction's not really been done before and would therefore feel fresher to a reader or viewer. Just a thought![199]

The other addictions grab all the column inches – let them! It's not a grief competition. I don't know why they think they have something to prove. And sure, maybe there's something glamorous about a boozeman swigging whiskey on a sidewalk or junkie 'chasing the dinosaur' in a squat, but take it from someone who knows: both physically and mentally,

---

195 The drink and drugs of the chapter title.
196 This paragraph is an edited version of a much longer passage, which the publishers felt borrowed too heavily from *Bouncing Back* (2002), available in second-hand bookshops in and around Norfolk.
197 This would have made more sense if the previous paragraph hadn't been edited.
198 It certainly is, Alan.
199 © Partridge.

confectionery addiction is the worst kind of addiction there is. Nothing comes close to the shame, desperation and unsightly weight gain of chocoholism.

So who's to blame? Me? Society? Kraft Foods? The Government? Pepsi or Shirlie out of Pepsi & Shirlie? In all honesty, it's probably a combination of them all, with a slight weighting towards Pepsi or Shirlie from Pepsi & Shirlie. You don't go pushing something as powerful as Toblerone on someone you've only just met. It's utterly irresponsible, and I'm absolutely furious with her. She could have bloody killed me.

27.
CHIN UP

***

I TOOK SOME TIME out after Dundee. People were very nice. Sue Cook called and offered to take me to the zoo one day. She never actually turned up but then she never does. That's just Sue, as she always says.

Bill Oddie was a real rock too. When he found out Sue had let me down, he swiftly agreed to come along in her place. We had a nice drive over there (he uses one of those booster seats so he can see over the steering wheel) but later in the day, when we went into the aviary, he seemed to tense up. A cloud seemed to descend. I pressed him on it.

'Are you alright, Bill?' I asked, as a bird of paradise landed on my head.

'Fine,' he grunted unconvincingly, as I shoved it away again.

'Well you don't seem fine,' I retorted, swirling my arms around my hand to try to keep the bird at bay.

He looked me in the eye. 'All these people watching birds without using binoculars.'

'What about them?'

'It's cheating.' And with that, the bird-mad Goodie strode off, partly because he was angry and partly because he only had five minutes to get over to the other side of the zoo for the seal performance.

Other people were there for me too. My assistant would pop round to the house every day to drop off food, do the dishes, flush the loo (I tended to forget). At my lowest point, she also offered to help me shower. But even with my swimming trunks on I think that would have been a bit weird.

Although technically my employee, I knew that she was doing all this as a friend, and that meant a lot. She came round so often, I'm surprised she had time to get any actual work done, and I think it was that as much as anything else that forced me to drop her down to a part-time wage for a while.

I did a lot of crying as well. I'm not ashamed to say that now, but at the time I found ways to hide it. Mainly by doing the bulk of it in the shower. That way people can't say what's tears and what's just hot water. Same applies in the bath. Just hold your breath, stick your head under and let the grief flood out. You'd be surprised how much better you feel.

To this day I still use Short-Burst Underwater Crying for all sorts of problems. I wouldn't cry at, say, an unexpectedly large MOT bill. But if I'd received an unexpectedly large MOT bill, combined with the death of a good friend, plus I hadn't eaten that day, then I might well weep.

I developed a complementary technique called Controlled Anger-Release Splashing, though it should only be used as a measure of last resort, and you will need to mop up afterwards.

Against the express wishes of Bill Oddie, I also tried therapy. It wasn't for me though. I didn't want someone to pick and prod at my troubled mind like a shopper fingering a piece of fruit in the supermarket. I wanted something that would allow my soul to heal in its own sweet time. And that's why I took up pony-trekking.[200]

It all stemmed from someone telling me I'd feel better if I exercised. They'd suggested jogging, but what appealed about pony-trekking was that you were basically in charge of a vehicle/being. Also, horses don't complain. They don't criticise you about viewing figures, play hard-ball over budgets or fail to re-commission your show. Plus they're grateful for a sugar cube.

I'd had a little experience of horses previously, not least on *Knowing Me Knowing You.* Show-jumper Sue Lewis had been a guest and had come on the show with her horse (see picture section). And I must say it made for pretty pleasing television until she shat on the floor (the horse).

But yes, clambering aboard my horse, Treacle, really was just what the Doc ordered. Mottled grey and measuring a good 15 hands, you could tell that she just 'got' me. I truly found peace in the gentle side-to-side bob of her trot, the quiet swoosh of her tail and the tender plippety-plop-plop of her shit hitting the dirt.

It wasn't all plain-sailing, though. Probably my lowest ever equine moment was when we were out one day and I fell badly

---

200 *Press play on Track 35.*

My best-ever blazer. It actually belonged to Lenny Henry but I stole it from his dressing room at *Comic Relief*. He came after me and demanded the jacket back, saying it was his. I simply stared him down and replied, 'Prove it.' 'I'm going to report this, Alan,' he called as I walked off down the corridor. 'Oh yeah?' I shouted, without even looking back. 'And who do you think they're going to believe?' The next year I decided to give it to a charity shop, but they didn't want it. So I just threw it in a bin. Easy come, easy go.

Above: When behind the Radio Norwich mic, I'd always be turned out in shirt, tie, buffed footwear, quality sweater. Just because you can't see the people you're talking to, doesn't mean your standards should drop. That's something I learned from my good friends the blind. It's equally important for TV newsreaders. They always look good up top but there are some who refuse to wear trousers – Trevor Macdonald (cut-down jeans); Kate Silverton (PE skirt); James Naughtie (Captain America).

Opposite top: The meeting of two chat heavyweights. Clive asked me back to his dressing room afterwards to reminisce about our best-ever interviews and take a shower with him. I declined the shower but we had a lovely natter.

Opposite bottom: Me, moments before staging a mock execution of Elton John. I shot the former Watford chairman straight in the mouth. It was probably the most realistic mimed celebrity assassination I'd ever pulled off. I'd slit the throat of Monty Don the year before at a Christmas party but it was nowhere near as convincing. Elton and I later went for cocktails where he spent the best part of two hours outlining the plus points of homosexuality. I'm still not convinced, Elton! Love the songs, though.

Below left: A Toblerone. This is a 750-grammer, one of the tastiest in the Toblerone range. Although I'm salivating profusely as I look at the photograph, I steer well clear of them these days. Have I given up Toblerones? Ha ha. No, you can never say you've given up Toblerones. I just say, 'I'm not going to eat one today.' And if I make it until bedtime without eating one, great. I'll then celebrate with half a Yorkie.

Below right: Still in the grips of my Toblerone addiction, this shot shows me sprinting to the corner shop, desperate for my next Swiss-choc high. By this point I've sunk so low that I don't even care that my groin is peppered with splash-back from a recent foray to the urinal. Incidentally, during this period I wore exclusively C&A. I found the cut of their garments wonderfully forgiving.

Above left: Attleborough Leisure Vehicles, the dealership that sold me my Delta static home. I got a discount for paying cash, although the guy got annoyed when the last twenty quid consisted of small denomination coins stored in a large whisky bottle. To lighten the mood I said, 'What are you going to do? Call the *coppers*?!' He didn't laugh but I knew I was on to something. I raced home and faxed the joke to Terry Wogan for his exclusive use on that year's *Children in Need*. I tuned in to see if he used it but quickly grew bored and flicked over to ITV to watch *What Women Want*. How Mel Gibson did not win an Oscar for his performance is beyond me. Not least because it was shot years before he became Australia's best-known anti-semite. Ironic really, because Mad Max was a Jew (CAN SOMEONE CHECK THIS?).

Above right: Me, in the caravan. In the wine rack is a bottle of plum wine given to me by a local farmer. It was one of the worst liquids my mouth has ever played host to. It was almost as bad as the time Michael spiked my coffee with WD40. I got him back by claiming I'd seen him inappropriately touch a female guest in the Travel Tavern car park. He was suspended for a month. Great days. (It was a lie, of course, but I didn't feel bad because I know for a fact he did once touch a woman but got away with it.)

Above left: On the right is my ex-Forces confidant Michael, with his 'thousand-yard stare'. I often practise this look in the mirror but just can't get the hang of it! In the centre, my former girlfriend Sonja. Our relationship was 80% physical, 15% small talk, 5% Don't Know.

Above right: Standing outside Classic House. In the top-right window, Michael can be seen peeping. During the building's construction I employed him as a security guard. He offered the ideal combination of military know-how and borderline post-traumatic stress disorder. He would do whatever it took to defend the property, and hang the consequences. Thankfully, the closest we ever came to a burglar was a fox that wandered in, lost. May it rest in peace.

Opposite top: My stall in Norwich train station, where I once spent a week selling copies of *Bouncing Back*. It's probably fair to attribute the lack of takers to poor literacy rates in Norfolk. In the more rural areas many kids are simply beyond the reach of the education system. It's rumoured that some go their whole life and never learn to speak.

Opposite bottom: When I wake up each morning, this is what I see: a new dawn, a glittering horizon, a vista ripe with opportunity. It really is one of my favourite posters. I take a sense of boundless optimism with me wherever I go. Along with mouthwash, a clean shirt and a piece of paper containing the phone numbers of my next of kin. Oh yes, I also like to think of myself jumping into that hammock to give the young lady a big kiss and a cuddle, whether she likes it or not!

Top: 10 kilometres, 20, 30! Here you can see me eating up the ground on a static exercise cycle. 40 kilometres, 50, 60! I'm throwing my weight behind a campaign to encourage cycling among fat kids. 70 kilometres, 80, 90! This was quality public-service radio but also compelling TV, thanks to the studio webcams I'd suggested we install. 100 kilometres, 200, 300! (No one knows how far I cycled that day. What we do know is that the campaign itself ran into funding difficulties and was discontinued later that month.)

Above left: This is yours truly with Sidekick Simon. He is a genuine original and an unbelievably funny man but lost his job on *Mid-Morning Matters* because he basically has an attitude problem. Also, many webcam viewers said they didn't like his beard – and I agree. It's too wispy and not a good colour. In this picture we're pulling funny faces, which was my idea. These impromptu moments of goofing around were an almost hourly occurrence before things turned sour. After I sacked him he threatened to take me to an industrial tribunal. But I put a big Jiffy bag of dog dirt through his letter box and he soon backed off!

Above right: Here I am at the North Norfolk Digital desk. I'm not actually on air; it's just a publicity shot. I keep a few autographed copies in my glove box at all times, in case I get accosted by a fan or need to bribe a bent copper. At the time of writing, I haven't needed to use them for either. I did once get stopped by a fan at some traffic lights but I just drove off.

off the pace. Soon I was totally lost. I began to panic. In an effort to relocate the rest of the riders I'd taken a short-cut across a dual carriageway. But it was then, as we tried to hurdle the central reservation, that something terrible happened. Treacle stood on a nail. On another day, she might have got away with it, but with the quite extraordinary weight of me on her back the rusty nail just slid through the hoof like a knife through hoof.

Over the roar of the onrushing traffic, I heard her whinny. But because I hadn't seen the incident, and because I knew almost nothing about horses, I assumed she was just laughing. The poor girl. By the time we got back to the stable her hoof looked like a split sausage.

She was fine in the end. Even more incredibly, she didn't seem to blame me in any way. She bore no grudge.[201] The dignity of these beasts. Mind-blowing.

After the rides I liked to stick around. I'd lean on the gate, unwrap a Twix and watch as the ponies got groomed. I'd marvel at the skill of the stable lads as they went to work with their hoof picks, shedding blades and dandy brushes. I really loved the fact that it was like a car-wash for horses. I really loved that fact.

Once one of the lads offered to let me have a go, but I got all shy and said 'no', even though I would have enjoyed it. Not a day goes by when I don't think about that moment. What an error.

Over time, though, I did pluck up the confidence to join in the chit-chat.

'Lovely grooming, John!' I might shout.

---

201 That was actually one of the titles I was thinking about for this book – 'She Bore No Grudge' – until I realised it made little or no sense.

'Thanks, Mr Partridge,' he might reply.

'Except for the fact that there's still shit on Prancer's under-carriage!' I might add. I had a smile on my face but we both knew it needed dealing with.

I don't ride any more, haven't done for a while. I stopped when *Brokeback Mountain* came out. I just didn't feel comfort-able. I do occasionally go on the stables' website though. I like to see if they've uploaded any new pictures of Treacle. I also 'friended' her on Facebook. I know it's not actually her that replies but it's still nice.

*****

Just as important as my mental health was my physical shape. Over the previous few years my body had become flooded with blubber. It was now home to over five stones of excess weight. There was no getting away from it, I was clinically chubbed-up. And it needed to change. I set about one of the most merciless exercise regimes in the history of Norwich.

In the last few years I estimated that I had spent somewhere in the region of £54,000 on Toblerone. That's more than most unhappily married men spend on prostitutes in their whole lives. My assistant said that wasting so much money on treat-food was immoral, especially with so much starvation in places like Africa and parts of Norfolk. She said the devil had got inside me, which sounded serious at first, but she says that about most people, especially John Craven.

But first things first – I had to round up all the remaining Toblerones in my house and get rid of them. Going through my cupboards was easy. The problem came when I needed to find the secret stash. I knew that in the fug of a previous Swiss choc high I had hidden a bar somewhere in the house. But where?

Never before had I been so badly in need of a metal detector adapted to detect Toblerone. Instead I had to search myself, through the medium of my assistant. I (i.e. she) began by checking the cisterns of all three toilets. Then I (she) checked the underside of all tables and chairs. And then I (she) checked in the loft, during which I (she) fell from the stepladder and cracked my (her) head on the wall. But I found nothing.

It wasn't until hours later that I (i.e. me – she'd taken the bus to casualty) found it, hidden in an air vent behind a wardrobe. It was just sat there looking at me, like some sort of confectionery Anne Frank. (God I hate the Nazis!)

I gathered what remained of my Toblerone supply into just six bin bags. I knew that the most cathartic thing to do would be to just give it all away. So that very afternoon I parked up at the local primary school, wound down my window, and handed bars out to the kids as they walked home. It was just a nice thing to do and the fact that the police were called says more about genuine paedophiles than it does about me.[202]

Finally it was time to commence the total annihilation of all the un-needed flab within the body of Alan Gordon Partridge. In terms of weight I effectively had a large midget wrapped around my internal organs. And I wanted him gone. I looked into liposuction but it was too expensive. Besides, while I knew it could do a good job on tummies and thighs, I wasn't 100% convinced of its ability to cure a fat back. I would have thought about the stomach stapling technique used to such great

---

202 The constables and I laughed about the confusion, though there's no denying that I looked like a paedophile, many of whom – like myself at the time – are paunchy. It's said they consume food as avariciously as they do explicit images of children.

effect by Fearne Cotton, but it was yet to be introduced at that stage. Probably still being tested on rats.

My only option was to hit the exercise, hard. I started with a regime I found in my assistant's copy of *Bella* magazine. She very kindly offered to do it with me, but when I thought about her in a leotard it made me feel all cold inside. I went for a drive to clear my head but at one point I nearly had to pull over because I was shaking. In the end we compromised. I would do the exercises and rather than be joined by her I would just watch *Oz Aerobics* on Sky Sports One. How that programme has not won awards I will never know.

The other big problem was the squat thrusts I was supposed to do. It was a simple question of physics. With the best will in the world, the only way my knees would have been able to cope with the sheer poundage was with the aid of a Silverline SE9 hydraulic jack.

I turned my attention to swimming, and it was fun for a while. We figured out that I displaced the same amount of water as half a Ford Fiesta! Not bad for a little lad from Norwich. Not bad at all. But soon enough the local kids started calling me Moby Alan. I gave the swimming up. It was the straw that broke the whale's back.

The thing is, I knew one of their mums and I'd seen her leaving a local hotel the other week with a man who wasn't her husband. Now I could have mentioned that to her catcalling child, but I didn't. Well I did, but it gave me no great pleasure.

My emphasis changed again, this time to running. I was a bit nervous as I hadn't been jogging for years and wasn't sure I'd be able to remember what to do. But as long as you keep telling yourself to move your right arm in time with your left leg (and vice versa) and to push off with sufficient propulsion to travel part of each stride airborne, you literally won't put a foot wrong.[203]

I used to run along the country lanes with my assistant driving behind like a Baptist kerb crawler. The idea was that if I went below a certain speed she would just blast the horn. The shock of it would lead to a sudden burst of acceleration. We called it the 'toot and shoot' technique. Yet such was the agony of running that I soon learnt to ignore the horn. (I only wish the same could have been said for the many, many horses that we spooked.)

No, we needed something more drastic, otherwise I would never lose the weight. With a heavy heart I decided on a new plan. If I consistently dropped below my target speed my assistant was to pull forward and slightly run me over. Well it worked famously. Believe me, when you've nearly been trapped under the front left wheel of a car driven by an unbalanced Cliff Richard fan, you soon speed up.

Once I got to grips with exercising, though, my excess baggage just melted just away. I was like a snowman in the sun. (One day I lost five pounds, although that was partly because I'd eaten some bad ham.) And within three months I was more or less back to my pre-Toblerone weight. It had been a slim-down as dramatic as it had been medically inadvisable. But I had succeeded.

How I longed to go back to the swimming baths and show those young boys my body. I used to lie in bed imagining them staring at me, my skin glistening under the changing room

---

203 There's no need to tell yourself this out loud, although as a habitual sports broadcaster, I found myself automatically providing a third-person commentary of my runs which buggered up my breathing patterns and gave me a painful stitch in my abdomen.

lights, my body covered in a veil of twinkling, chlorinated droplets. And it felt good, it felt right.

I would have done too, were it not for one thing – the sudden weight loss had left me with masses of excess skin. When I was clothed it wasn't a problem – I'd just tuck it into my jeans. But when I was naked, you couldn't miss it. I was half tempted to get on a plane to Papua New Guinea. Knowing that lot, they'd have cut it off and made crackling. Cannibals, eh? What are they like?!

Of course, in the years to come I'll probably be able to donate my skin to medical science. And the thought that one day a flap of my tummy might be grafted on to the face of a badly burned woman is a source of enormous comfort to me. Not just her face either. I've got enough skin to cover large parts of her body. She really can afford to be as clumsy with that chip pan as she likes.

To summarise then: my drink and drugs heck had taken me to places I never wanted to go. Mainly Dundee. I'd like to say that I came out of the whole ordeal older and wiser. But I'm not sure I did (though I concede that the age one is is hard to dispute). Yet it didn't matter because, by the spring of 2001, thanks to a hardcore diet and the love of a good horse (cheers, Treacle!) I was back. I had bounced back.

28.

BOUNCING BACK[204]

***

I'M NOT SURE I'D ever felt so proud. As I walked into the shop, I could feel my chest puffing out like a toad's throat. In front of me were rows and rows of books. And on the front cover? Yours truly. I reached out and tenderly fingered my glossy, smiling face. That might sound a bit weird, but it wasn't.

I span flamboyantly on my heels so I could look out of the window of the big-name high-street bookstore in which I stood. As humans of both sexes hurried and scurried about, I nodded in quiet satisfaction. Today Norwich Waterstone's, tomorrow the Booker Prize for Books!

---

204 *Press play on Track 36. I love the shiny black legs!*

Allow me to explain. To begin, you must join me as I return to the year 2PD (post-Dundee). Alan Partridge is in a tizz. He just can't figure out what to do with his experiences. He has been through a major male mind meltdown, surely there's some good that could come of this? Then one day in the bath tub – Ulrika! – it hit me. I'd translate them into a publishing deal.

As I searched around the soapy depths for my pumice stone, the idea began to take shape. The book would be called 'Bouncing Back'. (Incidentally the pumice made pretty short work of my calluses. It's no surprise that this tough yet light-weight material is also used to make insulative, high-density breezeblocks.) On the surface it would appear to be half auto-biography, half self-help manual. Yet it would be so much more than that. It would be a system to set free the limitless potential within us all, which just happened to be bound in hardback and sold in all good bookshops. Plus Tesco's.

I got so caught up in thinking about the book, that by the time I finally emerged from the bath, my skin was as shrivelled as an over-microwaved pea. But you know what? I didn't care. My only focus now was on *Bouncing Back*. And I have to confess, I loved the writing process. Sometimes I'd sit in my study and just pound away on the word processor. Other times I'd go jogging with a Bluetooth headset on and get my assistant to type the chapters up as I spoke them to her.

This run-writing worked very well. Unless I was going up a hill. In which case I quickly became too puffed out to talk. My assistant and I would simply maintain a comfortable telephone silence, save for the odd whinny of exertion from my end, until I reached the brow. Then I'd just make up for it by speaking at twice the speed on the descent. She'd really struggle to write as quickly as I was speaking, but that's not my problem.

One morning, though, I decided to do something differ- ent. I resolved to write in the park. I rose early and, just as dawn cracked, I found myself a nice little bench by the pond and began yabbering merrily away into my Dictaphone. This only lasted a couple of hours, though, because my audio kept getting polluted. If I learnt one thing in the writing of that book it was that the pained cackle of a swan in labour really does carry on the breeze. Disgusting.

After what seemed like an eternity, the book was finally writ- ten. It had taken three long weeks. As I typed the very last word – 'Allah' – I collapsed on to my keyboard. I was spent, every last drop of me had been poured into that book (save for a couple of anecdotes that I took from Russell Harty and re-badged as my own – and there's nothing he can do to touch me).

A wave of relief rushed over me as I began to dribble on the space bar. If pony-trekking had soothed my troubled mind, writing this book had been a full radiator flush, removing any traces of magnetite sludge from my system. My demons hadn't been exorcised, they'd been rounded up and shot. And now, as I bulldozed them into a mass grave with a fag in my mouth, I could move on with my life.

Of course there was still the small matter of finding a publisher. My previous work '*A Funny Thing Happened on the Way to the Stadium to Alan Partridge by Alan Partridge*' (a wry collection of amusing anecdotes about my experiences as a sports reporter) had been published by Peartee Publishing, the publishing wing of my now defunct company. (PP had gone under years before, after an injunction from former goalkeeper Ray Clemence who angrily questioned the validity of one of the anecdotes.[205])

---

205 'Clemence: practising goalie throws by hurling kids over hedge.'

So we needed to source a new publishing house. I'm told by my assistant that it only took about a month – after all, anyone reading the manuscript would quickly see that snapping up the rights was a total 'non-brainer' – but can't recall the exact details as I was drinking a lot of cider at the time. I don't really like cider but there'd been a very good deal on at Thresher's. And this explained my somewhat distracted response when she'd phoned with the good news.

'I've found you a publisher!' she squeaked.

'What?'

'For your book.'

'What about it? It's ace.'

'You asked me to find you a publisher.'

'For what?'

'The book, Alan. You asked me to find you a publisher for the book and I've spent the last month sending it to various companies and now one has come back and said they're willing to publish it!'

I hesitated. Was the news sinking in?

'Just get me some crisps.'

No, it wasn't. The next day, though, with all the cider now either drunk, spilled or thrown, I soon shaped up. And let me tell you, I was elated. My strategy of combining searingly honest admissions about my own life with a liberal use of the Roget's thesaurus, had worked a treat. I was to be published!

I immediately phoned Carol, before quickly hanging up when I remembered we were divorced. I know – Fernando.

'Son?'

'I'm just in the loo, Dad.' He was such a joker!

'Son, I'm to be published!'

'That's great, Dad.'

'The book will share my own life experiences and teach people a system for setting free the limitless potential within us all.'

'So like half autobiography, half self-help manual?'

'Kind of, but also so much more than that.'

'Great, Dad.' I heard a plop. Either he hadn't been joking about being on the loo, or he was dropping stones into a well.[206]

'Fancy meeting for a drink to celebrate?'

But the line went dead. In his excitement at my publishing deal Fernando had cut the call off. No matter, because I was still as pleased as the punch I would later make at home from whatever I could find in my drinks cupboard.

Fast forward a few months and it was launch day. It was ten minutes to opening time and I was explaining to the manager of Waterstone's where best – and in what quantities – to position my book in the store. I grabbed a nearby book (not one of mine) and tore out a blank page to quickly sketch a store map. I clicked my pen into life, its inky nose jutting obediently into view, and began to write.

'Biographies: 10; Health & Wellbeing: 10; Mind, Body & Spirit: 10; New Releases: 6; Bestsellers: 6.' (I knew this was cheeky, as the books hadn't even gone on sale yet, so I drew a smiley face after it to quell the shopkeeper's anger.) I also penned in 5 to go by the cash tills because I'd read something about Cadbury's Chomps doing the same to cash in on impulse purchases.

Next, I headed home and began sending copies to friends, family and a raft of BBC executives, past and present. This wasn't an attempt to show them that I'd bounced back from

---

206 He wasn't dropping stones into a well.

their rejection fitter and stronger than ever. No, it was simply because they all went to Oxbridge so I know they liked reading and didn't really watch any TV. Out of respect for the dead, I also sent copies to the widows of Tony Hayers and Chris Feather. It was a classy touch.

In the end there weren't that many left for friends and family, but I figured Denise and Fernando wouldn't mind sharing one, on the basis that they were siblings. And on the basis that we were now divorced, I decided my wife Carol could buy her own. Or, worst-case scenario, rent it from the library. (As I wouldn't be receiving a new royalty every time a copy was taken out, I suggested to Norwich City Council that I get a cut of any late fees instead. They didn't go for it.)

One thing that did thrill me, though, and I knew it would thrill the reviewers, was that I had managed to stretch it to over 300 pages. It had a real meatiness to it. I banged it down on the kitchen table so I could enjoy its undeniable thud factor. 'Thud,' it went. 'Thud,' I repeated, like a parrot trained to accurately mimic the noise of books.[207]

Yet my happiness was to be short-lived. Sales were disappointing. My refusal to dumb down (if anything, I had dumbed up) had cost me dearly. I received word via fax that a lot of stores were going to take it down from the shelves. I was absolutely thunderstruck (thanks, Roget's).

I marched into the offices of my publishing company and read them the riot act. 'There's only one course of action I will settle for,' I roared. 'A raft of nationwide TV adverts to give the book the push it deserves.' The subsequent silence that fell over the open-plan office told me that my message had got through loud and clear. You could have heard a pin.

---

207 *Press play on Track 37.*

As ever, though, there were logistical headaches to be addressed, so in the end we hammered out a compromise. Instead of running a series of nationwide TV adverts, they were not going to run a series of nationwide TV adverts.

By this point I was left with no choice. I had to take matters into my own hands. Sales needed to be boosted, and fast. I quickly formulated a plan of action. Every day for the next fortnight I would go down to Norwich train station, set up a stall and see if I could shift a few units myself. It would be stripped-down concourse retailing in its purest form. I launched myself into it like a small circus man being shot from a cannon. What a buzz! I'd literally flog to anyone. It didn't matter if they were travelling inter-Norfolk, trans-county or intra-Anglian, they were all fair game as far as I was concerned. I felt like I could sell coal to the Eskimos.

I was rigged-up with one of those cordless mics that you fix to your head. I loved it, with its sponge-covered microphone dangling in front of my mouth like a big black grape. When a sale had gone well I almost wanted to reach out and lick it! (Couldn't though – tongue too short. Oh to be a lizard!)

Better still, it gave me total mobility (within a radius of 20 metres). If I headed out to its distant eastern rim, the radius took me within spitting distance of WH Smith. (Literally, in the case of one chap who flicked me the Vs. I'll be honest, I lost it.) And this meant I had a captive audience. After all, what do we all do if we have time to kill before catching our train? We head to Smith's to browse the latest issue of *What Car* magazine, even though we've already got it at home. And possibly have a flick through *Cosmo* if someone's taken one out of the packaging.

It's safe to say that my maverick tactics caused quite a few sleepless nights over at WHSHQ (WH Smith HQ). They were petrified I was going to snaffle their customers. It's not that they came over to have a word, it's that they didn't. They tried to act like it didn't bother them. And in many ways I thought that was much more revealing.

I may have resembled a market trader, but in fact I was a bookshop without walls. And they knew it. The only thing they had over me was that I didn't do snacks, mags, chocs and pop. Although I was giving away a free Danko torch with every sale. And I know which I'd rather have. If the power goes while I'm tucked up in bed with a good book, I'm hardly going to be able to keep reading using a bag of Revels. No further questions, your honour.

I remember the first book I sold to a WH Smith customer. He was a man by the name of Warren. Before he'd been sucked into my sales tractor beam, he'd been innocently copying out a recipe for white bean stew from the BBC *Good Food* magazine. Yet within minutes he was writing me a cheque, £8.99 poorer but one *very* good book richer. And I remember that I did use those exact words.

It might seem weird that I remember the name of a man who bought a book from me almost 15 years ago, but in my defence he did have a lisp. Not that I realised at first. I thought he was just being silly. But the more I chatted to him, the clearer it became. There were no two ways about it – this man had a disabled mouth. Out of interest, I enquired if it entitled him to a badge for his car. It didn't. Justice? Not in this world, mate.

Good on him, though. He could have stayed at home, resenting his impediment, a cut-out of a big letter 's' on his dartboard. But no. Here he was, bold as brass, out and about. He may not have been able to say the word 'sausages'. (Or the word 'say', come to think of it.) But nothing – and I mean *nothing* – was going to stop him getting the 10.02 to Newmarket from platform nine. If memory serves, he needed a new Ethernet cable from PC World – something, he noted with a wry smile, that he could ask for safe in the knowledge that everyone involved would remain bone-dry.

And besides, if he did suddenly get a craving for sausages on his way back, he could simply bob into Morrison's and get them from the chill cabinets. He'd never actually have to say the 's' word. Unless he was insistent on buying direct from a butcher.[208] In which case, just point. I know for a fact that's what Mike Tyson does on his weekly shop. It's either him or Toyah Wilcox anyway.

No, I liked this guy. As I pretended to have an itchy cheek so I could wipe another fleck of his spittle from my face, I understood that we all have our crosses to bear. His just happened to be a chubby tongue. It was incredible to think that the letter 's', such a simple concept to even the youngest of children, was like a foreign country to this man. It was the enemy in a lifelong war his mouth was never going to win. Like a kind of oral IRA (pre-ceasefire).

Before he left he was good enough to take a photo of me, for posterity (see picture section). Sadly though, my one-man station-based sales frenzy only delayed the inevitable. Alas and alack (Roget's again), I had failed. I started to sense something might be wrong when I received an email entitled 'Bouncing Back is going to be pulped'. My god, this couldn't be real. What was being proposed was nothing short of literary genocide.

---

208 Richard Madeley is one such person. He'll never consume meat unless he's seen it be handled by a trained butcher first. And preferably been to – or seen a video of – its slaughter.

I picked up the phone to Henry Chesney, my contact at the publishing company.

'Henry, there has to be some sort of mistake here.'

'There's no mistake.'

'Damn you, man, we can turn this round! I know we can.'

'We're not doing a raft of nationwide TV adverts, Alan.'

'Okay then, a stunt. We'll make a house out of a thousand copies of *Bouncing Back*. Then bequeath it to the homeless. We'll be on the front page of every paper in the land (of Norwich). Though the structure may lose rigidity if it rains.'

'The book's being pulped tomorrow. It's over, Alan.'

'Henry, I'm begging you. I'm literally on my knees.'

'It sounds like you're driving.'

'Okay then, not literally. Just throw me a bone here, buddy.'

'Well if it's any consolation you're more than welcome to go along to the pulping.'

I hung up in an explosion of fury. Go to the pulping of my own book? How dare he? HOW DARE HE?!

I was deeply moved by what I saw at the paper mill the following day. (I did go after all. I decided to take some sandwiches and make a day of it. It seemed only right that I should pay my respects.) There was great dignity in seeing fourteen thousand copies of my own book being ferried along a conveyor belt to their certain death. As they jiggled and jaggled their way into the jaws of a state-of-the-art pulping machine, it was all I could do not to stand bolt upright and salute. Those poor bastards.

Of course this wasn't goodbye, though, it was just au revoir. After all, my fallen brothers would soon have an exciting new life as recycled paper. Sometimes, if I was feeling a bit blue, I'd sit down in my favourite armchair with a big mug of milky coffee, shut my eyes and imagine what could have become of every trounced copy of *Bouncing Back*.

I like to think me and the odd fragment have met again in the years since. Yes, I like to think that very much indeed. An A4 jot-book from Rymans? A love letter from one man to his troubled bi-sexual fuck buddy? Or maybe a ream of high-grade printer paper purchased by a thriving local business. Shoved into the tummy of a Canon iP 2000, it would bide its time, until one day emerging kicking and screaming into the world, caked in the latest set of company financials. Of those three, the one I'm least keen on is the fuck buddy.

The only option I'm not prepared to risk is toilet paper. That's why I insist on buying foreign these days, and hang the cost. If it's not been imported, it's not going within a yard of my exit chute. And if the shop only has British then I just make do with a wet wipe or a splash wash.

Never mind all that, though, because I actually had a really good day at the paper mill. I would say it was easily the level of a very good school trip. Ignore all those people who say pulping is just a matter of chucking loads of books into a big bin, then letting a massive mechanical fist duff them all up into a papery porridge. It is that, but it's also a highly technical industrial process.

By the end of my time there I felt I'd really come to understand it. 'If books really do need to be destroyed,' I screamed at the foreman over the deafening roar of machinery. 'This is definitely the most humane way of doing it.'

He didn't hear me but it didn't matter. I'd made my point. Call me an old softy, but as a memento I asked if I could take home a doggy bag of *Bouncing Back* slurry. To my delight, the foreman agreed and that bag now has pride of place at the back of my attic.

29.

GOOD GRIEF

***

I KEPT MY EMOTIONS in check during the pulping.[209] It wasn't easy, but you draw on all your experience and I'd been attending funerals since I was eight.[210] In recent years I'd been to the send-offs of Tony Hayers (chief commissioning editor of BBC Television), Chris Feather (chief commissioning editor of BBC Television), Mum and Dad (my mum and dad), and

---

209 *Press play on Track 38.*
210 The first one I ever went to was that of my dog, Barney the dog. He lost his life at the hands of an ice-cream van. I decided to bury him in the back garden but it had been a very hot July and the earth was rock-hard. I managed to dig a hole big enough for his head but then had to give up. It looked like he was digging for a bone; a bone that, sadly, he would never get to chew on.

[DON'T KNOW NAME] (the racist mother of the woman who works for me).

In the case of the latter, I immediately gave my assistant 36 hours off. I swung by the hospital to explain the terms and conditions to her.

'I'm giving you 36 hours off, whether you like it or not.'

She didn't reply, which could have been rudeness but was more likely to be because her mother's body was still warm, I reasoned.

'What was that? "Can all those hours be taken in one go?"' I knew she'd said no such thing, but I was keen to try to make this as interactive as possible. 'Good question,' I continued. 'No they mustn't be used all in one go. Instead the allotted hours may be taken at any time in the next month, but in units of no more than three hours.'

This system – flexi-grief, you might call it – may sound odd, but I knew the blues could strike at any moment. Just like a young chimp raised by humans, your grief can seem totally under control. But one day that grief will reach adolescence and dish out a frenzied and unprovoked simian beat-down, I explained as we accompanied Mum to the mortuary (her mum, not mine).

What would happen if a person took a straight 36 hours off but then grief hit when that person was back at work doing, I dunno, her employer's quarterly underwear shop?[211] You can't very well just wipe your nose on his ice-white cellular briefs and carry on as if nothing has happened. Marks offer a wonderfully forgiving returns policy but even they would draw the line at snotted grundies.

---

211 Always M&S, unless finances were tight. In which case, I'd cut the budget and send her to Next.

And how glad I was that I had insisted on spreading those 36 hours across the month, because we had problems a couple of weeks after the death. My assistant was busy double-checking my Sainsbury's receipt for any instances of over-charging. I just saw a flicker on her face. I leaned over.

'Are you okay?'

'Yes. I thought they'd diddled you on the kidney beans but ...'

'No, I don't mean that. You looked like you were about to cry.' I demonstrated this by doing a sad face then lifting my fist to my eye and waggling it.

'No, I'm fine.'

'Good. I just wanted to check on you,' I said in an 'arm around the shoulder' kind of way, although there was absolutely no physical contact between us. 'Because your lip was wobbling. It looked like you were, y'know, thinking of things you should've said.'

Suddenly my assistant burst into tears. So she had been upset after all. The little fibber! I didn't mind, though, she was a mum down. I pointed to a box.

'Tuck into those tissues. They're laced with aloe vera so you can be as rough on your nose as you want.'

In the end she found the whole thing harder than antici-pated. I'd said she could take 36 hours overall, but when we totted it up at the end of the month, it came to almost 40!!! In other words my assistant had loved her mum 12% more than I'd calculated. That was fine, though, not a problem at all. Ultimately, you can't precisely gauge amounts of sadness. And I actually wanted to help with the healing process. Not least because it was dragging me down a bit.

I got her straight back to work. To start the healing process, I had her buy and assemble, then disassemble and return, a gas barbeque.[212] What she didn't know was that I already had one, I was just trying to keep her mind off things. Namely her racist mum, or lack thereof. But every cloud has a silver lining, and I suppose my assistant's loss is the black community's gain. Not that life is ever quite so clear-cut. She may have been one of the most profoundly prejudiced people this side of Eugene Terre'Blanche, but she also cooked an excellent shepherd's pie. Shades of grey, everybody, shades of grey.

Both of my own parents are also thoroughly dead. I have to be honest and say I wasn't too cut up when Poppa[213] passed on. Our relationship had been so complex I could write a book on it. (What do you reckon, HarperCollins?!)[214] For a time I was determined not to shed a tear over him, so if ever I felt myself welling up – useful tip this – I'd just think of all the bad things about him. I soon felt better. It's not what he would have wanted, but in a way that helped.

The first and worst death of the lot was Mum's. It's hard to describe what it's like to lose your mother. But HarperCollins have insisted I try. Their suggestion is that I think back to how I felt at the time of her death and use words that relate to or convey those emotions. So where to begin? Well unlike someone else's mum, she certainly wasn't racist! She really didn't agree with any of that stuff. In fact she hated racists as much as she hated homosexuals.

---

212 A Phoenix Stainless Steel 4 Burner. It's actually a lovely bit of kit. And with a cooking surface of 70cm x 45cm it allows the adventurous host to try his hand at any type of food. Play it safe with sausages, or become the talk of the town with a delicious spatchcocked chicken? The choice is yours.

213 I never actually called him Poppa but it just looks cool on the page.

214 Seriously, let me know because I can easily turn round a mis-lit book: – e.g., *1968: Summer of Hate (For Me)* or *Locked in the Larder*.

My relationship with her went way back, although we weren't close right from day one. During those long hard months in the womb, she'd been less my mother and more my house. I didn't interact with her, I just lived inside her. And then when I'd made good my escape from her cervix (see Chapter One) she'd become less my mum and more my canteen. Although her teats weren't much of a chef – it was milk every day for goodness sake!

But it was as the years rolled on, as I began to crawl, walk and then express myself through dance, that things began to blossom. She was my friend, my cheerleader, my protector-in-chief. And we remained close until the onset of my difficult adolescent years. I remember we entered choppy waters pretty much as soon as my balls dropped. By the time I was 16 our relationship had broken down to such an extent that I'd rarely even let her do my blackheads.

Yet when I had asserted my independence and emerged from my mum's considerable shadow (I mean this metaphorically, although she was fat – the poor woman looked like someone had blown her up with a bike pump),[215] our relationship began to improve.

In my BBC days no one was more proud of my success. She would absolutely insist on watching *Knowing Me Knowing You* if she was at home when it was on. It was different when I returned to radio. She didn't listen to *Norfolk Nights* (on too late), *Up With the Partridge* (on too early) or *Mid-Morning Matters* (dead), but it didn't matter. I knew she only ever wanted the best for me. And I'm sure the same is true today. If there's a radio in heaven I'm sure she'll be up there

---

215 But she was fat in a nice way. She wouldn't have looked out of place on a packet of Aunt Bessie's Yorkshire Puds.

listening, providing my show doesn't clash with *Today, Start the Week* or *The Archers*, which is what God would listen to.

Sadly, I can't say the same for Father, who is probably in a different place.[216]

To preserve her dignity I'd rather not say what she died from, but suffice to say the family was forced to ask some rather uncomfortable questions about what she used to get up to in her spare time. When they'd finally brought her body back from Hull (don't ask) and the coroner had concluded his post-mortem (long story), we were free to arrange the kind of funeral we knew she would have wanted, minus the open casket (believe me, you don't want to know).

With Dad in no fit state to do anything, I agreed to say a few words at the service. I'd felt absolutely fine in the hearse. In fact I'd enjoyed the ride. It was a mint-condition Daimler Lauderlette Vanden Plas with slide-out occasional seats, allowing generous room for up to five mourners who would easily drown out the hushed whisper of the smooth straight-six engine. I would have loved to have seen what kind of speed it could have reached on the open road, but the undertaker was not to be persuaded. (And quite right too.) All in all, though, very nice. But as soon as I got into the church it all went wrong. I went to pieces like a dropped jigsaw.

After a few minutes of being cuddled by Great Aunt Susie, we'd managed to reduce my crying down to a manageable sob. Then it was time to give the speech. I took a deep breath, gritted (grat?) my teeth and just spoke from the heart.

'I stand before you all today to talk about a woman I can describe in just two words: my Mummy.'

---

216 Hell.

But when I started recounting how she used to let me lick the spoon when she was making cakes or gravy, it all got too much. I became so grief-stricken I barely knew what I was saying. For a while I thought I was broadcasting. Uncle Pete said that at one point I tried to introduce 'Cool for Cats' by Squeeze.

I can't recall much about the wake either. To be honest I was in a bit of a daze. I remember eating a great many chicken drumsticks and someone coming up to me and telling me I mustn't forget to have some fibre too. He said the last thing I wanted was to be bereaved *and* bunged up. And he was right. To this day that's advice I always pass on to mourners who I see failing to eat sufficient roughage in the immediate aftermath of the death of a loved one.

After the burial things slowly got better. For the first couple of days I used to visit the grave every day. My schedule soon got in the way, though, so then I'd start sending my assistant as my grave-side representative. She was visiting her mum anyway, and the bus connections between the two graveyards were really quite good considering how far apart they were.

Besides, I reasoned that, as a believer, my assistant derived more meaning from grave-side grieving than I did. Not that I'm a non-believer as such. I'm pretty open-minded about the possibility of an afterlife, although I always think of heaven as a kind of members club for do-gooders. White bean bags, 24-hour room service, fat babies with wings, pointing at other fat babies playing compact harps. Don't get me wrong, it's good stuff. If you find it comforting, go there.

I don't go down to the cemetery at all these days unless I happen to be passing. In which case I'll take flowers. The beauty of her headstone is that it's located on the main thoroughfare through the graveyard. So if I'm pushed for time I can open my passenger-side window and throw the flowers out without stopping. That might sound crass, but in many ways it's a tribute to Mum because she was a real stickler for punctuality. Not that the flowers always land in the right place. Quite often they end up on the grave of Dan 'loving father and loyal husband' Faversham. Occasionally other mourners will see this happening and frown. I can only assume they think I'm a predatory gay with a fetish for the dead. And I know that would have made Mum chuckle.

30.

CLASSIC HOUSE

***

BEFORE CHANNEL 4'S INSUFFERABLE *Grand Designs* programme, few people realised that it was possible or legal to build your own home. Apart from me. My project was in the works a full six months before the first transmission of the show, and I defy anyone to prove otherwise.

Unlike the deeply unpleasant couples who appear on *Grand Designs*, I wanted to create the perfect home rather than an art installation with a built-in toilet. So, working with a team of expensive architects, I asked them to duplicate exactly the design used by Redrow homes, with a soupcon of Barrett thrown in around the porch area. Imagine Henry 8th had commissioned, nay ordered, Redrow and Barrett to create a modern 21st-century house for a pre-renaissance fat king using the efficiencies of modern techniques combined with a Tudor brick quality (a sort of Hampton Court fit for a Norfolk Conservative), that's the effect I was going for.[217]

I could sense the architects were disappointed not to be able to flex their creative mind muscles, but Redrow and Barrett are experts in creating homes. Architects aren't.

Besides, as with advertising agencies, it's hard to think of architects as genuinely creative people when the best company names they can muster are a list of the owners' surnames: Beeden Allison Lyons or Humpleton Goggins & Fox. Or Tithe St John Crooks. Or Cannock Jones Scilly Andrews Haynes. Or Peterson Johnson Magnusson Hanson. Or Dennis Dennis & Dennis. Or Grigson Smith Oliver. Or Barrow McGuigan Bounder. Or Hiscox Greengrass Mitchell and Matthews. I could go on but I won't! If advertisers/architects were even a fraction as clever as they think they are (Swinson Shaw Lancashire – that would be another example), they'd call themselves Rock Steady (architects) or Pizzazz (advertising). The fact that they don't *proves* that they're either vain or thick.

They could (should) have taken a leaf out of my book. Long before the design was finished, I'd brained out a list of potential names for the property.

COLEMAN HOUSE
ATLANTIS
ACE HOUSE
ALAN HOUSE
THE COTTAGE

---

217 The finishing touch was to be a boot scraper outside the front door. When I see one of those outside a house I think, 'They know which way to vote at a General Election!'

THE OLD RECTORY
BARN COTTAGE
FOLLYFOOT
STEED MANOR
LORD HOUSE
ROCKFORD HOUSE
FLAMBARDS
BRIDESHEAD HOUSE
THE SKIRMISHES
APACHE
TOMAHAWK
SCEPTRE HOUSE
THE CINNAMONS (it's just a lovely ingredient)
CLASSIC HOUSE
THE CLASSICS
MANOR HOUSE
BENTLEY HOUSE
LARGE COTTAGE

That kind of thing. No, I was happy for my architects to mimic the Redrow boys wholesale, then I paid them handsomely and the building work began. But where to live in the meantime?

The Linton Travel Tavern had made it abundantly clear that I was welcome back at any time, but knowing that builders are often ex-offenders, I thought it best to stay on site where I could better observe/befriend/monitor them.

I would be staying in a static caravan (see picture section) – a 10-footer from the yet-to-be-bettered Delta range. I was comfortable with this (I'd be living in it for three years anyway, parked up in the garden of a kindly farmer.)[218]

---

218 One of the very, very few.

It's funny – when you move from a hotel or detached house into a 10-foot static home, people are quick to assume you're down on your luck financially.

Nothing could have been further from the truth. After all, for some time Jimmy Savile lived in a caravan and absolutely insists it was a lifestyle choice. Scruffy crooner David Essex also lived in one.[219]

My reasons had nothing to do with money. Caravanning had long been an ambition of mine. It gave me the opportunity to live out the holiday I'd always been denied in my harrowing childhood – minus the swingball. At the same time, I hoped it would give me a chink of insight into the mind-set of the travelling community, so that I might come to understand how they could even consider dumping a binbag full of used nappies in the ginnel next to someone's house.[220]

No, I was doing pretty fine, thanks. I was approaching my 200th episode of *Skirmish* and had learnt all there is to know about military strategy. I don't think it was in any way arrogant of me to offer my services as a consultant to the Ministry of Defence. (I revoked the offer when I realised it might mean travelling to London or Aldershot, but I'm confident they'd have literally bitten my hand off.)

At the same time, my other business interests were blossoming like the small flowers that grow on trees each spring. Peartree Productions had been a great success, having achieved everything it had set out to. And so, with its mission accomplished, it was placed into liquidation.

---

219 I may be wrong about this, but he looks like he could be gypsy. I'm not sure of his ethnicity but I'm reliably informed he once tried to put a curse on Leo Sayer after an argument over the bill in an Indian restaurant.

220 Still clueless over that one. *Animals.*

Instead, my efforts were focused on a new and exciting venture. The Apache Group of Companies® was aimed squarely at the canny businessman, a one-stop shop providing everything a business might need. Comprising six distinct brands – Apache Communications, Apache Productions, Apache Office Supplies,[221] Apache Media Training, Apache Risk Management ('Trust No One') and Apache Military Strategy – it was a welcome revenue stream that complemented Brand Partridge beautifully.

It was a tri-headquartered concern, with my business activities based out of the static home, the property-under-construction and Choristers Country Club.

Now a leading light in the local business community, I had taken membership of Choristers to provide some much-needed respite from the hustle and bustle and fustle of Norfolk life. As a haven for businessmen, Choristers was quite unique – with the Norwich club only complemented by the one in Bristol, another in the Roman town of Chester and one at Stansted airport.

Much like a masonic lodge, it provided a meeting point where the region's most important people could get together, share ideas and do each other clandestine favours. Unlike a masonic lodge, there was no snobbishness towards celebrity broadcasters. Nor was there any suggestion that members must sacrifice livestock and daub themselves in its blood while chanting. I liked it there very much, and enjoyed offering suggestions to the management as to how the staff could improve. (I'm still a member to this day. After several years of lobbying, I have managed to ban children entirely. There is now a heated outhouse for children with a light and running water.)

---

221 The name was registered but no business was ever conducted.

The Apache Group of Companies® had its fair share of work – some people think it didn't but they're wrong because it did. Trust me, Apache Productions made *quite* the name for itself and found a niche satisfying the easy-to-satisfy corporate market – whose idea of entertainment is generally limited to a Dilbert cartoon or the use of Comic Sans font in an otherwise serious PowerPoint presentation.

I did well out of it – my versatility and willingness to leave my principles at the door (for the right price) making me an attractive proposition for even the most toxic brands.

The only time I faced a slight moral twinge was when asked to give a motivational-presentation-plus-rock-music to a well-known cigarette brand. Tobacco was a sensitive subject area because I knew my assistant's racist mother had just died of lung cancer. Upset an employee for money or upset a lucrative paymaster? You can see the bind I was in!

I eventually agreed to do it. Even the most ardent do-gooder would agree that the £5,000 fee on offer made my assistant's feelings *pretty* inconsequential. Sometimes in business you have to be hard-headed.[222]

And the presentation? It went well, thanks. Ever the pro, I always made sure I gave the client exactly what they wanted.[223]

And so it was that later that week, I walked out in front an audience of 400 tipsy sales execs … wearing a gas mask!

After the 15-second blast of intro music[224] stopped, I began: 'I once had a teacher who smoked,' I said. 'Smoked his whole life, didn't miss a day's work. He died at 36! Ha ha.'

---

222 Postscript – it turned out my assistant's mum died of colon cancer anyway, so I was absolved/vindicated.

223 'Fail to prepare? Prepare to fail!' – as I once had engraved on the underside of a watch that I've subsequently never worn.

224 'Every Breath You Take' – The Police with Sting.

I was paid in full.

***

Like my now-completed home (I opted for the name Classic House), the Partridge that saw in the third millennium post-Christ was strong, impressive and had fully working plumbing. Yes, this was a good time for me. A very good time. People noticed that this incarnation was good. And they liked it.

That – the liking of other people towards myself – found itself manifested with all the clarity this sentence has in manifesting itself in front of yourself as you currently read.

For one thing, I was promoted to Radio Norwich's glamour slot, *Norfolk Nights*. It really didn't get better than that.

According to listener figures, it was only the third most popular slot on the station. But that's statistics for you. You can make statistics say anything. 'Statistics'[225] say that 80% of women under the age of 30 are either indifferent to, or actively dislike, my current show *Mid-Morning Matters*. That doesn't make it true!

My show came directly before the graveyard[226] slot of Dave Clifton. Despite our differences, I took no pleasure in having a much better slot than Dave. I mean, I enjoyed helping him out because – and he'd surely be the very, very first to admit this – he needed all the help he could get. Dave was drinking a hell of a lot by now and no amount of Polo mints could mask that. I'd like to say it wasn't affecting his broadcasting but that would be fraud. Dave wasn't able to muster anything like the

---

225 North Norfolk Digital Listener Survey, June 2011.
226 So-called because of the time of day it was broadcast and because that's where Dave was heading if he didn't cut down on the booze.

energy needed to carry a three-hour late night show, so I'd have to generate enough energy and momentum in the final hour of *Norfolk Nights* to carry the listener to the bitter end[227] of Dave's show.

It's similar to the slingshot technique used to propel the Galileo probe out into the solar system. They basically razzed it round the sun a few times to get its speed up and then they used that momentum to hurl it into deep space. That was what I did to my listeners in the final hour of my show, before pelting them into the atmosphere-free void of Dave's slot.

We've never spoken about it but I was doing him a massive favour. Still, I was happy to do it every night of the week for Dave because he was – and is – in a very bad place. (If I thought Dave minded me saying any of this, of course I'd not have committed it to print. I wouldn't dream of upsetting the guy, because I know he has a bit of a temper, although it's mainly directed towards women.)

In terms of making me feel good, this gave me a metaphorical 'hand-job'.[228] As did (less metaphorically) the new love in my life, Sonja, then 33.[229]

Yes, on top of a luxury abode, a successful business empire, a burgeoning television and radio career and membership of Choristers, I also had a girlfriend who was significantly younger than me. Fourteen years younger.

Sonja was responsible for awakening my dormant libido – and making it do press-ups! It had been a-slumber for a while. Apart from a truly distasteful dalliance with a menopausal

---

227 And it was always bitter.
228 Manual masturbatory relief by a consenting foreign hand.
229 *Press play on Track 39. Check out the video!!!!*

member of staff years earlier,[230] my sex life post-Carol had been as threadbare as the gusset of my 'Number One Dad' novelty briefs.

But Sonja changed all that – and how! I've heard of the phrase 'a healthy sex life' but this was ridiculous. I don't know if it's possible to be *too* healthy – Lance Armstrong maybe? – but that's what our sex life was.

Within reason, I loved every minute of my time with Sonja. She was introduced to me by Pete Gabitas, MD of BlueBarn Media. Sadly no longer with us, Pete had been a confidant, friend and lender of production facilities for over a decade.

Pete had a stunning Ukrainian girlfriend, a decade his junior, and arranged similar girlfriends for six or seven of us. Mine was probably the second best.[231]

Lithe, smooth-skinned and so youthful I'd started pubing before she was even born, I couldn't help but notice that she was a svelte, effortless size eight. In other words, she'd achieved through genetics and poverty the exact body shape that Carol had been fruitlessly striving for since she was 20. Just a thought!

And right from the off, it was an exciting time. I think I've mentioned what a lot of sex we had? Ever the joker, she bought a window sticker that said, 'If the caravan's rocking, don't come knocking!' And I made my own one that said, 'If it looks like we're having sexual intercourse in here, please respect our privacy!'

---

230 I won't say too much. I've no doubt she'll be reading this. She still sends me Christmas cards with glitter glued on to a picture of Our Lord with a sort of Ready Brek glow around him and inside the inscription says, For unto us this day a child is born (which is fair enough). But I've always found her continued correspondence a *bit* desperate.

231 My favourite thing about her? Her backside.

I was in two minds about whether to include intimate details of my sex life in this book, but I read a pamphlet in a dentist's waiting room which said that it was healthy and important to speak openly about sexual issues, so I will. If Carol is reading, that's her lookout.

Sex with Carol was all very sedate. It was effective – at least two of our copulations resulted in children – but sedate.

With Sonja, it was much more spontaneous. What I like to call smash and grab sex. Or a ram raid!! Sonja delighted in the spontaneity of our sexual salad days and relished my playfulness.

Using the full area of the caravan, I liked to pretend to be a KGB agent. But as a Ukrainian who had spent half of her life as part of the Eastern bloc, she'd rather pretend to be an East German gypsy, so I'd be the Stasi. I'd ask to see her papers before mounting her from behind over the twin hobs that were concealed beneath a work surface. She'd pretend to be confused and … I think you get the idea, gents. At that point we must draw down a veil.

Suffice to say it ended with us showering off, and me returning to my normal accent (Sonja had retained hers) before we'd both settle down to a quick boil-in-the-bag curry while watching a VHS of Taggarts and Magnums, the austere greyness of those Glaswegian skyscapes contrasting perfectly with the sunshine of *Magnum P.I.*, like a TV detective yin and yang.

But it was more than sexual. Apart from the lots of sex we were having, Sonja had plenty more to offer. She had a wonderful anti-ageing effect on me, like Oil of Olay has on a middle-aged woman's cracked, craggy skin. Energetic, boisterous and really very zesty,[232] she loved to laugh – boy, how she

---

232 NB – check word exists.

loved to laugh – and had a relatively infectious giggle. I'm glad to say that was the only infectious thing about her – I had her fully checked out before *anything* happened. (A lot of nonsense is spoken about germs passed from one to another. There's *nothing* more unsexy than talking about venereal disease – when I'm with a new lover, I merely casually suggest/insist that we take a hot bath together with three caps of Dettol, an activity that is sexy *and* hygienic.)

All in all, Sonja had that indiscriminate fun-loving quality that you often find with people from post-Soviet regimes. It's as if their people have cast off the state-imposed grumpiness of Communism and are now grabbing life with both hands. After a while, of course, it becomes incredibly tiresome. But Sonja's love of practical jokes, sex, laughter, chintzy homeware and relentless intercourse was a sometime source of periodic happiness for quite a while.

We broke up just hours after the house was completed. She was understandably miffed by this but, as I explained patiently in rudimentary English, it was a new build so I wanted shoes off at the door – and she was hopeless at remembering to do that.

You know that phrase, if you love someone set them free? I've always liked the sound of that – even if its logic is plainly horseshit. It's the equivalent of saying, 'If you like beefburgers, don't eat them' or 'If you hate London, go and live there.' Instead, I've adapted it slightly to read, 'If you don't love someone and don't want to hang around with them any more, set them free'. It just makes more sense.

Breaking the news to her wasn't easy. We'd been living together for a year and a half for goodness sake, and she'd often talked about marriage – ideally to me, but at a push anyone with UK citizenship. This was a big deal for her.

So I locked myself in the bathroomette and got my assistant to do it. She broke the news with some relish – a bit too much if you ask me. Of course, Sonja was devastated. She kept banging on the door and telling me to come out and face her. Knowing she was from a former Soviet country where human rights atrocities are commonplace, I had no idea what she was capable of, so I had no choice but to stay inside.

'Come out, Alan!' she was shouting.

Through the door, I could hear my assistant trying to placate/fib to her. 'He's not in there any more,' she attempted. 'He clambered out of the window and ran off.' I winced at her utter inability to lie and pledged to fine her £10 later on.

'Alan, I love you!' she kept shouting (Sonja, not my assistant – urgh). Poor kid, I thought as I did my belt up. (I was in the toilet anyway so thought I might as well make use of it.) But I became less sympathetic with each shout, because it was repetitive and, other than the theme tune to *Ski Sunday*, I don't like repetitive noises.

She stayed for absolutely ages. I found this irritating because I'd promised to send a showreel to Bid-Up TV and the post office was going to shut. After a few hours she calmed down and sloped off, but I'd missed the last post and never got that BUTV job. Shame, because it was one of my favourite channels and I used to practise the patter in the shower, imagining I was selling Radox or a bath mitt.

And so I moved into the house alone – a big space for one certainly, but I liked that, sometimes running around the building with a makeshift cape around my collar. It had four good-sized bedrooms and I used to alternate between rooms 1 and 4, leaving 2 (Fernando's) and 3 (Denise's) untouched in case they dropped by and needed to go to sleep. Still do!

And Sonja? Well, she and I are still very close – in the sense that she's now my cleaner. I wish things had turned out differently but I'm glad they didn't.

31.

FORWARD SOLUTIONS™

***

I AWOKE AT 3AM to find sweat pouring from all over my body. Something wasn't right.

But how could this be? I'd *bounced* back. I was in solid fettle. Slim, happy, professionally successful, I was a published author no less! Things were going fine for me. So what gave?

It wasn't until after I'd made toilet that things started to fall into place. Whether it was a brainwave triggered by the exhilaration of one of my best ever slashes, or the blissful relaxation engendered by crouching in the half-light, flannelling sweat from my undercarriage, I'll probably never know. But it was at that moment that my destiny took shape.

Yes, things were going fine for *me*. But, as I've always modestly insisted, it's not all about me. There are people out there who are lonely, weak, vulnerable, obese, not on the radio, poverty-stricken, drugged to the nines on smack pipes. Things were going fine for me, but what about them? The underpoor, the badlings, the shitsam and flopsam. What could I, Alan Partridge, do for them?

It was obvious. I had a responsibility to give. I had a god-given duty to help others. It was incumbent upon me, Alan Partridge, to summon up everything I'd learnt while bouncing back and run after-work Forward Solutions™ courses for a special corporate rate[233] of £299.98 per head, ex VAT.[234]

***

A man who does manual labour for a living once accused me of being arrogant. My crime? Taking my wisdom and sharing it with people who would never develop it off their own bat.

Is that arrogant, do you think? To genuinely help people less savvy than you? When Gandhi advocated non-violent resistance or when Moses parted the Red Sea, were *they* being arrogant? Well yes, maybe Moses was a little bit jazz-hands, but leaders need a little showmanship. It's what Jesus of Nazareth would have had in mind as he turned loaves and fishes into five thousand tuna butties.[235]

---

233 For those on a limited budget. The least I could do.

234 *Press play on Track 40.*

235 Of course, he didn't always get it right. Turning water into wine at a wedding isn't just showing off, it's irresponsible. As a miracle, it just doesn't work on any level. Impressing people who are already drunk, by magicking up more wine to get them pissed – how is that holy? That's what I'd ask the Pope if I met him. By the way, I'm not knocking God. He's a powerful man. Think about the recent earthquakes and tsunamis – he really does knock Al-Qaeda for six when it comes to killing the most number of people. For that alone, he deserves a quiet respect. That's why I never blaspheme.

So no, not arrogant. Helpful.

'It's not arrogant, it's helpful,' I said, wishing I'd never wound my window down to address him. He was holding a Stop/Go lollipop while his 'colleagues' spread gravel across one lane of the carriageway. You would not find a candidate more in need of night school and a shave. And, in a nice way, I'd said so.

I was in the early evangelical flush of Forward Solutions™ – keen to get out there and improve lives. So I'd slapped the door of the Lexus and suggested that if he improved his literacy and appearance he 'could drive one of these'.

What followed had been good Samaritanism thrown back in my face. So I explained that I was a force for good.

'Yeah, but only if folk want helping,' he spluttered, unintellectually. 'Tha's no right to come up t' folk and t' tell 'em wot's right and what's not, tha dunt. I'm happy as I am.'

He made me think about all the funny things Jez Clarkson says about the working class. I thought, 'Wow. If Clarkson could hear this spiel, he'd have a *field day*, laughing along with me at this guy's working classness.' No doubt we'd end up down the pub swapping stories about people with no money.[236]

'My friend,' I said, 'you're wearing a high-visibility jacket over a t-shirt that says "Rage Against the Machine" on it – the only machine here is that generator and if you were to rage against that, it'd be riding rough shod over basic health and safety. Not a good look, hombre!'

And with that quip, I revved my engine, ready to speed off. There was no traffic in either direction so I was ready to slam

---

236 God, I'd *love* to live in Chipping Norton. Brooks, Cameron, Clarkson, a Murdoch, quaffing champers and laughing our heads off at everyone else. Brilliant.

her into first and really let rip. You snub my advice, I'm going to deliver a quip and then drive past you fast – it's that simple.

But he just stood there watching me, the Stop side of the lollipop facing my way. I revved louder to let him know I was eager to drive past him fast but he seemed not to notice.

I started to become anxious. The more time that elapsed between my acid put-down and me driving off fast, the less it would seem like a conversational flourish – it'd just look irresponsible. I revved again. Still nothing.

I called out to him but he didn't seem to hear me. This was really annoying. On the off chance that he might be about to turn the lolly round I repeated the 'Not a good look, hombre' bit to give it proximity to my driving away. But then a full five minutes passed.

With my requests falling on deaf ears, I got out of the car and approached him.[237] I was just about to ask him to turn the lollipop to Go when he did just that. I trudged back to the car and pulled steadily away.

I learnt something that day. That *unsolicited* life coaching was inadvisable. If people don't pay for it, they don't appreciate it. Even during the Sermon on the Mount there must have been a couple of Sinai-based goat herders who wished Christ would just eff off.

Also, it's not a sustainable business model, and at least by charging a fee you cut out the true bottom feeders – who are probably beyond help anyway. My advice is more for amateur businessmen, shopkeepers, even people who rent out pedalos on a shallow man-made lake. It's not for single parents, asylum

---

237 I *really* hadn't wanted to do this, because I only had socks on. My assistant had taken my shoes to clean.

seekers, football hooligans, people in care, or criminals (unless white collar and sorry).

No, Forward Solutions™ was a potentially lucrative, potential helpful, potentially global life-improvement programme that, having helped me, could potentially help other people. I whipped it into the shape of a 60-minute presentation and, alongside my radio work, it became a source of real professional fulfilment that made me *feel* good (pride) and *look* good (image).

***

So what was Forward Solutions™? Perhaps it's easier to tell you what Forward Solutions™ wasn't.

1. It *wasn't* some attempt to boost my profile and secure lucrative television work. No, no. My TV days were dead to me and I was fine with that. Did I miss having my own parking space at Television Centre? Not really. Do I even remember that my face on the cover of the *Radio Times* once led to a 2% leap in circulation? Can't say I do. Did I used to enjoy the make-up girls referring to me as 'Mr Partridge' but calling Nicholas Witchell 'Nick'? Perhaps a little.

   But, just to reiterate, Forward Solutions™ was not and is not some presentation that could just be repackaged into a 12-part series of lifestyle makeover shows for BBC 1.

2. It *wasn't* some kind of clever-clogs psychobabble. The opposite! What was unique about my system was that it took science and plucked the good bits out and dismissed the rubbish. Science can really bog things down with blah-blah about research, tests, statistics,

facts and psychology. I didn't want to be bogged down. I wanted to be bogged up.

3. It *wasn't* just another self-help programme. Of course, there were a lot of people who were trying to do what I was doing. It was a very crowded marketplace.[238] Stuart Blender was just launching his Mind Muscle™ technique. David Els was generating plenty of attention for his Ladder of Legends™. And of course Solomon Baptiste's Rise Like a Phoenix™ programme was the big show in town.

But I had a considerable advantage in that, unlike the three I've just mentioned, Forward Solutions™ wasn't shit. I really was offering the best coaching around. Yes, Blender raises the interesting point that the hero is deep within us and all he needs is soul food. And yes, Els does offer a moving discourse about hope being a buddy who doesn't mind what time you call. And there's a certain entertainment value in watching Baptiste whoop and holler like he's got chillies in his unders. But could they compete with Forward Solutions™? No.

4. It *wasn't* all about personal happiness. It had real business benefits too. From day one, hour one, minute one, second one, I wanted to create something that was touching yet business-like: a presentation that would make you laugh and make you cry or (if better) make you stop laughing and make you stop crying.

---

238 To help you understand what I mean, imagine a place where you'd have a market, then imagine it's very busy, or crowded.

5. It *wasn't* just spoken passages culled directly from *Bouncing Back*. Although some bits did double up. It had taken a great deal of thought and consideration and thinking. Nothing was rushed – and boy, did that pay off. It was a presentation I developed very gradually in my bathroom mirror. What started out as me slapping my own face and saying 'You have to get through this' went on to become what *Winning Management* magazine describes as 'nothing less than the advertised hour'.

But there were still doubters – still are! In Britain, people are very wary of seeking help for problems that occur around the head, brain or mind.

Why? If your car breaks down, you call the AA. If your *mind* breaks down, I'd say, call the AP.[239] Actually, unlike the AA, AP doesn't discriminate against middle-aged men. Try phoning the AA when you're not a pregnant disabled single mother and see how much they value your call. You'll be there all night.

Last time my fan belt went, I was in the middle of Norfolk at 2am and I had to flag down a *woman's* car and demand that she make the phone call for me. She was really scared. But then so was I.[240] Why would a single woman be any more prone than a single man? Single men can be just as vulnerable to a

---

239 Alan Partridge.
240 See, that's another example of Forward Solutions™. I was stranded, bereft of hope (thanks to the lack of professionalism of Swaffham Vauxhalls). Did I spend three hours sitting on the kerb crying about it? No. A quivering lip gave way to strong, decisive action. I sought help by standing in the highway wielding a jack. There was no way she was driving past. No way.

crazed homosexual pest[241] or – and this is less likely – a very strong woman.

So now that it's clear what it wasn't – and I was certainly clear on that – I felt it was high time I shared Forward Solutions™ with the world.

***

Fast forward three months and a thrusting go-getter by the name of Alan Partridge is in the staff room of Richer Sounds in Norwich, wrapping up a well-honed presentation to a sales team that would outnumber the fingers on both hands of a fully able man.

'So you see, it's not about "self-help" or "self-improvement".' (I'm walking slowly up and down as I say this. You can't take your flippin' *eyes* off me.) 'What I'm talking about is "self-transformation".'

Oh, *now* they're listening.

'Self-trans-formation. The actions I've given to you – to you Daniel, to you Marvin, to you Sam, to you Andrew[242] – the actions I've given to you are nothing less than a Self-Transformation Diagnosis. Now I've given STDs to men, women, children in some cases ...'

They're smiling now.

'Actually I find that it's most pleasurable to give STDs to kids. The younger the better really. When I go into schools and give STDs to kids, I know that I'm really having an impact on the rest of their lives. And that excites me.'

---

241 I can hear all the PC brigade: 'Oh no, homosexuals never attack anyone, they just prance around Hampstead Heath picking flowers!' Get real – Dennis Nilsen, Jeff Dahmer, Boy George.

242 I'd *remembered their names* and kept using them again and again. It's a devastating technique, later stolen by Nick Clegg.

All of them laugh and, although I only later work out what the joke is and pledge not to acronymise Self-Transformation Diagnosis ever again, it's a nice upbeat ending to the session.

'Now go out there and attack the planet!'

Think this was a one-off? Think again. The Richer Sounds presentation was in December 2005. In the preceding seven months alone, I'd presented Forward Solutions to the staff of Clinton Cards in King's Lynn, to Fords of Norwich, to the entire company at Bulwark IT Security and to the staff at the Norfolk Mead Hotel.

I felt like a new person. Younger, fitter, wiser, louder. I took to wearing the three old reliables: stone-wash baby blue denim jeans, oversized white training shoes and a wearable microphone.

Quick digression for the AV nerds out there. I absolutely insisted on presenting with a Sennheiser 152 G2 Headset microphone. If any of you are in the market for a headset mic – aerobic instructors, business leaders, the people at the market who sell chipped crockery – let me give you a piece of solid gold advice. This is the Piat d'Or of headset mics. Used by the likes of Mr Motivator and – weirdly – Terry Nutkins, the Sennheiser is the official headmic for both product demonstrators at the Ideal Home Exhibition and Gabrielle.

I'm not going to go on about headmics, and bulk out my word count with technical details[243] – other than to say it's lightweight but packs a punch. And its supercardioid microphone produces crystal clear sound.

Some of the lesser headmics out there – I'm thinking of your Radnor CL-07s – muffle certain consonants so that an S sounds like an F.[244] I gave a version of this presentation to the

---

243 The publishers specifically asked me not to.
244 And vife verfa! LOL.

children of a local primary school and caused uproar by repeatedly using the phrase 'You can't teach your grandmother to suck eggs.'

So avoid the Radnor range. That's my advice.

I would also advise you to avoid wearing a headmic on one side of your head and a Bluetooth mobile phone headset on the other. Because during the same presentation, Carol called – she was angry that I'd cancelled a long-standing direct debit, suspending her subscription to BBC *Good Food* magazine. And the sound from the call vibrated through my head and was picked up on mic.[245]

I had bigger plans for the project than drafty staff rooms, though. My aim was to take the presentation on a tour of the major theatres around the country. Provisional chats were initiated with the Norwich Playhouse, but they said their only free slot was the Christmas season, and they normally fill that with a pantomime. Kein problem, I said! My presentation was loose enough that it could easily have been re-purposed to become a fun family-based show in the best traditions of the UK pantomime. For example, the hero would be on stage and he'd say to the audience, 'Where *aren't* my best years?' And they'd say, 'Behind you!!'

They never got back to me. No matter!

At least I was showing ambition. All you need to do is aim high. As Jimi Hendrix once said, 'Excuse me, while I kiss the sky.' And I echoed that. Of course, Jimi was found dead in his own sick shortly afterwards. He'd probably been listening to Stuart Blender's CD.

---

245 Thankfully the poor sound quality of the Radnor mic meant that all the audience could hear was her calling me a 'petty little suckwit'. Which is meaningless.

It's all about belief. I had a chap called Alvin visit me who'd struggled to hold down a job. He was in a hostel and at a low ebb. He believed he would one day learn how to travel forwards and backwards through time.

'In that case, you will,' I said. 'Just hold on to that belief. You can achieve whatever you want to achieve.'

'Really?' he said. 'My psychiatrist says I'm being weird. I've been prescribed pills.' And at that moment he looked so sad – his will crushed by medical science. I told him to lose the pills and follow his dreams.

And as a result of that advice, Alvin came on in leaps and bounds. He was soon dreaming of even greater feats – inter-galactic real estate deals, breeding humans with mermaids, an invisibility cloak, flying from one high-rise building to another.

Surprise, surprise, his psychiatrist pleaded with me to stop. 'It's irresponsible,' he said during one particularly shirty phone call. 'He can't travel through time.'

'Oh? Why?' I said. 'Because *you* say he can't? Because *society* has decided he can't?'

Defeated, he mumbled something about the laws of physics prohibiting it and hung up. And it's that attitude, that 'prohibit' word, that idea of 'can't' that I was trying to break down. You *can't* travel through time. You *can't* have a second series. You *can't* have time off your show to do a self-help tour. Bullcrap, all of it.

I decided not to devote too much of my time to Forward Solutions™, instead choosing to concentrate on my radio show. I quietly laid the programme to rest. I'd helped enough for one lifetime …

And Alvin? Hmmm. I had a funny feeling, he'd be aaaa-okay.

32.

NORTH NORFOLK
DIGITAL[246]

***

FREQUENCY MODULATION? WE'VE ALL heard of it. We all admire it. We all respect it. But what exactly is it?

You're the flippin' radio expert, Partridge! You tell us!

Well, off the top of my head: In telecommunications and signal processing, frequency modulation (FM) conveys information over a carrier wave by varying its instantaneous frequency.

And I think I'm right in saying: This is in contrast with amplitude modulation, in which the amplitude of the carrier is varied while its frequency remains constant.

Yes, it seems to me that: In analog applications, the difference between the instantaneous and the base frequency of the

---

246 North Norfolk's best music mix.

carrier is directly proportional to the instantaneous value of the input signal amplitude. Digital data can be sent by shifting the carrier's frequency among a set of discrete values, a technique known as frequency-shift keying.

And I'm just riffing here but: While it is an over-simplification, a baseband modulated signal may be approximated by a sinusoidal Continuous Wave signal with a frequency f_m. The harmonic distribution of a sine wave carrier modulated by such a sinusoidal signal can be represented with Bessel functions – this provides a basis for a mathematical understanding of frequency modulation in the frequency domain.

Oh, and: In radio systems, frequency modulation with sufficient bandwidth provides an advantage in cancelling naturally occurring noise.[citation needed]

So that's pretty much all I know. I'm sure there's more on the subject but I'd have to look it up.

What I think we can all say for certain is that FM was, at one time, the Gold Standard for UK radio. If you weren't on FM, you were nothing![247] But today the opposite is true.[248]

Now, FM is considered prehistoric isn't it? If someone said they were DJing on an FM frequency, you'd think they were on pirate radio, Sad FM, or were just an absolute idiot. You'd laugh at them and you'd be right to laugh at them. No, FM had had its day. It was as tired and lifeless as Chiles's eyes. Which is why I was so delighted when Radio North Norfolk lost its FM licence in 2006.

Radio North Norfolk? Say whaaaat, Alan?

Allow me to explain. It'd been a time of genuine upheaval for Radio Norwich. Since 2002, it had been a station in

---

247 5Live would be a good example.
248 With the exception of 5Live.

desperate need of stability. Which eventually arrived in the form of a steady downward trajectory of revenue and turnover.

Whoever was to blame – be it slovenly listeners or station management – morale was at a low. I, on the other, kept insisting on air that we were a damn good radio station and that the financial figures were bang out of order. I sincerely believed that and I was vindicated when we received the following email.

'Please read carefully,' read the subject line, which I thought was a strong hook, and it went on to say that Radio Norwich was to be sold to a fast-growing holding company called Gordale Media. We were hot property!

Now, that proved me emphatically right: people don't choose to buy something if it isn't good. It meant they liked us. We had something (or to use the corporate speak of the email, 'assets') that was worth buying (or 'stripping').

Lots of people were concerned about what they read but the tone of the email was, to my mind, unmistakeably upbeat: 'exciting times', 'improved offer', 'going forward', 'increased efficiency'.

Those Gordale boys didn't muck about. With little fanfare, they added Radio Norwich to their family of brands (six other stations were also in the Gordale hutch) and undertook an immediate review, making hard-headed decisions such as selling and leasing back the Radio Norwich studios and cancelling 'waste' such as refreshments and travel costs. And in personnel terms, did they ring the changes![249]

Dave Clifton was left to stagnate on Radio Norwich, shunted to *Norfolk Nights*. I was plucked for a kind of special fire-

---

249 Yes.

fighting role – one that removed me from Radio Norwich altogether and airdropped me into Radio North Norfolk, a sister station with a far more refined listenership but in need of a kick in the arm, in what I saw as a kind of Red Adair role. There I was (in my mind): top off, sweat dripping from my rippling torso, my glistening skin marked with soot as I strode through the burning station, salvaging a listenership here, capping the verbal diarrhoea spewing from some of the younger DJs there, while salvaging the reputation of the station, and drenching the place in a kind of radio foam made up of sodium alkyl sulfate and a crude fluorosurfactant, as onlookers watched and looked at me.

A memo from Gordale convinced me that this was a hugely radical step, and would represent an exciting chapter in both my career and the future of Radio North Norfolk. These guys were visionaries. Gordale, it said, was 'committed to making best use of its resources' (love that phrase) and had decided that when the station's FM licence came up for renewal in 2006, it would not be bidding. Instead, the station would become digital-only (only!!).

To the best of my knowledge, I'd never broadcast in digital before and was genuinely giddy at the prospect of my speech being delivered as a binary code. It would be transmitted as a series of zeroes and ones, reforming in the ear[250] as a crystal clear facsimile of my real-life voice.

This was no half measure. Gordale passionately threw its weight behind the move, rebranding the station as North Norfolk Digital[251] and spending a cool three grand on signage, mugs and t-shirts.

---

250 *Terminator 2*-style.
251 North Norfolk's best music mix.

There was a shake-up in the line-up too. Pop aficionado and Jonathan-King-alike Ben E. Parry was quietly moved on and I was invited to take over his post-breakfast-to-lunchtime slot.

And while other people who'd heard about Ben were saying 'No *way*' and 'Jesus Christ' and 'He used to go to my swimming baths' and 'Imagine his wife finding that out' and 'I knew there was something about him', I was punching the air, whooping and high-fiving like Obama after he'd just scored a slam dunk on the White House court, high-fiving his staff before doing a kind of funky walk around the court, saying 'Who da man' to everyone's delight.

Out went *Hits of Their Day* and in came a far more cerebral show. I envisaged it as a kind of 'idea melting pot', challenging but easily digestible for an audience of housewives and unemployed males. It was, I hoped, tonally equidistant between Nigel Pinsent's *In-Depth* and Wally Banter's *Junk Box*.[252]

I devised the name 'Alan's Show' as I felt that was the best name for the show. I was absolutely adamant that that's what the show should be called because I didn't feel that other names were as good as that one. I was fully prepared to walk if they didn't cede to my demand. But, after a conversation with effete station controller Frank Shears, I agreed that it should not be called 'Alan's Show'. As Frank pointed out, the name of the show would appear on a coffee mug and people might subconsciously think of me, Alan Partridge, as some kind of 'mug'.

Instead, I needed to devise a new name. I locked myself in my study – and like a scene from a US movie – I put on a

---

252 Regular NND listeners will know EXACTLY what I mean.

sweatshirt and walked around bouncing a tennis ball against a wall as I thought out loud.[253] I emerged three days later, having broken a window, an angle-poise lamp and a swivel chair, still no closer to a new name.

Then a brainwave! I thought back to a time of my life when I was at my most productive. When was I oozing with ideas? In what circumstances was I at my most fecund? I'd simply identify when I was at my best and then try to recreate that environment as faithfully as possible.

Which is how I came to spend a long weekend in the Aylsham Travel Tavern, dining each morning from the breakfast buffet and speaking into a Dictaphone while my assistant wrote down everything I said, like a human back-up drive.

We spent four days in that room together (not in an intimate way – she slept in the bathroom) until, exhausted and bleary eyed, we emerged. We (I) had devised a name that had gravitas, catchy alliteration, and was time-specific.

The second of these features was the most crucial. I love alliteration. I love, love, love it. Alliteration just makes everything sound fantastic. I genuinely can't think of anything with matching initials that I don't like: Green Goddess, Hemel Hempstead, Bum Bags, Monster Mash, Krispy Kreme, Dirty Dozen, Peter Purves, Est Est Est, the SS,[254] World Wide Web, Clear Cache.

My show would combine all that was good about its alliterative brothers listed above. It was to be called 'Daily Daytime

---

253 It should have been a baseball and pitcher's mitt but I didn't have one.
254 More the font they used than what they actually did, which was pretty awful.

Debate'. And as far as I was concerned that was absolutely final. I'd changed it once and I was *not* going to change it again.

In the end, it was changed to 'Mid-Morning Matters', which was a good name because it did 'matter'[255] and, running from 10am to 2pm, occupied a time that everyone would agree was known as 'mid-morning'.

I decided the show would combine music and chat, which effectively meant transplanting *Norfolk Nights* into a new daytime slot. This was reflected in a more housewife-friendly tone of chat, subsequently described by one North Norfolk blogger[256] as 'like a feral Lorraine Kelly' which I quite liked. Similarly, the mood of the music necessarily shifted from 'I love you' to 'Let's get things done'.[257]

Having completely bought in to Gordale's efficiency savings, I understood that there wasn't much in the pot to spend on marketing. Instead, I dug into my savings and had Prontaprint[258] make 2,500 flyers which I left in piles on the tables of Starbucks and Café Nero.

Then I began to broadcast.

'This is digital radio. Repeat: this is digital radio. Do you read me, North Norfolk? Do you read me?'

'*Alan, they read you,*' said a voice in my cans.

'Prepare your psyche for a new listening experience. Prepare for *Alan's Show* ...'

'*It's not called* Alan's Show.'

---

255 I enjoyed the double-meaning of 'matters' so much I'd sometimes pronounce it as a verb, and other times as a noun, and see if anyone noticed.

256 'Web logger'.

257 Essentially less Hot Chocolate and more Tears for Fears.

258 *Love* the alliteration. It's so clever!

'... for Alan's *new* show: *Mid-Morning Matters*. It's 10 o'clock in the morning – *or is it?* We want to hear from you if, like many farmers, you're simply not joining in with British Summer Time. I know Daylight Saving plays merry hell with milking patterns, so if you're a rebel GMT-worshipper, we want to hear from you. Also on the show, how long have you kept a fizzy drink fizzy for? Once the top's been opened, we want to know how long you kept the fizz and *how you did it.* And on the texts: we always hear the downside to female circumcision, but what about the upside? Send us your views in an SMS. Now ULTRAVOX.'

And so *Mid-Morning Matters* was born. And it was quickly apparent that listeners had warmed to this new Digitalan Partridge, with listening figures spiking in my first quarter by almost 2%. Why though? Just what is digital radio?

You're the bloomin' expert, Alan! Out with it!

Well, as far I know: The most common meaning is digital radio broadcasting technologies, such as the digital audio broadcasting (DAB) system, also known as Eureka 147.

I'm pretty sure: In these systems, the analog audio signal is digitised, compressed using formats such as mp2, and transmitted using a digital modulation scheme.

If you're interested, I'm *relatively* au fait with the aim of digital radio: The aim is to increase the number of radio programs in a given spectrum, to improve the audio quality, to eliminate fading problems in mobile environments, to allow additional datacasting services, and to decrease the transmission power or the number of transmitters required to cover a region.

But that's all I can remember right now.

33.
A SIDEKICK

***

IN OCTOBER 2010 I broke one of the most sacred covenants of
Brand Partridge. I decided to start broadcasting with the aid
of a sidekick. No consultation, no forward planning. I just did
it. BAM! Yet even to me his arrival – like that of a baby whose
parents weren't responsible enough to use protection, be it a
condom, the coil, or whatever – was completely unexpected.
So what the hell was I playing at?

The story begins on a Tuesday night.[259] Wearing flannel
slacks and a tossed sweater, I'd driven over to my local hostelry.
It was a warm evening and I was hungry for the 2.5 units of
alcohol to which, as a driver, I was legally entitled. I locked my

---

259 *Press play on Track 41.*

car by casually pointing the keys over my shoulder – *boop beep*[260] – but before I had advanced more than a few metres something stopped me in my tracks. It was one of the loudest peals of laughter since sliced bread. And it was coming from the snug.

It's no exaggeration to say that it nearly blew me back against the car. It might very well have done so too, were it not for the fact that my calf muscles had recently been beefed up by a Runton to Matlask power ramble. (If you're in the area by the way, can I urge you to drop in at The King's Arms in Barningham? Excellent guest ales and a very welcome zero tolerance policy on dogs in the bar. And I do mean *zero* tolerance. If you're blind, don't bother.)

I picked up the pace. The only person I'd ever heard cause such an uproar in that snug before was, well, me. Phil Shepherd had them crying with laughter in the saloon bar one night last year but, like I say, that wasn't in the snug. I couldn't imagine who it could be. Hmmm, I mused, curiouser and curiouser.

As I entered the pub I instantly spotted the source of the mirth. It was a man in his early 30s wearing an 'out there' Hawaiian shirt and sporting a beard that was a sort of gingery browny gingery browny ginger. His name was Simon Denton and – *Understatement Alert!* – he was *seriously* funny.

The joke he was telling when I walked in was an absolute groin-wrecker (is that a phrase?). But it was also wholly unsuitable for publication, touching as it did on the rather delicate subjects of race, sexuality and Phil Shepherd's mum. Me and the guys took it in the spirit in which it was intended, but if the PC Brigade saw it in print they'd have an absolute eppy. The

---

260 Love that noise.

second and third gags were just about fine, I thought, but HarperCollins disagreed so I can't share them with you. Let's just say that what I regarded as gentle joshing of the opposite sex, they regarded as plain hateful to women. Ditto a handful of Jew jokes. Ah well.

But petty questions of taste and decency aside, the point is that me and Denton hit it off large-time. We were like Siamese twins separated at birth by a combination of surgery and adoption. We both enjoyed a drop of real ale. We both had the same views on artificial insemination. And we were both absolute naturals at that thing where you lean on the barstool in a way that means you're sitting and standing at the same time.

More than anything else, though, we were just funny guys. As I drove home that night I thought my brain was going to short circuit. Had I been a robot,[261] I think it probably would have done. What the hell had just happened back there? Who was this guy? It was back at *Chez Partridge* later on as I drank a pint of tap water in just three gulps (a new PB) that it occurred to me. Why not invite Denton to become part of *Mid-Morning Matters* on North Norfolk Digital?[262]

Of course! It was so obvious. Comedy was the only thing the show hadn't nailed. Everything else was there by the bucket-load – music, guests, sound effects. We had a whole phalanx of killer features too: Alan Describes Art, A Partridge in a Pun Tree, Creed Crunch, Word Scramble, Gender Thrash.

Yet every night in bed, there was a nagging doubt in my mind. I'd lie there absent-mindedly tossing my ball bag from one hand to the other, and I knew something was missing. What we were lacking was the truly big laughs found on, say,

---

261 The Terminator, for example. Or Metal Mickey.
262 North Norfolk's best music mix.

Bedtime with Branning or the aforementioned Wally Banter's *Junk Box.*

Not that it was my fault. I was forever bringing a wry smile to my listener's ears, but there was only so far I could go. As one of the most trusted voices in Norfolk,[263] I had a responsibility to be taken seriously. It wouldn't do to have spent the entire show speaking like a quacking duck (which admittedly would be very funny) if I then had to read out an urgent newsflash about a dirty bomb going off in Wisbech.

So that was where Denton would come in. Not specifically for the quacking (in fact, least of all for the quacking – animal noises were a glaring weakness of his), but just to be the person whose sole job it was to bring the laughter. But my thinking was even bolder than that. I wasn't envisaging that Denton would come and go like a weather girl or a traffic and travel person. Instead he would be by my side throughout, free to lob in a gag at literally any time.[264] It would bring a real freshness to the show to have this unique comic mind chucking in dry comments the second they popped into his head.[265] And a bonus: thanks to (a) the webcam and (b) his striking resemblance to Clyde from *Every Which Way But Loose,* even the deaf could enjoy him.

Not that I was talking about a co-host. That would be taking it way, way, way, way, way, way, way too far. I'd already betrayed the trust of my digital devotees by introducing a sidekick at all. To go any further would have been insane. I like risk, but I'm not a dick. To make that point crystal clear I decided to enshrine his role in his on-air nickname, *Sidekick*

---

263 North Norfolk.
264 Provided he had first sought permission from me.
265 So long as he'd run the ideas past me during the previous song.

Simon. His job would be to enhance the show, not to share it. Never to share it. Not ever. No, that wasn't going to happen, pal.

He would be the polish to my car, the buff to my shoe, the sun cream to my back. Just to be certain I was making the right decision, I consulted my assistant. She seemed unsure that a lowly lab assistant could cope in the pressure cooker atmosphere of digital local radio. This was good enough for me. I hired Denton there and then.[266] At many of the pivotal points in my life I've found that the best way to reach a decision is to find out what a Baptist would do, then do the opposite.

Yet 'Sidekick Simon's' first show did not go well. I'd given him the perfect tee-up, advising listeners that major laughs were guaranteed: 'If you're standing, sit down. If you're driving, pull over. And if you're in a wheelchair, for god's sake keep away from the top of the stairs.'

In the event I wished I'd kept my mouth shut. Denton didn't just let me down, he let himself down too. He was riddled with nerves, his usually hilarious asides turning into little more than muttered rubbish. I'd advised to him to have a couple of drinks before he came on, to loosen himself up a bit. But he hadn't. He said he didn't want to start drinking when it wasn't even ten o'clock. I was absolutely furious. It was so unprofessional.

Time after time I was forced to intervene and send my audience into fits of uncontrollable laughter after another one of Denton's gags had fallen horribly flat. It was easy enough for me to do this, but that wasn't the point. That night I thanked my lucky stars that the Wisbech nuclear scenario had not come to pass. I'd had an incredibly lucky escape.

---

266 Unpaid.

We limped on for the rest of the week, but on Sunday I told him to meet me for brunch. It was a session we'd go on to repeat many times in the future. I'd canter in with the Sundays under my arm and plonk myself down by the fire. There'd always be a tussle over the motoring section, which I would invariably win, either through brute force or just by invoking the Paper Purchaser's Prerogative (my capitals, my whole phrase actually). Yet this particularly Sunday, it was serious. It was time for showdown talks.

I made my position clear. The nerves had to be dealt with. He was free to do as he wished at the weekends, but as long as he was appearing on my weekday show, I needed to know that he had been drinking. I obviously wasn't going to enforce this with a daily breathaliser test (couldn't get hold of a breathaliser) but, believe me, I would just know.

Happily it was a solution that seemed to work. He got over his nerves and I survived with my reputation intact. Other than those moments when I have either punched or shot people live on air, the name Alan Partridge has come to be a byword for broadcasting excellence, and I didn't want that to be compromised.

Denton's morning drinking did end up costing him his driving licence, but despite his incessant moaning both he and I knew that he could still make it into the station by using as few as three buses. While he and his fellow passengers could just sit back and effectively be chauffeured into work, the rest of us had to undergo the daily headache of changing gear, looking in our mirrors and turning the steering wheel.

I liked having a sidekick, though. It was a rush. It took me back to my days at hospital radio. I didn't have a wingman as such, but we used to do a feature where any child that was recovering from an operation could be wheeled down to the studio. They'd pick a few songs and read the traffic and travel (subject to their voice having the requisite clarity and authority). It was a really lovely part of the show actually. And while the music played they'd have the chance to tuck into Alan's Cookie Jar (a 'biscuit barrel' in old money). Of course, kids will never say no to a sugary treat, so they used to love this, though I did have a strict rule of no more than two biscuits per child. The last thing they needed was to be brought back into hospital the next month for a gastric band or a filling.

Plus, they didn't come cheap. It's not like biscuits grow on trees (note to self: possible film idea). You might think that buying a bag of broken bourbons from Norwich market doesn't cost much, and you'd be right, but when it goes on for week after week after week, the financial burden can become pretty crippling. If they'd served a medical purpose I would have turned a blind eye, but with the best will in the world, it's not like biscuits can heal broken bones (note to self: possible film idea).

Denton and I became moderately firm friends outside of work too. Despite being a lab assistant he was actually an okay guy. His B in chemistry, C in biology and B in physics (all at GCSE) had left him with some pretty amazing knowledge. The speed at which he could tell you the colour any given metal would turn a Bunsen burner flame was nothing short of incredible. As I found out one memorable night in the pub …

'Barium?'

'Light green.'

'Potassium?'

'Lilac.'

'Sodium?' This is me asking the questions, by the way.

'Orange.' And that's Denton answering.

'Calcium?' Me again.

'Brick red.' Denton again.

Of course he could have been lying. After all it's not always easy to trust the bearded. Not since Peter Sutcliffe anyway. I find it's easier to trust a man with a moustache. In modern times those with upper lip coverage seem to have been pretty good eggs, with the exception of Saddam Hussein, Joseph Stalin, Adolf you-know-who and several others. Freddie Mercury seemed alright, though, despite his tendencies, ahem!

***

Denton is no longer my sidekick of course.[267] The trajectory of our working relationship – from strangers-in-pub to partners-in-crime in six days – was clearly unsustainable, and so it proved.

I felt that Denton began to develop ideas above his station. Don't misunderstand me – I wasn't expecting him to pucker up each morn and kiss my rump, but I would have liked a little loyalty and gratitude. Sadly, these basic Partridgian values are commodities – like Sterling, or leaded petrol – that the public has deemed dispensable in recent years.

The warning signs appeared when Denton began to turn up late. On North Norfolk Digital, this ain't on. (I still have the internal memo that makes that very point.)

Me, I have a routine. Although my show doesn't start until 10am, I try to get to McDonald's for 7 (otherwise you don't get the booth by the window) with a pencil and pad. Before I do *anything*, I work out the tracklisting for the show and come up with scripted chat that I'll pass off as spontaneous quipping when I flag in the final hour of the slot.

---

267 *Press play on Track 42.*

A couple of coffees and seven hash browns later, I'm in the toilets putting my shirt back on after a good wash before brushing my teeth and grabbing another coffee on the way out. I'm beeping my horn outside Denton's flat no later than 8.50am.

Within weeks of being granted sidekickhood, Denton's punctuality became a problem. He'd keep me waiting for two, sometimes three, minutes, before rolling into the car without a word of apology. His foul breath told me he'd recently woken and the cakey orange build-up in the corners of his eyes was a sure-fire sign that waking early and/or washing had *not* been on his to-do list.

I said nothing of course, preferring to make clear my disdain on air – by quelling my laughter, talking over him or making him explain his 'jokes' in great detail.

I'm a forgiving man – I even returned a prized album of family photos to Carol after she left, going as far as gluing the torn shreds back together with Bostik and drawing in bits that had been lost – but I felt that Denton was pushing his luck enormously here.

The final betrayal, when it came, was still a shock. I was woken one night by a text from my assistant. 'Emergency,' it began, but then it always does. 'NND now. Not home.'

I ignored the message, temporarily forgetting that when she texts 'home', she more often than not means 'good'. I am continually staggered by her failure to grasp T9 predictive text, despite having used it for a decade.

So it wasn't until the following day that I realised the news was bad, and that I would be bidding 'home' riddance to my sidekick in a matter of weeks.

Turns out Denton had been moonlighting for *Bedtime with Branning*, supplying wry observations and wacky character-led monologues to a presumably bemused late-night audience.

Well, this was a clatter in the chops! Bang! I mean, I'd not demanded that Denton sign an exclusivity agreement, as his humour seemed so suited to mid-morning, but even without a legally binding contract, I'd have thought it obvious that he was mine.

Apparently not. And so with the relationship visibly curdling by the hour, we limped on for another few weeks, before we decided to call it a day.[268]

His departure gave the show a new lease a life – you'd have to be deaf not to recognise that – and my listeners were grateful that they were getting more Alan in their mid-morning diet. I pledged never to allow a sidekick to eclipse, obscure or impinge ever again. I've stuck to that pledge too – although, on occasions, I've shared mic-space with a girl whose name, I think, was Zoe.

And what of Denton? Well, we bumped into each other in the King's Arms three weeks ago, eyeing each other warily from across the bar, peeking out now and then from behind a strip of Scampi Fries.

With them in my eye-line, it was inevitable that I'd buy a packet and, once opened, I offered one to the woman I was having a drink with.

'Would you like one Scampi Fry?' I asked.

'Just one?!' she replied, greedily eyeing up my full bag of fish crunches. It may be that she'd forgotten that taking more than one would almost certainly compromise her appetite, which wasn't really on given that I was buying dinner.

---

268 I basically just stopped picking him up.

But no sooner had she eaten her Scampi Fry than Denton piped up with a joke about her having 'fishy fingers'.

On the face of it, it pertained to the distinctive aroma of scampi, but Denton and I both knew it had vaginal overtones. And while the woman was unimpressed, Denton and I *fell* about. It was a reminder of what genuinely good comedy sounds like and we've been fairly inseparable since then. In a recent raffle, I won an afternoon driving saloon cars around Brands Hatch and Denton has asked if he can come and watch.

And when the day comes, I might swing round to his place and pick him up. Yes, I think I will.

34.
HANGING UP THE
HEADPHONES

***

EVERYONE HAS A SHELF-LIFE – whether they're a finely tuned athlete, a surrogate mother, or a lady newsreader. Disc jockeys are no exceptions.

The last thing you want to do is plough on long past your sell-by date, trading on past glories (Simon Mayo) or pretending to like classical music (Simon Bates). The dignified approach is to recognise when your magic is gone, and serenely slip away, having negotiated a handsome severance package and delivered a stinging broadside against younger DJs and station controllers (also Simon Bates to be fair).

I'm perpetually analysing my relevance and fitness for purpose, angrily quizzing my assistant on the quality of each day's show and sending tapes to Denise and Fernando to flag up anything that sounds dated or fogey-like. So far nothing has come back.

But sometimes there are whispers, nagging doubts, worries. I'm a human being – a good one, but human nonetheless – and the creeping concern that I am outstaying my welcome has lived alongside me in recent years, like a quiet wife or a sidelined application for planning permission.

This has taken on new badness in recent months, culminating in a bounce-back to where I was before I bounced back. I found myself walking through the valley of no confidence towards the desert of deep despair.

You see recently there have been whispers that the Partridge is past it. Naturally the naysayers haven't had the testes to say this to my face, but you can just sense these things. Plus I've had my assistant sit behind them in the staff canteen and listen in to their conversations.

From whence did these hushed conversations arise, you ask (or at least, I do)? Well, it was all triggered by an incident in May. Craig Kilty, aka The Monster, a DJ from rival station Orbital Digital, had tricked his way into my studio and duped me into saying the words 'I listen to Orbital Digital.' Far from this being a clever publicity stunt, however, most people just ended up thinking he had learning difficulties. Which to my mind, he definitely does.

Yet it seemed that the chattering classes around North Norfolk Digital had seen it differently. To them it was a sign that I was letting my guard down, that I was losing my hunger, my sharpness, my 'joie de broadcast'. Of course this was cobblers/fucking bullshit. But it still needed answering, and the only way to do that was to stage the kind of one-off radio event that people would be talking about for a generation, certainly in my household anyway. Which is how I came up with the idea of 'Mid-Morning Matters, mid-air'.

***

Whoosh! Legs together, arms by my sides, I shoot up into the air, my body spiralling like a drill bit. 'Shiiiiit!' I scream in terror as my beloved Norfolk disappears beneath me. Up I go, higher and higher, climbing like a bird (that flies vertically). Two feet, three feet, four. God knows how many Gs I'm pulling.

Then suddenly the ascent seems to stall. 'Norwich, we have a problem,' I quip, deep inside my own head. But of course we don't have a problem. It's just Old Lady Gravity getting her way. (She always does in the end, the bitch.) And so here I go, beginning my long descent back to earth. Four feet, three feet, two. As I gather speed, my side parting lifts off my scalp. 'I can fly!' it must be thinking. How wrong it is. How wrong it is.

And then – ka-boom! – 13 stone, 8 ounces[269] of pure Alan Partridge crashes down into the forgiving embrace of soft, inflated plastic. A broad Cheshire cheese smile lights up my face. I really do love a bouncy castle.

It's August 2011 and you join me at the annual Fun Day of North Norfolk Digital.[270] A million miles away from our dark, cramped studios, the Fun Days are all about glitz and glamour as we broadcast live from a large field or car park. It's a rare chance for us radio professionals to do our stuff in front of a real-life audience, and I for one love it. Reading the travel news into an unresponsive studio mic is one thing, but

---

269 A bit less if I go to the toilet before I weigh.
270 North Norfolk's best music mix.

announcing a tailback on the A47 while staring deep into the eyes of a local granny as she nervously tries to calculate the implications for her journey home? Well you can't beat it.

I like to spice things up with a gimmick too. Last year I broadcast wearing a full suit of armour (hot, but worth it). The year before I didn't do anything. (I was going to dress up as David Beckham, but in the end I didn't as I was in a bad mood on the day.) And this year, I've trumped the lot. A first for digital radio anywhere in Norfolk,[271] I've decided that part of my show will take place mid-air, as I catapult myself up and down on a bouncy castle.

People have tried to talk me out of it of course – some concerned that the jumping will compromise sound quality, others believing (wrongly) that the castle is only for the use of under-10s. But there's no way I was going to be dissuaded, because this year of all years, with rumours circulating that I'm past it, I need to make my mark.

A few practice leaps have banished the nerves that kept me awake for much of the night. And as I look out into the small but high-quality crowd I can feel myself basking in the warm glow of relative confidence. I breathlessly clamber aboard the castle (having first removed my shoes) and quickly scare away any remaining children. Yet barely have I finished my first mid-air 'Hello, Norfolk!', than things go horribly, catastrophically wrong.

As I reach the high point of my first ascent, I can just make out something odd going on below. A grubby man has rushed forward and is shoving the castle out of the way. Suddenly there's nothing to cushion my fall but cold, hard car park. My whole life flashes before me (it really would make a good

---

271 North Norfolk.

film).[272] But before I crash to earth I notice who the perpetrator is. It's none other than my DJing nemesis, Dave Clifton.

With an hour to kill before opening time he's clearly decided to come and make mischief. Yet this time he has badly miscalculated. What he is attempting won't just leave me a bit red-faced, there is every chance it could lead to paralysis on a truly Perry Masonesque scale. And there is no way I am prepared to spend the rest of my life in a wheelchair, even though I have always been curious about the turning circles of the motorised ones.

I shut my eyes and prepare for the worst. But instead of the crack of bone on tarmacadam, what I hear is more of a squelchy thud. Because Clifton has failed to get out of my way and has effectively broken my fall. Better still, his recent thyroid problem means that, to land on, there's very little actual difference between him and a bouncy castle.

Yet as we lie there in a tangled heap of DJs, I realise I haven't totally escaped injury. My left ankle is badly sprained. As the pain courses up my body I yelp like a shot dog. Clifton is pretty badly hurt too. Blood is glugging from a cut in his knee like a big squirt of leg ketchup.

I'm sorely tempted to spit in the bastard's mouth, but don't. I'm worried it might be taken as a sign of affection by any sexual deviants in the crowd. As my mind scans its database for a plan B, he leaps up and starts to run away. Instantly I'm hurled into the belly of a dilemma. What do I do now? He's pushed it too far this time, but I'm still a professional, I've still got a show to do. My fans are expecting three hours of quality

---

272 Starring Charles Dance as Alan Partridge, and sound-tracked by 'You Can Call Me Al' by Paul Simon, which I think is quite cheesy but still good.

radio, delivered mid-air. I may have a bust ankle, but there's no reason I can't get back on that castle and hop.

But then I look out into the (small but high-quality) sea of faces. My god, people are laughing at me. Worse, on the front row I see Craig Kilty, aka The Monster, and a man who looks very much like Tony Hayers but isn't Tony Hayers because Tony Hayers is dead. What I wouldn't give to wipe the smiles off their faces, especially the face of Craig Kilty aka The Monster because it is actually him, whereas the other one isn't Tony Hayers (because Tony Hayers is dead).

If I just let Clifton get away with it even more people will think I'm past it. Even more people will think it's time to put me out to pasture/stud. Instantly my mind is made up.[273] 'Sorry, guys,' I say, 'show's cancelled.'

***

Two hours later the pursuit is still in full swing. Struggling with different but identically debilitating injuries,[274] we're locked in a dramatic low-speed chase. Thankfully for me, Clifton has been unable to stem the bleeding from his knee. Even if I temporarily lose sight of him I can always tell which direction he's headed because he leaves a small trail of blood. He's like a large, menstruating snail (with a drink problem).

By this point my ankle has swollen to roughly the size of a child's head. There's no way I can give up, though. To make matters worse, he's goading me.

'You'll never catch me, Partridge.'

'I wouldn't bet on that,' I counter, as a pregnant woman overtakes me.

---

273 *Press play on Track 43.*
274 Me: sprained. Him: cut, fat, drunk.

'Well I would,' he replies, his ridiculous mid-Atlantic accent hanging on the breeze like a bad trump.

'Oh yeah, how much?'

'How much have you got?'

'Depends if you mean cash or assets. If we're going down the assets route then we're talking house, car, antique Toby jug, which is chipped but not badly ...'

Suddenly something hits me. This entire conversation has been nothing more than a smokescreen. With me distracted he's hobbled on to a number 23 bus and is getting away. Overcome with rage I flick him the Vs (both hands). A young boy misunderstands and thinks I've aimed the insult towards his mother. Keen to defend her honour, he flicks his wrist to and fro in the international gesture for 'masturbator'.

I flick my head effortlessly to the right and see another bus pulling in. Hauling my kiddy's head of an ankle aboard, I pay my fare (£1.50 for a single!) and fix the driver square between the eyes.

'Follow that bus!' I bellow, my face puce with frustration.

'Jesus, what happened to your ankle?' he asks, leaning his head out of that little cabin they sit in.

'Bouncy castle fall only partially broken by bad man,' I answer, concisely. 'Now drive!'

He steps on the gas and with a massive cloud of dust we wheel-spin out of the depot, our back end bucking like a bronco. But at the lights, disaster. Clifton's bus turns left, mine goes right. I ding the dinger, but as I leap from the bus and on to the pavement I've forgotten about my ankle. The sudden throb of pain makes me understand what childbirth must be like. Except I'm feeling it in my lower leg rather than my vagina (which is presumably more sensitive).

'Are you okay?' says a passing French woman who's obviously learnt to speak English. I totally ignore her, partly out of pain, partly because I'm still angry at her countrymen for taking part in the Vichy regime.

I scan my surroundings. If I can cut across the retail park I should – *should* – be able to head him off at the junction. It's a long shot but it's the only shot I have. I make my way past Boots, JJB Sports and Blacks, who I notice have got 25% off all waterproof trousers. This is handy, not only as I need a new pair of waterproof trousers but also because I always aim to get them at a discounted rate rather than pay full price.

But when I look back over to the junction, the bus has gone. Clifton has eluded me! 'Noooooooooo!!!!' I shout, tossing my head back and firing my scream into the sky (although some of it will inevitably have spilled into the nearby Burtons). I trudge on in a daze, making it a few more paces before collapsing to the ground in a tangled heap of DJ.

***

When I finally come round – how long has it been? A few seconds? A few minutes? A few hours?[275] – I realise where I am.[276] I'm lying in a disabled parking bay outside Morrison's. Yet this isn't just any old Morrison's. This is the site of the copse where I'd stood all those years ago, an eight-year-old marvelling at a simple maple, bowled over by its class and its spunk. The same site to which I make pilgrimage once a year, to remember that tree and take stock; to remember who I am and re-engorge my sense of self.

---

275 Answer: a few seconds.
276 *Press play on Track 44.*

But today feels different. Today the tree/parking space feels blank, impassive, solemn. Rather than replenishing my self-esteem, being here seems to be sending me a far more poignant message.

As a child this is where I'd looked ahead to the rest of my life, where my hopes and ambitions had taken shape. And now I am here once more, at the tail-end of my career, bested yet again by a rival DJ. The message is clear – I really am past it.

Try as I might, I can't ignore what this tree[277] is trying to tell me. I feel tears welling in my two eyes for I know what I must do. I must go into North Norfolk Digital[278] in the morning and announce my retirement, effective immediately.

As the enormity of my decision dawns on me, I bring my arms into my body, tuck my chin on to my chest and roll away to the left (as a disabled guy wants to get into the parking space).

*   *   *

That night I sit alone on my sofa and prepare to write a good-bye speech to my listeners. Armed with nothing other than a pad of paper and one of those biros that writes in different colours depending on which button you flick down, I set to work.

Memories, people from my past, significant achievements dance before me, like I imagine they would if I was sitting at a fire after drinking the potion in some kind of voodoo ceremony.

I will myself to write my goodbye. But that night's Bid-Up TV is so enjoyable that four hours later I realise I haven't done

---

277 Patch of ground approximately where a tree once was.
278 North Norfolk's best music mix.

anything (other than make a winning bid for a 12v automatic hammer with soft-grip handle).

I turn off the TV and head into the kitchen to treat myself to a bowl of Coco-Pops with hot milk (heavenly), and as I'm slurping down a mouthful of sweet brown cereal, I fall sound asleep. I wake at 7, with a bit of milk on my face but also with a genuine sense of clarity and certainty. 'No time for McDonald's today,' I say loudly, 'I have to say my goodbyes: to my colleagues, to my listeners, to the profession that has been my love for the best years of my life.'

I telephone my assistant to tell her the news. I'm obviously not interested in what she has to say, so when I've finished speaking I press the buttons on my phone in order to drown out her protests with the keytones. Then I hang up.

I start the drive into work, manfully trying to operate the brake, accelerator and clutch with only one functioning foot. It's not easy, but I'm confident that if I move my good foot quickly enough, while slinging my bad one over the gear stick, it can be done. A close shave with the local lollipop lady tells me I'm wrong. I clamber aboard my crutches and begin the long walk to work. It will at least give me time to marshal my thoughts.

Some hope! As I struggle to pole-vault my body gradually towards the studios, my concentration is crumpled by interruptions.

'Excuse me, love,' a bespectacled woman asks from the driver's window of a Renault Espace. 'I'm trying to find the Millennium Library. I think it's Ethel St?'

'It's Bethel Street,' I mutter, my eyes fixed on the pavement ahead. 'It's just past the end of Earlham Road but there are tailbacks from the roadworks on the Grapes Hill roundabout, so you're better off taking Dereham Road and heading for St Benedicts St.'

'Thanks!'

I must concentrate. This is a seminal moment in my life. I need this to be right. But a shout from a nearby doorway halts my train of thought.

'Lovely day!' says an old cardiganed woman, towing a tartan shopping trolley and dead-locking her front door behind her as all old people obsessively insist on doing.

'Yeah, for ducks!' I holler. She laughs, and I explain. 'The weather's going to take a turn any minute. Massive chance of rain today. Massive.'

She stops laughing and, deep in thought, heads back indoors to collect a coat or buy her shopping online.

I arrive at North Norfolk Digital[279] still clueless as to how I'll announce my retirement. Just before I enter the building, the security guard catches my eye. He looks a bit down – or rather, more depressed than usual – so I engage him in a quick bit of chat, instinctively focusing on topics someone like him he will relate to, such as football or the lottery.

I get inside and crutch myself to the bathroom. Standing at the mirror, I observe my reflection: my eyes still dance and sparkle (of course they do) but my hair is mottled grey, my eyes are riddled with wrinkles and my skin has developed a blotchy quality that I never discovered the source of.

'The time has come for me to retire,' I mumble to myself. Yes, something simply feels right. I hear a snigger from a toilet cubicle and curse silently. My colleagues really are *twats* sometimes.

After splashing my face where it had been stained with milk, I leave the bogs and order a couple of less senior people

---

279 North Norfolk's best music mix.

to assemble everyone in the foyer. And then I drop my bombshell. 'I'm calling it a day. I wanted you all to know first, but in a few moments I'll share the news with my listeners. "I've had some great years with you all," I shall say. "But the time has come for me to retire."'

A hush falls over the room. They can't believe it. At the back, I think I see someone faint. I start the process of shaking every member of staff by the hand. It's only a small gesture but I know it'll mean a lot. Some people have got palms even clammier than my own (including a worryingly high proportion of women), but I don't tell them – now's not the time, I'll just give my hands a good wash later.

In the end I have to do the shakes increasingly quickly as I've noticed people have started to drift away (no doubt intent on returning to their desks to switch off their email, take their phones off the hook and give themselves a few minutes to get their heads straight).

By the time I get to the last few it's barely even a shake, it's more of a grip-and-release. I'm in such a hurry I end up pressing the flesh of a couple of people who aren't even on the payroll – one is a DHL courier, the other isn't.[280]

I'm so determined not to miss anyone out that I even head back into the toilets (first the men's, then the women's, then the disabled's) to mop up any stragglers. By now however it's five[281] to ten. The time for shaking hands with people in toilets, no matter what their gender or handicap, is over.

I glance out of the window and see an old woman looking up at the window, through the driving rain. But I've no time to worry about lady pensioners. It's show time for the final

---

280 *Press play on Track 45.*
281 Minutes.

time. I enter my studio, for the final time. I sit on my seat, for the final time. I warm up my voice, not for the final time (at this point I'm still toying with the idea of joining a gospel choir).

As I have done for every one of my broadcasts over some 30 years, I quietly run through my pre-show checklist. Headphones – on. Throat and nasal passages – clear. Fingers – ready to push buttons and slide sliders. The breakfast show has chosen to end with 'It's My Life', the 1992 hit by Dr Alban. It seems somehow appropriate, even though it's been used to advertise tampons.

My moment has arrived. Alban stops, his husky European rap-singing slowly fading in the crisp morning air. And then …

Nothing. Silence. I've frozen. I'm committing the biggest sin in radio: dead air. But it's not that I've lost my bottle. Me? No way. Get real. I'd made my mind up after all. It's simply that I can't muster the will to speak. Something has grabbed my brain like the jaws of a distempered police dog. It's the old lady I've seen from the studio window, moments earlier.

It's only now I realise: this wasn't just any female pensioner. It was the woman I'd spoken to earlier this morning. This time she was wearing a coat, carrying an umbrella to protect her body from the drench. And when her eyes had fixed on mine she'd been mouthing something. 'Thank you,' she'd been saying. 'Thank you.'

I'd helped that woman. I had genuinely helped her. In providing a simple weather update, I'd helped her to avoid both the downpour and – who knows – perhaps a fatal dose of hypothermia.

And it wasn't just her. The travel bulletin I'd given to the bespectacled driver had helped her to (I imagine) return her library books in time, saving her money that she could use to feed her children, and all thanks to a detour away from the inevitable jam-back at Grapes Hill. And then there was the security guard. He'd been at a low ebb, but my chat, my breezy demeanour, my easy way with people had given him a chuckle, a moment of levity, a sign that someone cared.

I shake my head. No time for sentimentality, Alan. I need to get back 'on-message', as Tony Blair would say. But still I'm dry-mouthed and unable to propel the words towards the foamy orb of the mic.

By now word has spread that I'm drying up live on air. People are pouring into the studio that faces mine. Others are peering in through the little round window in the studio door. It's only a small window but I count at least 3.5 faces.

But still, I can't do it. Because I'd helped people, I'd amused, I'd chatted. Help, amuse, chat. And those qualities – help, amuse, chat – are qualities that broadcasters spend a lifetime trying to perfect. Yet on the limp to work I hadn't even had to think about it – it was like breathing, or going for a wee in the night. It had all come so naturally. It was just Alan being Alan, Partridge being Partridge, me being I.

But shouldn't I be saying 'sod them all'? Sod the mockers, the naysayers, the bouncy-castle saboteurs? Whatever they think of my broadcasting, isn't it my audience that matters? I mean, for them I am doing a good thing, day in, day out (except weekends). Help, amuse, chat. Help, amuse, chat. I look back to the window. Now my assistant is there. She's holding up a plastic bag with some sandwiches in. Is this a sign? No, probably not.

Suddenly the producer is in my ear. 'Speak, man.' His voice seems to go into slo-mo. 'Speeeeeaaaakkkk maaaannnn!!!' I go to loosen my tie but realise I'm not wearing one. So instead

I just end up scratching the bit below my Adam's apple. As I drag my nails back and forth across the base of my gullet, the producer is back in my ears. 'Snap out of it, Alan.'

Dozens of eyeballs peer at me, thousands of ears strain to hear. I lean towards the mic and finally, *finally*, I speak:[282]

'This is Alan Partridge with *Mid-Morning Matters*. And on the day that 67-year-old Norwich resident Mary Leese has woken from a three-year coma, we'll be asking – what's the best night's sleep you've ever had?

'We're also looking at the *law* and asking: are you legally allowed to draw a line down the back of a photograph and use it as a postcard? Now, though, the best band ever to come out of Liverpool – it is, of course, China Crisis.'

A deafening roar goes up around the station as people realise I've shelved my retirement plans. I go to shield my ears from the noise, but suddenly an ecstatic throng of well-wishers is flooding into the studio. As two oldish receptionists struggle to lift me on to their shoulders, dozens of others reach over and hug me (although there is absolutely no physical contact between myself and my assistant).

Instantly everything feels right again. I am back where I belong. I am I, Partridge.

***

So, dear reader, our time together is over. All that remains is this short epilogue. And anyone who thinks it's designed solely to haul me over the minimum word-count specified by my publisher is very, very, very, very, very, very wrong.

---

282 *At this point Track 45 should really kick in. If not, you're not reading at the right pace. Re-read the section and back time the start of the song to the right point (if you can be arsed).*

Instead it's a chance for us to reflect. Having read this book I'd like to think you've come to know me a bit better. Because in a funny kind of way I feel like I've come to know you. Shall we be friends? Yes, I think we shall. In a spiritual sense anyway, please don't come to the house.

It's my belief that in the previous 309 pages we've been on a journey – literally in the case of those reading this on the train or bus, less so for those on the sofa, in bed, or reading aloud to a blind friend or lover.

Now, however, as I ask that you play track 46,[283] the time has come to bid you farewell. I have been through much in my life. I have scaled the highest highs[284] and I have plumbed the lowest depths.[285] And though I sit here today with a heavy heart and a weary soul, my eyes still burn brightly. They burn for a better tomorrow, for a world without famine and war and the BBC. But more than anything they burn for a million-plus sales of the hardback version of *I, Partridge: We Need to Talk about Alan.*

---

283 *Press play on Track 46. When it comes to an end, the book is finished.*
284 Witnessing the birth of my first child, witnessing the birth of my second child, marriage, getting my first job with the BBC, finding out that *Knowing Me Knowing You* had been commissioned for radio, finding out that *Knowing Me Knowing You* had been commissioned for TV, securing a lucrative deal to be the face of military-based quiz show *Skirmish* on UK Conquest, being awarded a Burton's Gold Card.
285 Dundee.

TRACKLISTING

***

1. Theme from *Harry's Game* – Clannad
2. Down in the Park – Tubeway Army
3. Nights in White Satin – Moody Blues
4. Anything by Keane
5. Smalltown Boy – Bronski Beat
6. Thank God I'm a Country Boy – John Denver
7. First Time Ever I Saw Your Face – Roberta Flack
8. Fernando – Abba
9. Poppa Joe – The Sweet
10. Jump – Van Halen
11. Theme to *Ski Sunday*
12. Solsbury Hill – Peter Gabriel
13. Tusk – Fleetwood Mac
14. Love Is a Battlefield – Pat Benatar

15. Amateur Hour – Sparks
16. If I Was ... – Midge Ure
17. Japanese Boy – Aneka
18. Licence to Kill – Gladys Knight
19. The Winner Takes It All – Abba
20. Knowing Me, Knowing You – Abba
21. Is It a Dream? – Classix Nouveaux
22. On the Wings of Love – Jeffrey Osborne
23. Brothers in Arms – Dire Straits
24. Alone – Heart
25. Stop the Cavalry – Jona Lewie
26. Alright Now – Free
27. Équinoxe Part 4 – Jean Michel Jarre
28. Be With You – Mr Big
29. Wishful Thinking – China Crisis
30. The Race – Yello
31. Mamunia – Wings
32. Anything by Keane
33. Axel F – Harold Faltermeyer
34. Fade to Grey – Visage
35. Cake Walk into Town – Taj Mahal
36. Single Ladies – Beyoncé
37. Babooshka – Kate Bush
38. Drive – The Cars
39. Satisfaction – Benny Benassi
40. Pipes of Peace – Paul McCartney
41. Iko Iko – The Belle Stars
42. Poison Arrow – ABC
43. Theme from *The Saint*
44. Theme from *Harry's Game* – Clannad
45. Fix You – Coldplay
46. Portsmouth – Mike Oldfield

INDEX

***